The Offense of Poetry

By Hazard Adams

poetry:
The Farm at Richwood and Other Poems

fiction:
The Truth About Dragons
The Academic Trilogy
   The Horses of Instruction
   Many Pretty Toys
   Home

nonfiction:
The Academic Tribes

literary criticism:
Blake and Yeats: The Contrary Vision
William Blake: A Reading of the Shorter Poems
The Contexts of Poetry
The Interests of Criticism
Lady Gregory
Philosophy of the Literary Symbolic
Joyce Cary's Trilogies: Pursuit of the Particular Real
The Book of Yeats's Poems
Antithetical Essays in Literary Criticism and Liberal Education
The Book of Yeats's Vision: Romantic Modernism and Antithetical Tradition
Four Lectures on the History of Criticism and Theory in the West
The Offense of Poetry

Edited by Hazard Adams
Poems by Robert Simeon Adams
Poetry: An Introductory Anthology
Fiction as Process (with Carl Hartman)
William Blake: Jerusalem, Selected Poetry, and Prose
Critical Theory Since Plato
Critical Theory Since 1965 (with Leroy Searle)
Critical Essays on William Blake

The Offense of Poetry

HAZARD ADAMS

A Robert B. Heilman Book

University of Washington Press
Seattle and London

The Offense of Poetry was published with support from a generous bequest established by Robert B. Heilman, distinguished scholar and chair of the University of Washington English Department from 1948 to 1971. The Heilman Book Fund assists in the publication of books in the humanities.

© 2007 by the University of Washington Press
Printed in the United States of America
Designed by Renée Cossutta
12 11 10 09 08 07 5 4 3 2 1

University of Washington Press
P.O. Box 50096, Seattle, WA 98145 U.S.A.
www.washington.edu/uwpress

Library of Congress Cataloging-in-Publication Data
Adams, Hazard, 1926–
    The offense of poetry / Hazard Adams.
      p.   cm.
    Includes index.
    ISBN-13: 978-0-295-98742-2 (acid-free paper)
    ISBN-10: 0-295-98742-1 (acid-free paper)
    ISBN-13: 978-0-295-98759-0 (pbk. : acid-free paper)
    ISBN-10: 0-295-98759-6 (pbk. : acid-free paper)
    1. Poetry.   2. Poetry—History and criticism.
I. Title.
PN1031.A284   2007
809.1—dc22   2007023877

The paper used in this publication is acid-free and 90 percent recycled from at least 50 percent post-consumer waste. It meets the minimum requirements of American National Standard for Information Sciences—Permanence of Paper for Printed Library Materials, ANSI Z39.48–1984.

Pages 109–10: "This Is Just to Say," by William Carlos Williams, from *Collected Poems: 1909–1939*, vol. 1, © 1938 by New Directions Publishing Corp. Reprinted by permission of New Directions Publishing Corp.

For

Sim, Wendy, Jacqueline, and Perry

. . . and then if no new poets should arise to create afresh the associations which have been thus disorganized, language will be dead to all the nobler purposes of human intercourse.
—P. B. Shelley

What shocks the virtuous philosopher delights the chamelion poet.
—John Keats

I, too, dislike it: there are things that are important beyond
                all this fiddle.
        Reading it, however, with a perfect contempt for it, one
                discovers in
        it after all, a place for the genuine.
—Marianne Moore

Contents

Preface

This book proposes that traditionally poetry, in the larger sense of imaginative writing, has been offensive and that its offense is the ground for its cultural value. My use of the word "poetry" includes literary works usually classified as prose, while at the same time I regard poetry, in its usual sense of verse, to be closest in spirit to the center of what I am talking about. This book is not concerned with offensiveness of subject matter but rather with poetry's fundamental nature as one of the principal forms of human expression. The offenses I present are those of gesture, drama, fiction, and trope. The aim is not to offer these offenses as something startlingly new but to remind of their continued important presence, given the relatively recent theoretical emphasis on political content. In two of the chapters in Part III—those on Joyce Cary and Seamus Heaney—I try to show how through these offenses the literary produces what I call an "antithetical" politics. The concept of the antithetical, which I derive from my earlier studies on Blake and Yeats, I describe here in chapter 1. Poetry has a very important social and political dimension, but when it is most clearly perceived, it is often antithetical by its various nature to social and political fashions. The reason for this is that both are constituted by poetry *inside* and *by* its way of thought and expression. Poetry is offensive to some people because of this. My aim is to try to get to the bottom of its offense and to claim that its offense is the best ground for its defense and that poetry's offense should be taught.

In my own career, I have spent much time teaching the history of literary criticism and theory. I believe it is an important subject, properly belonging to the comparative history of ideas. But I must confess that in some respects it is a history of cyclically returning error, in which formal concerns vie with concerns about religious or political morality. Usually this opposition has created on all sides isolation and acts of condescension or worse. Cyclicity has recently revealed itself again in theoretical discourse. A sign has been the intense concentration of theory on itself and the subsequent use of literature, when considered at all, as source of examples endorsing or failing to endorse an ideological position. This movement followed cyclically, partly by reaction, on what had become in academic teaching about poetry a sterile formalism. Another and more serious sign is the near disappearance of the experience of lyric poetry among students. In my courses in the history of literary criticism and theory, there have been undergraduate literature majors who had never taken a course devoted to verse. Poetry is often thought difficult, tiresome, and irrelevant; often when it is taught, it is not brought alive but deadened in reductive fixed interpretation. My book deliberately offends against this situation. Part of the reason for the decline in the teaching of lyric poetry is that verse tends to resist or even to defy easy readings of supposed content.

In some ways, this book tells an old story. The four kinds of offense I discuss in Part II are, no doubt, familiar (though perhaps in other terms) to readers of poetry. I turn to these offenses without apology and often to past critics who, though they do not explicitly use the word "offense," have been valuable to my understanding of it. Thus I do not claim theoretical originality for the offenses I discuss. Rather, I try to reinvigorate interest in what has always been there, though from time to time (sometimes unintentionally) suppressed.

My thanks go especially to David McCracken and Robert L. Montgomery, both of whom carefully read the manuscript and made very helpful suggestions. Thanks also to those students who have expressed their interest in poetry as an art, especially those in a seminar at the University of Washington in which the subject was poetic offense A few parts of chapter 8, revised, appeared in an article on William Blake's *Jerusalem* in *Studies in Romanticism*. Part of an article on Blake and Joyce in *The James Joyce Quarterly* appears here in chapter 9. A few sentences about Joyce Cary in chapter 10 are derived from an essay that appeared many years ago in *The American Scholar*. Chapter 11 is revised, expanded, and then contracted

from an earlier version in *Critical Essays on Seamus Heaney*, edited by
Robert F. Garratt (New York: G. K. Hall, 1995). Some parts of the book
have been given as lectures in various places.

Hazard Adams
Seattle, 2007

The Offense of Poetry

1

Introduction: Scandal and Offense

In his interesting and entertaining *History in English Words*, Owen Barfield remarks that the Greek *scandalizien* and the Latin *offendere* mean "to cause to stumble," but for us today "scandalize" and "scandal" "merely hint at the liveliness of an emotion," while "offend" and "offense" convey "a sober warning of its probable results."[1] I am going to adopt the words not only in the ancient metaphorical sense of "stumbling block" or "obstruction," from which they are derived, but also and simultaneously in the senses that Barfield assigns to "scandal" and "offense," for both senses apply to my subject. Is there something offensive and scandalous about poetry? It appears so from the number of attacks on it and defenses it has inspired over the centuries. Has the alleged cause of offense been the same thing or many things throughout history? Have the apologists tended over time to make the same kinds of arguments? Have the arguments been adequate? Is it a good thing, this offense? These are some of the questions that I hope to answer, in passing, as I argue that poetry's main value is, in fact, its offensiveness, that some of the principal or usual characteristics of poetry are in themselves offensive, and that in our time poetry should be defended *as* offensive.[2] Further, I argue that poetry's potentially ethical nature is part and parcel of its offensiveness, but this ethic cannot be expressed as a message of a set of moral principles or even ultimately in interpretation. Indeed, this fact about poetry is its ultimate scandal and offense.

My title takes "offense" in an additional way beyond those indicated above. Offense the reader may take to include defense, and the best defense must include, as I indicate, offensiveness. So I am proposing to write here

---

1. Owen Barfield, *History in English Words* (London: Faber and Faber, 1962), 96.
2. My argument is quite different from that of Anthony Julius's *Transgressions: The Offences of Art* (London: Thames and Hudson, 2002). Julius is concerned with a specific period in art history that he calls transgressive (roughly the past 150 years) and not with offense in my sense.

an offense of poetry as well as write *about* its true offensiveness, accusations against it, and the defenses that have been made of it. Most important for me is not, however, defense in the traditional sense but the twofold meaning of offense mentioned already, which I identify with the Greek *scandalon* as it appears in the Bible.

Biblical and Secular Offense

My colleague David McCracken has written a very interesting book called *The Scandal of the Gospels: Jesus, Story, and Offense*, and because both story and offense are important to my argument, I shall steal from him here at the outset as much as I can without, I hope, unbearable offense.[3] McCracken points out that *scandalon* is variously translated in the Revised Standard Version as cause for stumbling, cause for sin, difficulty, hindrance, hindrance in the way, pitfall, stumbling block, temptation, and temptation to sin (7). This is an impressive array, and the Bible, as McCracken argues, is serious as well as emphatic about the importance of offense, indeed the necessity of offense for faith. Jesus's acts, his very being, and even the Bible itself are scandals. Jesus continually puts in the way of his disciples stumbling blocks in the form of puzzling parables, other sayings, and acts. Furthermore, his very existence in the Bible as the incarnate Son of God is an offense to reason, as is the Bible itself. Jesus is a scandal and an offense, and he requires that the disciples and anyone else who comes along, including the Bible's readers, must confront the *scandalon* and pass through it to active faith. For faith to occur, according to McCracken, there must be the possibility of offense (167).

It is the Bible as narrative that interests McCracken. Indeed, it is the Bible's narrative nature that is part of its offense. He makes a distinction between narrative and a verbal vehicle that carries a message. The former is as confounding as it is revealing, and interpretation that reduces it to a message (for instance, a moralism) misses the point, for one must enter into

---

3. David McCracken, *The Scandal of the Gospels: Jesus, Story, and Offense* (New York and Oxford: Oxford University Press, 1994).

the story and gain its experience by imaginative involvement. Jesus's parables and the stories about him are of this narrative sort and often illustrate inside themselves their scandalous defiance of interpretation. McCracken observes that there has been a tendency for biblical interpreters to suppress the offensiveness of the stories and parables in order to "domesticate" them and "nullify [their] dangerous powers" (6).

Hans Frei takes the view that early readings of the Bible were realistic, that is, literal and historical; but there came a time when, among interpreters, a break occurred between the literal and the historical. From then on, the biblical stories had to fit external history, whereas at an earlier time, history was put into conformance with the biblical story. Figural or typological readings, which gave to the Bible a single narrative shape with beginning, middle, and end, fell out of favor—thus the title of Frei's book, *The Eclipse of Biblical Narrative: A Study of Eighteenth and Nineteenth Century Hermeneutics*.[4] There was left for interpreters either the way of moral allegorization or as much of external history as could be salvaged. One might say, then, that the Bible first contained history, but history later contained the Bible.

McCracken gives attention to a number of parables, each of which is a narrative within a narrative. He notes that frequently the disciples, to Jesus's displeasure, do not understand his parables. Often the parables are offensively obscure. McCracken discusses the well-known story of Jesus's encounter with the Canaanite woman, an event in which Jesus gives offense. I quote it in full in the Revised Standard Version as it is told by Matthew (5:21–28):

And Jesus went away from there and withdrew to the district of Tyre and Sidon. And behold, a Canaanite woman from that region came out and cried, "Have mercy on me, O Lord, Son of David; my daughter is severely possessed by a demon." But he did not answer her a word. And his disciples came and begged him, saying, "Send her

---

4. Hans Frei, *The Eclipse of Biblical Narrative: A Study of Eighteenth and Nineteenth Century Hermeneutics* (New Haven, CT: Yale University Press, 1974).

away, for she is crying after us." He answered, "I was sent only to the lost sheep of the house of Israel." But she came and knelt before him, saying, "Lord help me." And he answered, "It is not fair to take this children's bread and throw it to the dogs." She said, "Yes, Lord, yet even dogs eat the crumbs that fall from their master's table." Then Jesus answered her, "O woman, great is your faith! Be it done for you as you desire." And her daughter was healed instantly.

Like McCracken, I am interested in the passage's narrative reading. He quite rightly sees the central issue of the passage as one of a collision with offense that produces faith undeterred by the offense. He points out that interpreters have frequently refused to recognize the offensiveness of what Jesus says to the woman, whom he calls, in effect, a gentile bitch. Moreover, Jesus is twice offensive in that he proceeds to attribute greatness of faith to her while, in an almost immediately previous passage, the disciples tell him that he has offended the Pharisees by accusing them of lack of faith. Furthermore, Jesus appears to have been offensively irritated at the disciple Peter for failing to understand what he has said, causing Jesus to have to interpret his own words.

McCracken remarks that other interpreters see in the passage a play of wit by the woman that appeals to Jesus and leads him to work the miracle. This reading need not conflict with the theme of offense and faith (or, rather, faith achieved by passing into and through offense). Indeed, it is tied up with it. As I see it, the woman by her response extends the narrative situation in a dramatic way and thus enters into Jesus's offense. When she responds, she does so actively, whereas, previous to Jesus's meeting with her, Peter responded passively to a parable. There the narrative simply ended, and Jesus's reply to Peter was an allegorical interpretation of his parable, to which there is no dialogical answer or continuation. There can be only passive obedience or negative disobedience to the message of the moral law. There is no entrance into the event. It should be no surprise that after Peter's failure Jesus is said to have gone "away from there," subsequently meeting the Canaanite woman. The woman's active response in extending the metaphor of the dog is an imaginative act as well as one of faith, and perhaps the Bible is committing an offense in making one equal to the other. In any case, it seems that we find here the Jesus of whom William Blake wrote in a deliberately offensive poem,

> I am sure this Jesus will not do
> Either for Englishman or Jew[.][5]

It is interesting to observe that Blake here makes Jesus offensive to both sides of an imagined opposition. This is a stance that I shall later characterize as "antithetical."

In the story of the Canaanite woman, the reader has to confront a narrative action of considerable drama, not an abstract idea or message. For the reader, there is the risk of collision with offense, not just the offensive words of Jesus, but the offense of narrative, of a certain gesture, and of metaphor.

The notion I shall try to develop, paralleled by that of offense in the Bible, is that great poetry is itself offensive and that readers must confront and pass through the offense, which is a moment of challenge, crisis, and decision generated out of the prevailing cultural view of language, its appropriate uses, and its characteristics.

If one misses the offense of Jesus and the Bible or is simply offended and nothing more, one has not grasped the nature of Christianity. The offense of poetry is, of course, a secular one, in and of time and history. One cannot say that poetry has always been and ever will be offensive or that all poetry is offensive. But the most intense and concentrated is; even some very bad poetry has a certain value as doubly offensive, as chapter 12 will show. Poetry challenges readers with a manifold of offenses, documented as such in attacks on it over centuries. Teachers of poetry, especially poetry written in verse, can attest to its offensiveness simply by reporting on the results of dislike and impatience among their students—active hatred, sullen resistance, passive obedience to academic demands for paraphrase and interpretation, or active avoidance when it is announced as the subject of a course of study. Poetry's secular challenge to readers might seem to be, initially at least, its difficulty, often referred to as obscu-

5. David V. Erdman, ed., "The Everlasting Gospel," *The Complete Poetry and Prose of William Blake*, rev. ed. (Garden City, NY: Anchor Press/Doubleday, 1982), 524.

rity.[6] But difficulty has a very broad range. It is not always the source of offense, and an offense is not always a difficulty. In Part II, I offer what I regard as certain principal forms of offense—gesture, drama, fiction, and trope—and discuss difficulty briefly by way of conclusion. Each of these forms can be described as contributing to the *presentational* character of poetry. The term "presentational" I find first used in connection with forms of art by the philosopher Susanne K. Langer.[7] I use it to indicate that poetry does not speak, that we readers speak *about* it, and it is present, as Wallace Stevens suggested, as a "nature" to be spoken about. As with drama, it presents itself as something that happens. It evokes *our* speaking, if only to ourselves. It evokes active mental response. There is a sense in which poetry is not ethical and a sense in which it is. It is not, in that it does not speak but presents. It is, in that it challenges us to confront and pass through offense to active mental involvement. Each of the offenses I discuss is and has been a stumbling block in a cultural history that has privileged the abstract verbal concept over poetic forms of particularity, has had a deep suspicion of drama as falsity, has opposed fact to fiction, and has wanted its language straightforward and free of unnecessary ornament. It is fair to say that these views are ingrained (to various depths) in all of us, even though they may not be commonly recognized as such. Poetry does not come to annihilate such views, which are products of a cultural development no one should want to obliterate. They have their value. Rather, poetry provides within that development a necessary active opposition. But more of that later.

Writing and reading may have been the vehicles, even the causes, of the emergence of the views that poetry opposes. Story-telling and audience preceded story-writing and story-reading. Plato reverts to story when he has a character in *Phaedrus* deplore the invention of writing in fear that people's memories will be severely weakened if information is stored in books rather than in the memory. Perhaps, however, the loss that should

6. On difficulty from the point of view of the problem of teaching, see Alan C. Purves, ed., *The Idea of Difficulty in Literature* (Albany: State University of New York Press, 1991). It includes my essay "The Difficulty of Difficulty," 23–50.

7. Susanne K. Langer, *Philosophy in a New Key* (Cambridge, MA: Harvard University Press, 1942), esp. chapter 4.

have been most feared was the loss of human immediacy and relation when a text replaces a teller. Perhaps the result was readerly suspicion and eventual distrust of the characteristics of story itself.

In the history of attacks on poetry, perhaps from the time that stories were transferred to written texts, these objects of distrust—gesture, drama, fiction, trope—have been confronted and found offensive. However, as I shall try to show in my survey of attacks in chapter 2, the attacks have often displayed or masked a certain ambivalence, indicating suppressed respect and sometimes even affection. Unfortunately, the defenses that have been mounted, subjects of chapter 3, have often been unable to escape encompassment of their language by that of the attackers. My proposing an offense of poetry would resist the inadequate vocabulary of past defenses.

Secular offense challenges readers to confront these stumbling blocks and pass through them. One of the first literary theorists in the West offered a psychological version of such a passage. Aristotle spoke of a *catharsis* of pity and fear undergone by the viewers of tragedy and implied the setting in of a resultant calm. Although Plato was certainly not talking about the experience of poetry in his famous allegory of the cave in *Republic*, the movement he described from shadows to the light has something of the same shape, as the person going into the light is at first blinded. But, for Plato, the poets were at the very least complicit in the making of the shadows. What are the shadows that readers of poetry face? Among them are the notions that there is something primitive, threatening, and purely emotional about poetry and its refusal to accept certain commonsense assumptions: that fact is always superior to fiction, that there is a real life and a false life (the latter being identified with drama and deception), that language is adequately defined as a tool of communication, and that tropes stand in the way of clarity and are at best only rhetorical decorations. The offenses of poetry exist *as offenses* because of these aged cultural prejudices and poets' stubborn insistence on mounting offenses against them.

Poetry's offenses are challenges to a way of thought that too narrowly circumscribes experience. The secular passage through and beyond them is not into religious faith, but it is similar in that it enlarges for the imagination the grasp of what is truly desirable and what is not. Teachers of verse know that these offenses have barred many readers from this experience, but they know also of those whose attitudes, affections, and capacities for knowledge have been changed by the confrontation.

For such teachers and readers there is, however, like the test of faith achieved, the danger of dulled familiarity with a poem, resulting perhaps in the failure to sense the tension of confrontation with it that demands renewal with every reading, perhaps a willing half-suspension of experience. Or perhaps earlier readings had been unsuccessful in some way and later ones dulled by familiarity. John Keats wrote a sonnet about facing an experience of rereading:

On Sitting Down To Read King Lear *Once Again*

O golden tongued Romance with serene lute!
    Fair plumed Syren! Queen of far away!
    Leave melodizing on this wintry day,
Shut up thine olden pages, and be mute:
Adieu! For once again the fierce dispute,   5
    Betwixt damnation and impassion'd clay
    Must I burn through; once more humbly assay
The bitter-sweet of the Shakespearean fruit.
Chief Poet! And ye clouds of Albion,
    Begetters of our deep eternal theme,   10
When through the old oak forest I am gone,
    Let me not wander in a barren dream,
But when I am consumed in the fire,
Give me new Phoenix wings to fly at my desire.[8]

This poem begins with expression of desire to leave the romantic world, the mythical "old oak forest" of Keats's earlier poetry, to be consumed and reborn as a different kind of poet. It appears that he is driven to do this, but with some reluctance, even perhaps fear, which must be met by deter-

8. My transcription is from Clarence DeWitt Thorpe, ed., *John Keats: Selected Poems and Letters* (New York: Odyssey Press, 1935), 208.

mination. The catalyst for this change is to be his rereading of *King Lear*.[9] It is as if he had recognized poetical power in his first or earlier readings, but apparently there was not then the result that he now seeks. He had passed through the fire, both a torment and a purgation, of the play, but he seems not in any larger sense actually to have gained from the experience. He no longer sees it merely as a test of his ability to endure the fire. He now recognizes the play as an offense against an earlier self that he has come to identify with serenity and perhaps innocence. The word "assay" of line 7 suggests attempt, judgment, and testing; and it has a history of identification with the analysis of precious metals. It offers strenuous difficulty, but also reward. Earlier, he seems not to have met this test. The poet's whole being will now be put at stake. I suggest that the primary offenses of this poem about offense are its drama of uneasiness, difficulty, and desire and the implication that the reading of a fiction can have so profound an effect. But more of specific offenses in chapters 4 to 7.

I would like to offer here a perhaps more problematic test case of offense. I have deliberately chosen what seems to be a relatively simple poem to illustrate poetic offense. It is a poem that at least used to be taught in secondary schools. No one to my knowledge has charged Edwin Arlington Robinson's "Richard Cory" with obscurity. Perhaps it has been declared to be about an enigma, but not obscure about it. We might well remind ourselves of Blake's remark that there is a great gulf between simplicity and insipidity.

> Whenever Richard Cory went down town,
> We people on the pavement looked at him:
> He was a gentleman from sole to crown,
> Clean favored and imperially slim.
>
> And he was always quietly arrayed,   5
> And he was always human when he talked;

---

9. "Rereading" has for some time been a tiresome cliché among academic critics, who can't seem to admit that they haven't read everything at least once. Apart from this, "rereading" has come to mean putting the work through the grinding mill of a currently fashionable theory and its terminology.

But still he fluttered pulses when he said,
"Good morning," and he glittered when he walked.

And he was rich—yes, richer than a king—
And admirably schooled in every grace: 10
In fine, we thought that he was everything
To make us wish we were in his place.

So on we worked, and waited for the light,
And went without the meat, and cursed the bread;
And Richard Cory, one calm summer night,   15
Went home and put a bullet through his head.[10]

The gesture here, as always, has to do with what is not said but presented verbally nonetheless. There is the appearance of detachment in it, as if the speaker views himself as only a reporter, thinks that the facts can speak for themselves and that they need not be ornamented by even the least amount of hyperbole. This is not true, of course, for the poem is actually shot through with it: Cory's *imperial* slimness, the *fluttering* pulses, his being *richer than a king*. These are clichés or close to being so, appropriate because part of a public view of the man, the speaker being both one person and many. The most prominent trope is "glittering," a liberty taken with the word's literal sense. It is a kind of fiction.

The usual view of fiction, going all the way back to Plato, is that there are facts and truth and there are fictions, untruths, lies, illusions. But poems oppose this distinction between fact and falsity *with* their fictions. As in the form of all metaphors, Richard Cory glitters and does not glitter, and this apparent contradiction is an accurate representation of the way the poem's people see him. One has to pass beyond the opposition of fact to fiction as untruth into the realm of fiction itself and accept that fiction is not inferior to fact. Falsity is.

The speaker of the poem offers no answers, no psychological expla-

10. My transcription is from Edwin Arlington Robinson, *Collected Poems* (New York: Macmillan, 1924), 82.

nation, and no explicitly personal response to the story he tells. Nevertheless, his is a dramatic performance in its very refusal to be dramatic in the expected sense. This seems to have the effect of heightening the intensity of the not quite suppressed class resentment of lines 13 and 14. Is there something offensive about the detachment (as far as it goes)? I think so. The detachment, which some would call irony, is unsettling because, first, it doesn't seem to respond in shock to a shocking event but instead passes the shock on to us, and second, it does not deliver explanation. It is a gesture that leaves us momentarily incapable of analysis. We are challenged. There is no relief, even though the poem closes formally and certainly powerfully. A likely response would be to provide the conclusion that we might think the poem ought to have been required to give us—some moral truth: appearances are deceiving, wealth does not make happiness. I suspect that the academic demand for interpretation has often evoked such student responses. But that is to ward off the poem's offenses and reject the clash with enigma. The classic example of comment on a situation like this is Coleridge's remark to Mrs. Barbauld that he feared his "Rime of the Ancient Mariner" obtruded moral sentiment too openly on the reader. He was, of course, referring to the last few lines of that poem.

I seem to have been speaking of prejudices. I think the prejudices against offense are not only inevitable but also necessary to the moments of confrontation and passage. Furthermore, they should survive somewhere in the mind. A world run entirely by poetic imagination would be just as intolerable as one run entirely by whatever we call its enemy.

Contraries and Antitheticality

Poetry's special kind of offense is what I call its "antitheticality," a term I have stolen from W. B. Yeats, though he did not coin it.[11] One of the sources

11. Yeats employs the term in *A Vision* (New York: Macmillan, 1938). Harold Bloom, in *The Anxiety of Influence: A Theory of Poetry* (New York: Oxford University Press, 1973), uses "antithetical," and his use is also derived principally from Yeats but differs from mine in two ways. First, it comes out of Yeats's notion of the poet as an antithetical type of personality (as opposed to a primary one). Second, it is not identified with contrariety in Blake's sense. Bloom sees what he calls "strong" poets as antithetical to their poetic predecessors

of the Yeatsian antithetical is Blake's notion of contraries, mentioned in scattered passages in Blake's work. It first appears in *The Marriage of Heaven and Hell*, where reason is declared contrary to energy, being its "bound or outward circumference" (34), the form that energy takes at any given time. But reason and energy can be debased into good and evil respectively by those religious and secular authorities with the power to suppress. Under these conditions, reason becomes dominant and controls what is to be declared good and evil. Along with this come systematic accusation of sin and the threat of eternal punishment against the energetic. Energy becomes offensive. In *The Marriage*, Blake's energetic devil therefore sides with evil. He also defends the body against the soul. Later, in his poem *Milton*, Blake enlarges his concept of contrariety and considers the oppositions soul-body, good-evil, and object-subject to be "negations" or "cloven fictions," in which the first of each of these dyads dominates at the second's expense. True contraries would have to express opposition to these negating oppositions. To embrace the second term of the dyad would not be enough. This new kind of contrariety would not seek the tyrannical victory over and even annihilation of its "cloven" opposite but would recognize it as a fiction and

---

in misinterpreting them through "revisionary ratios." He offers six, among which are interpretive "swerves" and "completion" of the predecessor's work by a kind of opposition to it. Each misinterpretation also inevitably affirms a relationship to the predecessor. Bloom's theory is a psychology of the poet, or, rather, poets, since for Bloom the poet has no identity in the usual sense. The theory is one of the travail of modern (roughly post-Renaissance) poets in a Cartesian world of subjectivity and alienation. My use of "antithetical" comes also out of Yeats, but it is not based on Yeats's view of the poet's personality. (I take no position on this matter.) Instead, it emphasizes how poems, as in Blake's notion of "contrariety," are antithetical to the primary dualistic assumptions of the tribe, one of which is that of subject and object, secondary and primary (in John Locke's terms). Poems may or may not exhibit Bloom's neo-Freudian "anxiety of influence."

Bloom argues for an antithetical criticism that would have three phases: (1) reading the predecessor poet as his great descendants did, (2) reading the descendants as if we were their disciples, (3) measuring the first swerve against the second. This means that we cannot really read the descendants until they have "disciples not ourselves."

Criticism in this theory tends to become prose poetry. Bloom's theory is "strong" in his sense of that term, and I cannot do justice to it here. In my view, criticism is or should be ironic about itself, knowing that it fails to read with finality but keeps the conversation going for the sake of cultural life.

stand in intellectual warfare, which is intellectual conversation, with it, thereby opposing the domination of either side, even its own.

In Blake's *Milton*, this third force is called (in a parody of John Calvin) the "reprobate," which arrives to oppose the corruption of reason and the suppression of energy. The corrupters are the "elect," fixed in their view, who would condemn those Blake calls the "redeemed" (really the redeemable) to damnation. The reprobate's contrariety to and pressure on negating power allow the possibility of energy's expansion of the boundary that reason continually puts around it. In Milton's final speech in Blake's *Milton* (2: 40[46]–41[48], 142–43), which is Milton's own self-redemptive act, the reprobate is identified with inspired poetry, as against the elect, who can do no more than merely pretend to election. Milton declares that he returns to earth from heaven "to cast aside from Poetry, all that is not Inspiration" (142). The elect do not disappear, but their power is energetically opposed. They are not redeemed but "Created continually" (1: 5, 98) in the historical process. With the reprobate and the redeemed, they remain one of the three classes of men. These classes are, as Blake says, the "Two Contraries & the Reasoning Negative" (98). The elect are the negative suppressive force. The reprobate and the redeemed are the contraries, the reprobate being the offensive redeemer. The redeemed are capable, but with difficulty, of passing through the offense of the reprobate. This merely scandalizes the elect. We readers are either elect or redeemed in the fire of the poem.

For Blake, reason and energy are never resolved into one. In *The Marriage of Heaven and Hell*, they appear also as "devourer" and "prolific," and Blake says of them, "These two classes of men are always upon earth, & they should be enemies; whoever tries to reconcile them seeks to destroy existence" (40). They are the analytical divisive user and the creative provider. Later, Blake distinguishes between two kinds of enmity, one of physical warfare, which is negation, and the other of conversation (or dialectic), which is true contrariety. In *Milton*, Blake writes that there is a place where "Contrarieties are equally True" (129). He does not mean that they are synthesized. Rather, each is perfectly itself. This place Blake calls Beulah, the land of marriage in the Bible and in Blake the source of poetry in imaginative dreaming, a fictive area where no negation can come.

The refusal of synthesis marks an important difference between what has been called Blake's dialectic and that of Hegel. Hegel's ultimate synthesis shows poetry giving way to the pure abstractions of philosophy. For Blake, contrariety is perpetual and stands against Hegelian history, which would be for Blake a cyclical process to be identified as negation. For Blake, so-called synthesis is always going to be a situation in which one side of an opposition becomes dominant and oppressive, imposing a "system," the very thing that he would have thought Hegel attempted to do. Thus, for Blake, any annihilation of oppositions by a transcendent third term merely repeats the crime of negation and suppression. Blake's reprobate stands for what we might call "antisystem" against system, which always negates by exclusion. It also stands for poetry.

Blakean contrariety is opposed to the form of opposition to system that we find in the movement known as Deconstruction. This is true insofar as Deconstruction emphasizes the differential nature of language at the expense of sameness. Blake would have seen this as a negation much as he would have seen Plato suppressing difference in favor of the same. In Blake's view, language was originally and is still fundamentally poetic, capable of producing new possibilities (prolific), which are then taken up and used (devoured) by the culture. The problem here is to maintain prolific power in the face of culture's tendency to use up linguistic formulations, eventually stultifying intuitions into abstractions that lead to fixities of law and cessation of intellectual movement. This is why Blake resists allegory when it is personification of abstract ideas.

Contrary opposition to the object's negation of the subject is expressed frequently by Blake with one of his fundamental tropes, that of "center" and "circumference," "contraction" and "expansion." A center represents the shrinking of the imaginative containment of one's experience to a situation in which that experience is entirely outside oneself in the form of an epistemological object or unsympathetic nature. The subject becomes passive, and the object dominates in the form of an alien, imprisoning, external force. A circumferential position signifies the bringing of one's experience into oneself or the extension of oneself outward, breaking down the alienation of self and other.

It should be clear that Blake's identification of inspired poetry with the reprobate advocacy of contrariety is an offense and a scandal in much the same way that Jesus's acts and parables are offenses, and that the Bible, which Blake called the "Great Code of Art" (274), resists interpretation. Interpretation makes the moral law, and Blake says of this, "If Morality was Christianity Socrates was the Saviour" (275).

This brings me to Yeats's antitheticality. In *A Vision*, Yeats thinks of Blake as an antithetical personality and identifies Blake's contrariety with the antithetical, which he sees as contrary to what he calls the "primary." Yeats apparently got the term from John Locke's *Essay Concerning Human Understanding*, in which Locke calls objectivity primary and subjectivity secondary, thereby (in Blake's terms) negating the latter. Yeats's antitheticality, though sometimes he uses "subjective" for it, is contrary to this negating opposition and is identified with artistic temperament and a logic opposed to system.

The only work known to me that employs if not a similar, at least an almost parallel sort of terminology is Virgil Nemoianu's provocative *A Theory of the Secondary: Literature, Progress, and Reaction*.[12] It is a work with which, it will be seen, I have sympathy, though a few differences. It is itself a defense of literature, to some extent against the eager systematization of recent literary theory and criticism. Nemoianu distinguishes between what he calls the "principal" and the "secondary." The principal is all that is central to culture and its needs: "social justice and economic progress, control of the natural environment and salvation of the soul, sexuality and hunger, cognitive expansion and actualization of potentialities," also various "explanatory systems," by which I assume he means physical systems or even literary theories (xii). The secondary, which includes literature, enacts the drama of relationships such as "hegemony and subjugation, revolt and harmony, anarchy and order" (xii). He goes on to claim that any hegemonic regime will find literature to be an "irritant, even a *scandalon*," and he identifies literature with "irrationality and randomness . . . surprise, rejection, and dispersion" (5). It is this last part of his argument of which I am skeptical, in part because it identifies the irritant

12. Virgil Nemoianu, *A Theory of the Secondary: Literature, Progress, and Reaction* (New Haven, CT: Yale University Press, 1974).

almost wholly with subject matter or content, while I identify it with a way of thought and expression.

Nemoianu's "principal" and "secondary" seem to bear the trace of John Locke's epistemological distinction between primary and secondary qualities of experience, objectivity, and subjectivity. Nemoianu is not the first to identify the secondary with irrationality, an identification I do not accept. But his interest is not epistemological. It is historical and theoretical, and he sees the secondary in its manifold manifestations as opposed in a reactionary way to history, by which he means the flow of events and its supposedly (on the whole) progressive movement. His ironic view is that historical progress would exhaust itself without the reactive opposition of the secondary, which allows it to escape entropy by introducing something other into the system, making possible a new progression.[13]

But after identifying literature with one side of a dialectical opposition (history and art), Nemoianu goes on to characterize literature as trying to "strike a balance between the chief clashing ideologies of the age." It is a "compromise," a "balance of oppositions" (9).

Here I disagree with him, and I believe Blake is with me. It appears to me that Nemoianu is struggling to make a two-term system do work that requires three or maybe four terms. Just as Locke's secondary-primary opposition is for Blake a negation, in which one side gains ascendancy at the expense of the other, so does Nemoianu's principal-secondary opposition risk the same cyclicity. But Nemoianu is too sophisticated to allow this cyclicity quite to rule, so he must displace the secondary from itself, so to speak, to a role in which it never gains the ascendancy but instead provides periodic incursions that give new life to the principal. On the other hand, he sometimes, as I have indicated, sees the secondary as a mediating force between competing ideologies or between history as progress and the messy potentialities of things in general. There is also a third Nemoianu who declares that there can be no rapproche-

---

13. His view seems to recall Blake's statement in *The Marriage of Heaven and Hell*, "Without Contraries is no progression" (34), and would seem to explain Yeats's attack, in *A Vision*, on the "happy counter-myth of progress" (262).

ment: "Literary discourse as dissent must be not only an alternative and a reservoir but a road block [more than a stumbling block, I think]; it does not modify, it denies" (16). This doesn't sound at all like mediation, and there is no passage through a road block to the progress promised by the reactionary force that for him literature is, at least according to his first position above.

What I call the antithetical is the third term that arises to oppose but not negate all systems of two-term cyclicity, all the two-term negations that Blake opposed, and more. I would go so far as to declare that there is a fourth, which is the *form* or *relation* of the opposition (Blake's "mental fight" or intellectual warfare) between the antithetical and the negations. This opposition cannot be resolved. The antithetical can stand against negations in an effort to redeem them and revive "progression," but it cannot annihilate them or gain hegemony. This would be to repeat the crime of suppressive negation that it came to oppose. Nemoianu comes around to saying something like this when he declares that the secondary cannot become the principal.[14]

Nor can the negations ever quite annihilate the antithetical, though from time to time cries of fear that this will occur are heard. For Blake, such a moment would be that in which everything reaches the limits of "opacity" and "contraction," absolute condensation like that represented by Dante's Satan in a block of ice at the center of the earth. This is Nemoianu's "entropy."

In my view, the reader of poetry must confront and pass beyond the stumbling block of poetry, pass through offense. That offense has been generated by a long history of suspicion extending into our own time and tacitly if not explicitly taught in the form of criticism of poetry's lack of usefulness, often its obscurity, and its disregard for empirical truth. Barfield describes collision with poetic offense when he speaks of "'a felt change of consciousness,' where 'consciousness' embraces all my aware-

---

14. However, there must have been a time when the present secondary *was* the principal—in what came to be called "mythical cultures." See my remarks on Vico in chapter 8.

ness of my surroundings at any given moment, and 'surroundings' includes my own feelings. By 'felt' I mean to signify that the change itself is noticed, or attended to."[15] The refusal of attention is the refusal to pass through offense.

The demand for attention, which may, in fact, seem to the reader a repulsion, may be poetry's ultimate offense. It is akin to destabilization, expressed by Arthur Koestler as "bisociation": "the perceiving of a situation or an idea . . . in two self-consistent but habitually incompatible frames of reference."[16] It requires thinking on more than a single plane, or confronting a second plane so that "the balance of both emotion and thought is disturbed" (36). Koestler is discussing mainly the moment of humor and laughter, but he also offers as an example the *Oedipus*, in which two notions of the love of the mother (if we read as Freud did) clash unexpectedly. This brings the imagination to crisis, requiring a third plane antithetical to but not negating the strife of the two.

Criticism and the Reductive

Before I pass further into my argument, I must take note of some books pertaining to my subject. In 1995, Mark Edmundson published the only recent explicit and extended defense of poetry known to me. In it, he discusses almost exclusively literary theory of the last forty years. There are detailed treatments of the work of Paul de Man, Jacques Derrida, Michel Foucault, the New Historicists, and Harold Bloom. Prior to these discussions, he argues that in many respects the literary theory of this period comes out of Plato's attack on the poets. He adds that some theorists, including all of those just listed, apply principles to literature that are not often critically examined, are generally reductive, and do not permit rebuttal: " . . . most literary criticism now begins by assuming that the questions that ought to be its chief matter for debate—questions about the relations between literature and variously insinuated languages—are already resolved. Criticism now often assumes that the correct procedure exclusively entails the appli-

---

15. Owen Barfield, *Poetic Diction* (1928) (New York: McGraw-Hill, 1964), 48.
16. Arthur Koestler, *The Act of Creation* (1964) (New York: Dell, 1967), 35.

cation of various vocabularies, often social-scientific in provenance, to the concept at hand."[17]

Edmundson observes that literature is "never simply innocent" (66), but he holds that criticism should address "the power of poetry to resist assimilation to fixed terminologies" (238), should not just apply theories to literary works but "create rejoinders" (235) on their behalf, and show how literature provides "resources for answering our worst doubts about it" (66). I am in agreement with these views, and I have not discussed in my chapters on attack and defense the recent theorists to whom Edmundson gives attention. Edmundson finds conscious friendliness and unconscious enmity toward poetry among the critics he studies and in most of the criticism that follows out of them. As I show, the history of ambivalence toward poetry does not begin in recent times.

I have proposed that poetic offense is potentially ethical or can result in the ethical. Another book of 1995 addresses the question of the ethics of narrative. Adam Zachary Newton is interested in the ethical power of an "interactive" relation binding "narrator and listener, author and character, or reader and text."[18] His location of the ethical quality is different from mine, though not in contradiction to it. He says of the criticism of narrative what Edmundson says of the criticism of poetry: "To truncate narrative discourse by fitting it to a scientific model it overreaches is to impoverish it" (54). He approaches the notion of offense in the remark, "It is ethics . . . which becomes the 'perturbatory' element rather than the 'resolving' one" (54) in literature. It seems to me that both of the books I have mentioned show that there is a turning away from reductive theory and the criticism growing out of it. I am more than willing to identify what follows with that turn.

More recent books brought to my attention when this study was substantially completed continue to make this turn. They head in a direction

---

17. Mark Edmundson, *Literature Against Philosophy, Plato to Derrida: A Defence of Poetry* (Cambridge: Cambridge University Press, 1995), 195. The title is a bit of a misnomer. Edmundson does not discuss criticism between Plato and Derrida and discusses much that postdates Derrida's early influential work. Nor does Edmundson discuss poetic texts, but then most past defenses don't.

18. Adam Zachary Newton, *Narrative Ethics* (Cambridge, MA: Harvard University Press, 1995), 13.

similar to mine, though they offer different arguments and concern themselves with different theoretical and literary works. Frank B. Farrell's densely written *Why Does Literature Matter?* (2004) takes a phenomenological tack. He notes that modern Western thought has first dissolved the world to "mind or subjectivity"; then the epistemological subject has in turn been "dissolved into language"; and later the linguistic has been dissolved into "social practices, into patterns of social power."[19] In each of these cases, there has occurred, according to Farrell, a "reduction and thinning out" of meaning of literary works. He is particularly concerned with reduction in the procedures of cultural studies. He sees no reason to "endorse that process but rather to bring into view experiences that resist it, that refuse the glib shallowness that the turn to theory and to cultural studies may encourage in the reading of literature" (45).

Farrell's argument, if not specifically "antithetical," appears to have similar ends. In my view, a theory ought to *emerge* from the direct experience of literary texts rather than proceed from an established view to which they must conform or fail to measure up. Except for his emphasis on subjectivity, as in phenomenology, I am in agreement with Farrell when he argues, "Meaning cannot be accounted for, whether in epistemic space or literary space, without a commitment to richer versions of the world and of subjectivity than these radical turns can allow for."[20] I applaud his call for "a more internalist account of literary space, that is, one that supposes it to be a privileged space whose power depends more on its particular arrangements than on the social context" (9).[21]

19. Frank. B. Farrell, *Why Does Literature Matter?* (Ithaca, NY, and London: Cornell University Press, 2004), 5. I presented a similar history in the introduction to my anthology *Critical Theory Since Plato*, rev. ed. (Fort Worth, TX: Harcourt Brace Jovanovich, 1992), 3–8, and again in the 3rd ed. (Boston: Thomson/Wadsworth, 2004), 2–6.

20. My concern about phenomenological language is that its use of "subjectivity" drags along a latent notion of an epistemological subject that requires an object to which it is secondary. Subjectivity, after its long history, might best be dispensed with in phenomenological analysis.

21. Farrell's use of "space" throughout his book does not refer to a spatial content but rather to something like a "symbolic form" as in Ernst Cassirer's *Philosophy of Symbolic Forms*, trans. Ralph Manheim, 3 vols. (New Haven, CT: Yale University Press, 1953–57) and *An Essay on Man: An Introduction to a Philosophy of Human Culture* (New Haven, CT: Yale University Press, 1944).

In the same year, Angus Fletcher published *A New Theory for American Poetry* and asserted, "We need to rescue poetry from an uncritical belief (very strong among academic ideologues, both left and right) that literature is covertly an arm of ideological affirmation."[22] What Fletcher describes as Walt Whitman's use of "phrase" is similar to an aspect of what I call "gesture," and he invokes drama with respect to Whitman when he refers to "a drama of the poet's own thinking" (107) in a way that suggests my treatment of a poem as a dramatic presentation.

This notion also appears in Statis Gourgouris's *Does Literature Think?* with the author's attempt to appropriate the term "theory" for literature itself by claiming that literature thinks theoretically.[23] This "intrinsic theoretical capacity" (11) is for him a "performative matter," that is, it is fundamentally, as I think of it, dramatic. Gourgouris refers to Pierre Machery's idea of "staging" in support of his view.[24] Because literature is performative, it is "against the law"(79), which Gourgouris identifies with the antimythical against the mythical character of literature. These are terms that I offered in *Philosophy of the Literary Symbolic*.[25] He goes on to argue that literature "must pose its object each time anew—to instantiate it performatively—so it cannot be judged in terms other to it . . . " (80). Thus it violates the law of antimythical thought. Gourgouris writes out of a modern European tradition and employs different sources and, on the whole, a vocabulary different from mine except for the myth-antimyth distinction.

All three of these books work toward ends that at a high level of generality do not clash with mine. They propose that literature can offer an ethical vision easily lost without attention to literature as a symbolic form with its own nature.

As for the offenses that I discuss, they all seem to me able to contrib-

22. Angus Fletcher, *A New Theory for American Poetry* (Cambridge, MA: Harvard University Press, 2004), 79.

23. Statis Gourgouris, *Does Literature Think? Literature as Theory for an Antimythical Era* (Stanford, CA: Stanford University Press, 2003).

24. His reference is to Machery's *The Object of Literature*, trans. David Macey (Cambridge: Cambridge University Press, 1995), 234.

25. Hazard Adams, *Philosophy of the Literary Symbolic* (Tallahassee: Florida State University Press, 1983). Gourgouris does not cite this book. I do not employ myth and antimyth in the present study.

ute to a specifically poetical ethical vision. In my view, gesture can be ethical in carrying words beyond what is usually regarded as their fundamental capacities. Drama can be ethical because it shapes and calls attention to particular moments of import. Fiction can be ethical because it can imagine beyond our selves to a vision of the ends of human desire and the depths of repugnance. The trope is ethical because it speaks moments of identity. The antithetical stance is ethical because it provides necessary opposition to the dominating negations of the culture. The ethical arises in presentation, demanding imaginative involvement, a challenge to pass into the particularity of events, other minds, sympathetic identification, or active repulsion. Gesture, drama, fiction, and trope, of course, can all occur in writing we do not think of as poetry, but in poetry each has a different kind of role.

The rest of this book is divided into three parts. In Part I, I offer a compressed historical survey of attacks against and defenses of poetry over the centuries. One of my conclusions is that the attacks are often ambivalent, as if the attacker may feel a little embarrassed or even guilty. Another is that most defenses have been trapped in the terms set by the attackers. Though well-intentioned, they fail to make a positive and necessary claim for offense. In writing the chapters of Part I, I wanted to show how repetitious and even ingrained over centuries the attitudes behind attack and defense have been.

In Part II, I study four characteristics of poetry that have been regarded as offensive, the aforementioned gesture, drama, fiction, and trope, and then, at the end, poetry's difficulty or obscurity. Together they do not and are not meant to define poetry or the poetic, but they are some of the properties of poetry, as poetry uses them, that give offense. A certain subject matter chosen by a poet (sometimes leading to censorship) gives offense, but this is not what I am concerned with. Anyone can be deliberately offensive in this way or avoid it, but poetic offense seems to me inevitable by the very nature of its presentational medium. The poet cannot escape committing the offense of one of the four characteristics I mention and still write a successful poem, and poets usually commit all four. By poetry I mean more than those literary objects usually anthologized as such. I include works of prose fiction and plays that approach close to the center of poetic intensity. The poetry-prose distinction, a type of Blakean negation, has always been trouble for literary criticism; and the definitions known to me tend to enclose poetry in a fixed boundary and suppress poetry's power to offend. Poetry evades the definitions most often given to it and is constantly offending against them. It is, I think, fair to say this much: that it is best considered as a way of verbal making, with a logic resisting the confines of logic as we usually think of it. This itself is an offense.

In Part III, I offer some examples of antitheticality that have on occasion puzzled, mystified, irritated, or even in some cases angered critics. In order to illustrate the range of the antithetical, I have deliberately chosen to discuss a philosopher and philologist (Vico) who wrote in behalf of the poetic against the grain of philosophy, a writer of a long poem in verse (Blake), two quite different writers of prose fiction (Cary and Joyce), if that is what one can call Joyce's *Finnegans Wake*, the criticism written by a poet whose criticism fits my notion of the antithetical (Heaney), and finally the odd offense of certain great bad poetry.

Virgil Nemoianu makes an interesting point relevant here when he observes that, in effect, all discourse aspires to the "status" of literature, that is, "towards the privileged enjoyment of liberty, self-referentiality, and a putatively inexhaustible substantiality as expressed in multiple meanings and openness" (185). If Nemoianu is referring to the tendency of language to assert on its own a certain freedom from the intentions of its users, that is one thing. But the human aspiration of much discourse seems to me to have been the opposite. There have even been movements that take as their model for language something approaching the mathematical. I am thinking of logical positivism among those that have left little room for the poetic. But discussion of that matter will have to come later. Nemoianu also reminds us that some texts thought to be literature today were not always so regarded. They achieved that status when their original purposes had been exhausted. It is then that what he calls their poeticality was liberated. This is a complicated matter, and I do not intend to get into it. But, as a coda, I shall discuss poems almost universally regarded as bad and argue that certain offensively bad poems are so heroically bad that they must be regarded as great bad poems. Thus they commit a double offense: the usual one against the reader and one against poetry itself.

I. Historical:
Attack and Defense

2

Attack

Friendly commentators on poetry who are self-confidently on the offensive are less numerous than one might expect. Generally they have been preoccupied with its defense against certain frequently expressed complaints. It is also true that many of those on the attack, though usually earnest, have in one way or another been ambivalent about the very attacks that they have mounted. This ambivalence is present in the best-known and most influential surviving attack, if indeed it can finally be called an attack, that made by Plato's Socrates in *Republic*, and the ambivalence survives in many later writers. If not ambivalence, attackers have often displayed condescension or grudging respect. Because the Platonic attack has been so important in the history of literary criticism and theory, I intend to discuss it and its ambivalence at some length.

The Socratic Attack

Much of the time in Plato's dialogues, Socrates seems to be acknowledging the authority of the Muses of Poetry, whose presence on occasion he invokes. Indeed, poetry seems to be as imbedded in Plato's and Socrates' imagination as it was in Ancient Greek culture generally. Furthermore, in many situations, Socrates' aim seems more to encourage thinking than to lay down a final judgment. Yet through the centuries, Socrates' suspicion of poets, expressed mainly in *Republic*, has been enormously influential, even though more than an equal number of critics have actually invoked Plato or some aspect of Platonism in poetry's defense. Both attackers and defenders have been selective where Plato is concerned. Although Plato on poetry has been much discussed, it is necessary here to look again, keeping in mind that, in *Republic*, at least, it is Socrates who is making the criticisms. The reader must decide whether Socrates is simply Plato's mouthpiece or a fiction of Plato's poetry from whom the author may have some distance.

Socrates' attack is threefold. First, he accuses poets of being third-remove imitators (and thus distorters) of the truth of the Platonic ideas (or forms). To this extent, the attack is an outgrowth of Plato's metaphysics and rises or falls with it.[1] There are moments when Socrates seems somewhat disturbed or at least regretful that he must disparage poetry. The second attack, more telling, perhaps, than the first, is that poets are irrational and thus untrustworthy. Socrates' ambivalence is expressed mainly in making this argument, but there is a connection between this one and the others. The third attack follows directly out of it: poets are liars.[2] Particularly are they impious liars about the gods. It is their untrustworthiness that identifies poets with those objects of Socrates' contempt, the sophists and rhetoricians, people who play with words at the expense of truth.

This view was hardly new with Plato. If we can trust the secondhand (or more) reports of Diogenes Laertius, Pythagoras, when he returned from his descent into Hades, said that "he saw the soul of Hesiod bound fast to a brazen pillar and gibbering, and the soul of Homer hung on a tree with serpents writhing about it, this being their punishment for what they had said about the gods."[3] Heraclitus, too, attacked Homer for the same reason, claiming he "deserved to be chased out of the lists and beaten with rods" (2: 407). To this we can add alleged derogatory remarks by Xenophanes (2: 427), although Diogenes notes that Xenophanes recited poems of his own.

Any mimetic art is, Socrates says in *Republic* (10: 598b), "far removed

---

1. Plato's twofold use of "imitation" is important to note here. The first, metaphysical use involves the relation of idea (form) to its artistic copy. The second, technical use refers to a type of poetry in which the poet does not speak in his own voice, all speakers being dramatic characters. All plays belong to this type. In the first sense, all poets are imitators. In the second, only playwrights are pure imitators; epics are "mixed" forms that include some imitation, as in *Odyssey*, where Odysseus narrates some of his adventures. Lyric poems are not imitative in this second sense, being regarded by Socrates as spoken entirely by the poet.

2. "The Greek words for 'lie' are wider in range of meaning than 'lie' in English and need not imply intention to deceive, but the authority of the teacher-poet depended on his reliability. 'Fiction,' 'imagination,' 'literal (poetic, psychological) truth' are among the terms which the Greeks lacked in discussing literature: 'lie' had come to cover everything from factual error through literary invention to deliberate deceit." Rosemary Harriott, *Poetry and Criticism Before Plato* (London: Methuen and Co., 1969), 112.

3. Diogenes Laertius, *Lives of Eminent Philosophers* (Loeb Classical Library), trans. P. D. Hicks (London: William Heinemann), 2: 339.

from the truth, and this, it seems, is the reason why it can produce everything, because it touches or lays hold on only a small part of the object and that a phantom."[4] It is a delusive copy of a copy. Yet Socrates will allow some poems not imitative in the technical sense into the State as long as they can be of service to it. Lies on behalf of the stability of the State are acceptable. Such poems must not be dirges or lamentations (3: 398d); they must have rhythms appropriate to order (3: 400d), and they must imitate good characters (3: 401b). Imitation, therefore, is not limited to subject matter but includes also the manner of presentation. Or, to put it another way, for Socrates, form always has content, certain rhythms, for example, imitating certain emotions. This kind of imitation may indeed be to his mind the most dangerous, since in his view it speaks to the feelings, and for him the feelings are irrational.

It is interesting to notice the conclusion to one of the attacks in *Republic* (3: 398a–b), where the technically imitative poet, described as a clever deceiver, a wearer of disguises, is ushered from the State. But some poets of the non-imitative sort are not subject to banishment:

> If a man, then, it seems, who was capable by his cunning of assuming every kind of shape and imitating all things should arrive in our city, bringing with himself the poems which he wished to exhibit, we should fall down and worship him as a holy, wondrous, and delightful creature, but should say to him that there is no man of that kind among us in our city, nor is it lawful for such a man to arise among us, and we should send him away to another city, after pouring myrrh down over his head and crowning him with fillets of wool, but we ourselves, for our own souls' good, should continue to employ the more austere and less delightful poet and taleteller, who would imitate the diction of the good man and would tell his tale in the patterns which we prescribed in the beginning, when we set out to educate our soldiers. (3: 398a–b)

---

4. Edith Hamilton and Huntington Cairns, eds., *The Collected Dialogues of Plato* (Princeton, NJ: Princeton University Press, 1963), 823. All quotations from Plato are from this collection of translations.

Socrates knows well enough that the poets who are allowed to remain are not good poets but rather those who might well be subject to the ridicule directed at poetasters or, in our time, the official work of the poets laureate. That before he is exiled, the mimetic poet is to be worshiped as holy and wondrous as well as delightful suggests Socrates' considerable attachment to the old ways even though he is being ironic, or half-ironic, if such a description may be permitted. That attachment could be called superstitious. It is as if Socrates' statement is designed to placate the Muses of Poetry even as they are dismissed in a moment of humor tinged with regret. It appears that there will not be much fun in Socrates' commonwealth, but there is quite a lot in its inventor.

In other places, Socrates pays similar respect to poets. Later in *Republic*, he announces that he must "speak out, though a certain love and reverence for Homer that has possessed me from a boy would stay me from speaking. For he appears to have been the first teacher and beginner of all those beauties of tragedy" (10: 595b–c). In *Symposium*, the respected Diotema remarks, "Wisdom and all her sister virtues, it is the office of every poet to beget them, and of every artist whom we may call creative" (209a); and Socrates says that he agrees with her. It is difficult to believe that only the "more austere and less delightful" poets are included here. The early Greek poets are referred to as "children or prophets of the gods" (*Republic*, 2: 366b) and in *Meno* as "divinely inspired" (816). Nor does Socrates refrain from calling on the Muses for aid (*Phaedrus*, 273a), though his invocations of and references to the Muses sometimes have a degree of irony directed back at himself. His statements of this sort seem somewhere between belief and disbelief.

That is the problem, because possession does not obey reason. It is radically irrational; its voice is not its own. Worse, there is no criterion to determine whether the poetic inspiration is from the Muses or is demonic. The effect may be deleterious because in reading the poets, especially Homer, we tend to abandon ourselves, that is to say, abandon our reason, which identifies us as human (*Republic*, 10: 605d). We end up experiencing pleasure in things it is better to be ashamed of and to avoid.

In *Phaedrus*, however, Socrates takes a different tack. The matter of imitation does not come up, and the emphasis is on divine madness. The kind of madness that here interests him most is that of the lover, and the poet is mentioned merely to illustrate one type of madness among several, each given a different source: prophetic madness from Apollo, mystic madness from Dionysus, that of the lover (whose inspiration is the highest) from Aphrodite and Eros, and poetic madness from the Muses (*Phaedrus*, 265a–b). According to Socrates, poetic inspiration

> seizes a tender, virgin soul and stimulates it to rapt passionate expression, especially in lyric poetry, glorifying the countless mighty deeds of ancient times for the instruction of posterity. But if any man comes to the gates of poetry without the madness of the Muses, persuaded that skill alone will make him a good poet, then shall he and his works of sanity with him be brought to nought by the poetry of madness, and behold, their place is nowhere to be found. (245a)

These spirited remarks, some of the language of which Socrates wryly says is deliberately poetic to please Phaedrus (275a), suggest considerable respect for what poets might utter (though not necessarily respect for poets themselves). But all of these poetic inspirations involve "divine disturbance of our conventions of conduct" (265a–b), and we cannot be sure of the source of all of them. Furthermore, no poet has succeeded or ever will succeed in singing worthily about "that place beyond the heavens" (247c), for only reason can behold it. But can reason do so by the preferred way of dialectic? I shall return to this question when I consider Socrates' habit of recourse to stories (myths, allegories) at critical moments in his argument.

   Despite the identification of poetry with divine madness and the odd respect implied, Socrates classifies poets with the detested sophists and rhetoricians. This leads to the accusation, which has a flourishing later life, that poets are liars. In Plato's system, anything thrice removed from truth is a sort of lie or deception, but particularly dangerous are the poets' impious lies about the actions of the gods. Such a falsehood Socrates calls "a copy of the affection in the soul, an afterrising image" (*Republic*, 2: 382b). Socrates adds that these images are not totally false in that they can reveal an unpleasant truth; he compromises somewhat his own notion of imitation as falsehood.

Yet elsewhere, Socrates concocts, and advocates the telling of, a fundamental lie for the good of the State, that of the cthonic origin of the guardians (*Republic*, 3: 414b–c), and, of course, the stories Socrates tells are, on his own terms, lies.

The emphasis on lies about the gods reveals that Socrates is, among other things, a religious reformer and that his targets are those who corrupt religious poetry by means of stories that foment false beliefs in the young. Since poets are possessed, at least they escape the accusation that their lies are deliberate.[5] This cannot be said of the sophists and rhetoricians, and it is unfortunate that Socrates identifies poets with them. In *Gorgias* (502c–e), he asserts that if you strip poetry of its music, rhythm, and meter, you have remaining only speech. Thus poetry without ornaments is a kind of public address. Put the ornaments back on and you have rhetoric. Rhetoricians and the despised sophists work in the same sphere and on the same subject matter (465c). Rhetoric is persuasive, but it is not instructive of right and wrong, nor is it an art. It is a "routine" that "produces gratification and pleasure" (462b–c), but pleasure should be for the sake of the good and not the other way around. As I have mentioned, in *Phaedrus*, Socrates ironically admits that in his praise of the god of love, "some of its language was poetical to please Phaedrus" (257a). Whether this pleasant language is offered for the sake of the good is not clear.

The poet is also classed with speechwriters and law writers, all rhetoricians according to Socrates. The poet is "one who has nothing to show of more value than the literary works on whose phrases he spends hours, twisting them this way and that, pasting them together and pulling them apart" (278d–e). Once so observed, the poet can be deemed little different from the sophist, who can "make the same things appear to his audience like and unlike, as one and many, or again at rest and in motion" or

---

5. In *Protagoras* (347e), Socrates says, "No one can interrogate poets about what they say," indicating that dialectic cannot engage them. He goes on to remark, " . . . most often when they are introduced into the discussion some say that the poet's meaning is one thing and some another, for the topic is one on which nobody can produce a conclusive argument." There is no way to determine a poetic intention. It is not merely a question of writing as against speech, as in the story told by Socrates in *Phaedrus* (275–77) that emphasizes the untrustworthiness of writing. The problem is also the poet's madness.

"make trifles seem important and important points trifling by the force of [his] language" (261d). So the poet's lying, even if beyond his control, exhibits a disregard for truth. The purpose would seem to be persuasion, the means pleasure, despite the poet's being unaware of any purpose. It appears, though Socrates does not come out and say this, that the poet's device, employed to make things appear both same and different and thus false, would be the trope of metaphor, one of the offenses I shall later discuss.

Despite the grounds for attack that I have mentioned (leaving aside for later the matter of ambivalence), some scholars of Plato have regarded him as a defender of poetry. The most vigorous of these efforts is that of Julius A. Elias.[6] As did several predecessors, Elias points out that Plato is himself a poet and that his poetry is the myths (stories, fictions, fables, allegories) that he (or, rather, Socrates for the most part) tells. These stories Elias divides into two types, and they constitute by implication the ground for what Elias regards as Plato's defense of poetry. The first type, which underlies what Elias calls the "weak" defense, is the moral fable, an elliptical presentation of something that might be offered in another way. Under this would fall some forms of allegory. The defense is weak because for purely intellectual purposes the fables as such would be unnecessary. Their interpretation would be sufficient. For persuasion and delight, however, they might be useful. Arguments for poetry as didactic usually belong to the weak defense. It is not difficult to imagine Plato advocating this type of poetry, since allegories present relatively little opportunity for deviant interpretations. They reduce story to moral principle. Some later defenders of poetry, Sir Philip Sidney, for example, actually attribute this view to Plato.

Elias's main interest is in the "strong" defense, which is represented by myths in which Plato "imbeds fundamental propositions which cannot be asserted as true because they are indemonstrable axioms of his system" (208). They are "so far from self-evident . . . that they can be advanced only in mythic form so that there should be no misconception that they are dogmatic assertions" (119). Further along, Elias claims that they are "such expression as we can give to an otherwise ineffable order of being"(144).

6. Julius A. Elias, *Plato's Defence of Poetry* (Albany: State University of New York Press, 1984).

Thus *poiesis* is a form of speculative expression of the "indemonstrable." Such expression need not be subterfuge. Plato's myths, the good ones anyway, occur when discursive logic is incapable of making a convincing demonstration. The myths do not contain necessary truths, but they are necessary in order to go beyond the limits of dialectic. In Elias's view, Plato's search by deductive means failed, and poetry had to take over because of the "limitations of human reason, but not because of its bankruptcy" (81): "It falls to *poiesis*, broadly conceived, to furnish the foundation on which the positive program of science and statecraft can be asserted" (81). If *poiesis* grounds reason, reason in its turn becomes the scrutinizer of *poiesis*, the critic of the hypothetical models it creates. Plato considered myths the harbors of premises that could only be hypothetical; indeed, for him, a first premise had to be hypothetical.

Of course, some myths have "bad effects" (213), and these, according to Elias, are the ones Plato attacks in his accusation that the poets told lies about the gods. Elias notes that, in contrast to our restricted definition of "poet," poets in Plato's time were "the physicists, cosmologists, moralists, legislators, politicians, religious leaders, and patriots" (213). This is to say that they were the mythmakers and fomenters of belief. He notes that Plato was relatively uninterested in lyric poetry but had great interest in mythic or bardic poetry because it was this kind of work that presumed to offer fundamental truths. Cosmologies like his own *Timaeus* have the scope that would attract his attention. They strive to go beyond the limits of dialectical knowledge.

Every Platonic myth is only the best story possible; or, as Socrates says at the end of *Gorgias*, "Now perhaps all this seems to you like an old wives' tale and you despise it, and there would be nothing strange in despising it if our research could discover anywhere a better and truer account, but as it is you . . . cannot demonstrate that we should live any other life than this" (527a–b). It is the best story possible as long as it cannot be rationally refuted.

This defense seems to me one that saves poetry for philosophy or, rather, would save philosophy. I do not think it saves poetry for poetry, which becomes a philosopher's substitute for philosophy where there is an embarrassing gap.

There is, however, an additional implied defense in Plato that suggests his ambivalence. Plato's works, as Elias observes, often have inside themselves myths; but it is also true that his works are themselves dramatic in structure, either imitations or mixed forms, to use his own terms. Plato's attack on poetry is, first of all, an attack made by a character in a mimesis and not explicitly Plato's. Further, as we have seen, Socrates exhibits ambivalence toward his attack, which is part of the drama of Plato's work. It is not the status of Socrates' stories as myths that is definitive here, though it is significant. It is the fact that the Platonic dialogue is structured as a poem or what Aristotle called a poetic whole. Plato has Socrates assert (*Republic*, 10: 607b) that there is an ancient war between philosophy and poetry. Elias's Plato has poetry save philosophy to war another day, but his account of poetry removes its offensiveness. I believe that Plato, when most successful as a poet (some of the dialogues cannot be regarded as successful poems or even poems), commits the offense of poetry against philosophy. He dramatizes the ancient war to which he refers. This offense is the dramatization of the violence of philosophy's failed attempt to swallow poetry and poetry's success in opposing philosophy, even to the extent of swallowing pieces of it, for it appears that there can be philosophy in a poem but no poetry in philosophy.

But let us read Plato as an imitative poet and see what we have. *Ion* is one of Plato's more dramatic dialogues. It is a pure mimesis, not a mixed form (as some of his dialogues are). It is, of course, necessary to distinguish between drama and dialectic. The Platonic dialectic can be dramatic, but there are long stretches where the dialectic, seen as conversation, has no dramatic quality. There is little drama where a character merely answers Socrates with the briefest of affirmations. But even here there may be the drama of Socrates' presentation, and on occasion there is the interior drama of intellectual search going on inside Socrates, as seems to be the case, for example, in *Cratylus*. This last can be said to characterize a good many philosophical and other texts that we would not call dramatic. I think of Kant's critiques, in which one senses a continual search for the right formulation, in contrast, say, to the *Summa* of Saint Thomas Aquinas, with its statements and counterstatements. As for rhetorical presentation, it seems more dramatic when there is a fictive audience made explicit in the text, though less explicit audiences, as sometimes in Nietzsche, also occur. This brings us back to the first point, where there is a dialogue with both speakers really engaged and both characterized. This does not, of course, mean that there must be equal time or equal intelligence.

Ion is particularly interesting for our purposes, because it is almost always included in anthologies of literary criticism (along with selections from *Republic*) as an example of Plato's attack on the poets.[7] It would be more accurate, of course, to describe it as an attack on interpreters, or rhetors; for in *Ion*, the attack on poets is a sort of by-product.

It is easy enough to see that *Ion* is dramatic, for the dialogue is not mechanical with the repeated affirmative answers often found elsewhere. Further, both Socrates and Ion are characterized in a certain situation, and there is a beginning, middle, and end. Socrates meets the Ephesian rhapsode Ion, flushed from his victory in a competition at the festival of Asclepius at Epidaurus. He predicts his victory at the Penetheniac as well. Playing on Ion's vanity, Socrates begins an inquiry into the nature of his art, raising the question of whether his expertise extends beyond Homer to other poets. The dialogue proceeds through what might be called four crises for Ion, at each of which he is presented an opportunity to unsettle Socrates' relentless line of questioning. But on none of these occasions does he rise to respond effectively. Although this rather silly man seems at the end happy enough, we readers (at least we modern readers) confront Ion's crises with mounting frustration.

The question as Socrates puts it is whether, when he recites Homer, Ion is a rational expert or instead possessed by a divinity. Socrates first presumes the existence of an art of poetry as a whole and therefore a mode of inquiry into it. Ion agrees, but on Socrates' terms. He does not respond by claiming that since there is an art of poetry, there must be such a thing as a poem, that is, something that would have to possess its own idea or form. Socrates treats poetry and poems merely as vehicles for imitations of phenomena with no acknowledgment that a poem is other than a congeries of such imitations, a transparency. This being the case, Ion cannot claim expert-

---

7. Renaissance critics frequently missed or ignored Socrates' ironic treatment of Ion, and the dialogue was sometimes invoked simply as a Platonic defense of poetry as divinely inspired.

ise on poems as such but only on the things poems imitate. That Socrates should state that there is an art of poetry and then insist, as he does, on the ephemeral nature of both poem and poetry would seem to be a contradiction that a more astute Ion could have noticed. Had he done so, the dialogue would have had to take another (and more interesting) turn toward inquiry into the being of the idea of poetry and poems. Socrates would have had to defend his notion that there can be an art without an ideal object before ever getting to the poet's and rhapsode's alleged divine madness.

On three more occasions, Ion has the opportunity to make this point (536c, 538b, 539c), but he becomes more and more enmeshed in Socrates' web of questions about his expertise on the various subject matters of Homer's poems. Finally, in desperation, he claims that his expertise is identical to that of a military general because he would know what a general should say to incite his troops.[8]

In this process, Socrates himself abandons the notion of an art of poetry. He does not need it any longer. Ion, by his own admission, is no expert on poetry or on any poets except Homer. So Socrates can offer, without argument from Ion, the conclusion that both the poet and the rhapsode are possessed by the Muse, who

> first makes men inspired, and then through these inspired ones others share in the enthusiasm, and a chain is formed, for the epic poets, all the good ones, have their excellence not from art, but are inspired, possessed, and thus they utter all these admirable poems. So it is also with the good lyric poets: as the worshipping Corybantes are not in their senses when they dance, so the lyric poets are not in their senses when they make their lovely poems. (523c–24e)

8. This response is, of course, silly; but it is not quite so silly when we note the story that Diogenes Laertius tells about Solon: "Solon, feigning madness, rushed into the Agora with a garland on his head; there he had his poem on Salamis read to the Athenians and roused them to fury. They renewed the war with the Megarians and, thanks to Solon, were victorious." Diogenes also tells us that Solon "prohibited Thespis from performing tragedies on the ground that fiction was pernicious." *Lives of Eminent Philosophers, with an English Translation by R.D. Hicks* (London: W. Heinemann; New York: G. P. Putnam's Sons, 1925), 1: 49, 61.

If there is a defense of poetry in *Ion*, it is in Socrates' expression of wonder at the possessed poet ("a light and winged thing, and holy") and Plato's use of the dramatic form. This defense is hardly straightforward, however. The same can be said of the attack. Can all rhapsodes be as puffed up and doltish as poor Ion? Is there, after all, an *art* of poetry?

Socrates repeats his criticism of poets in *Apology*. The matter of instinct or inspiration (but not wisdom) is mentioned, and the evidence is that poets are incapable of explaining their poems. Furthermore, Socrates observes, poets are arrogant: " . . . the very fact that they were poets made them think that they had a perfect understanding of all other subjects, of which they were totally ignorant" (22b–c).

After the arguments against poets, after the confession of love for Homer (a love that Socrates implies he should overcome), after the expression of guarded respect for, even awe at, poetic inspiration, there is the odd dismissal of the poets in *Republic* (10). Socrates then makes an offer to poets and lovers of poetry. There is something a little wistful here, as if Socrates' dialectic has worked him into a corner and he needs help lest he prove without a doubt that he must abandon his feelings: "But nevertheless let it be declared that, if the mimetic and dulcet poetry can show any reason for her existence in a well-governed state, we would gladly admit her, since we are very conscious of her spell. But all the same it would be impious to betray what we believe to be the truth. Is not that so, friend? Do you not yourself feel her magic and especially when Homer is her interpreter?" (10: 607c). The offer next becomes more specific and more odd, given what we have read. Socrates wonders whether poetry may justly return to the State if she can plead her case successfully, "whether in lyric or other measure." The statement, we note, is put in the form of a question. It is an odd offer because it would seem, from what has gone before, that a defense in "lyric or other measure" would have irrational elements and might represent the very sort of danger Socrates has worried about.

Reflected here are the results of Socrates' identification of poetry with rhetoric, considered as a "routine" of persuasion. It is not entirely consistent with the attribution of divine inspiration to the poet. On the one hand, poetry is a deviant form of persuasion and its use of tropes untrustworthy. On the other, the great tropes of divine madness would seem to transcend the division of poem into statement and ornament. It is difficult, if not impossible, to resolve this matter, if indeed Plato intended it to be resolved.

I think he did not. It appears that the drama of Socrates' dialectical search is more important than any straightforward argument. The drama sets off a chain of speculation, as does the drama of *Ion*.

In *Republic*, there is a statement echoed for centuries by those who would defend poetry against the very attack that Socrates mounts. "And we would allow her advocates who are not poets but lovers of poetry to plead her cause in prose without meter, and show that she is not only delightful but beneficial to orderly government and all the life of man" (10: 607d). Delight and benefit, the latter of which was interpreted as usefulness and teaching—these are the two virtues attributed to poetry by the many poets and critics who would later seek to answer Plato. The question of benefit to orderly government was often, but not always, ignored. The answers were for a very long time circumscribed by the terms Socrates set forth. As a result, the poem was bifurcated between the usefulness of rational content and the delightfulness of ornamental form.

We must not leave Plato without noting certain stories about him. Apparently, in his youth, before meeting Socrates, he studied painting and wrote both lyric poetry and tragedies. The meeting with Socrates seems to have been, by Diogenes Laertius's account, a sort of conversion: " . . . when he was about to compete for the prize with a tragedy, he listened to Socrates in front of the theatre of Dionysus, and then consigned his poems to the flames" (1: 281). But, as we know, whether this story is true or not, Aristotle is reported by Diogenes to have remarked that the style of Plato's dialogues was "half-way between poetry and prose" (1: 311).[9]

At what has been called "the crossroads of the Classical and Medieval worlds,"[10] the suspicion of poetry, and yet ambivalence toward it, was reflected in terms similar to Plato's. A good example is *The Consolation of Philosophy* by the Roman politician and scholar Anicus Manlius Severi-

9. Plutarch reports that Socrates himself put some fables of Aesop into verse. *Moralia* (Loeb Classical Library), trans. Frank Cole Babbitt (London: William Heinemann; Cambridge, MA: Harvard University Press, 1927), 1: 83.
10. V. E. Watts, Introduction, *The Consolation of Philosophy*, by Anicus Manlius Severinus Boethius, trans. Watts (London: Penguin Books, 1969), 7.

nus Boethius (c. 480–c. 524). Imprisoned in exile, ill, and awaiting savage execution, Boethius wrote a contemplative work famous for centuries, a mixture of genres, including poetry and dialogue. It is surprising, although there is an explanation for it, that the work begins with a poem, proceeds to a dialogue in which the Muses of Poetry are attacked, and goes on to include thirty-eight more poems. They are interspersed in a dialogue between Boethius himself and the Muse of Philosophy. The poems are uttered sometimes by one, sometimes by the other.

The *Consolation* begins with a poem in which Boethius laments his pitiful condition. He speaks of having been in youth an eager and zestful poet, though now he sings only songs of grief. The Muses of Poetry remain faithful comforters, and even as he writes, they are present at his bedside. But, having composed this poem, Boethius becomes aware of another, more impressive figure standing over him. This proves to be the Muse of Philosophy. With anger, she observes the Muses of Poetry, who surround him, and she speaks: "Who has suffered these seducing mummers to approach this sick man? Never have they nursed his sorrows with any remedies, but rather fostered them with poisonous sweets. These are they who stifle the fruit-bearing harvest of reason with the barren briars of the passions; they do not free the minds of men from disease but accustom them thereto."[11]

With her emphasis on the poisonous sweets of irrationality, Philosophy's attack on the Muses of Poetry comes right out of Plato; but immediately after this outburst, Philosophy launches into a poem of her own. It describes Boethius's mental state and comments that now it is time for healing. Another poem, uttered later on by Philosophy, is followed by her questioning Boethius as to whether he has understood the poem or is a donkey deaf to lyric poetry.

As we know, epic and dramatic poetry were the principal objects of

---

11. *The Consolation of Philosophy*, ed. and abr. J. J. Buchanan (New York: Frederick Ungar, 1957), 3. The text is based on the W. V. Cooper translation, but revised. The sentence referring to seducing mummers is in the Latin as follows: "Quis, inquit, has scenicas meretriculas ad hunc aegrum permisit accedere." "Scenicas meretriculas" might be more literally translated "theatrical wenches" or "wenches of the theater." The more easily available Penguin Classics translation (see footnote 10 above) loses the connection to the theater and thus to imitation by rendering the words "hysterical sluts" (36).

Socrates' attack, but there was a broader Platonic definition of imitation that would have included lyric. The poems of the *Consolation* are lyrics, and Philosophy criticizes the Muses of Poetry for inspiring the first lyric of the book. This poem, a lament, is the sort of thing that Socrates thought the potential guardians of the State should not hear. Presumably the thirty-eight poems that follow, or at least some of them, would be acceptable to him. Is a poem kept under the control of Philosophy acceptable? If this is so, any rapprochement between the Muse of Philosophy and the Muses of Poetry would have to be one in which Poetry ends the ancient war by submitting. Indeed, the history of allegorical interpretation of Homer and the classical poets was long one of such submission.

Ernst Robert Curtius argued that philosophers attacked poets as perpetrators of falsities of religion, Greek theology having been shaped by poets. However, in the tradition of allegorical interpretation of Homer, a kind of settlement occurred, though at the expense of making poetry a decorated, coded philosophy.[12] Boethius could regard the Muse of Philosophy as presiding over a higher form of poetry. But there is a passage in the *Consolation* that might have led, had its thought been developed further, to a different view of poetic value. A wedge would not have been driven between surface appearance and morally acceptable hidden meaning. Philosophy is upbraiding Boethius for his interest in objects of ownership and identification of the self with such allegedly beautiful or prestigious objects: "What an obvious mistake to make—to think that anything can be enhanced by decoration that does not belong to it. It's impossible. For if there is anything striking in the decoration, that is what is praised, while the veiled and hidden object continues just the same in all its ugliness" (Watts translation, 68). Although Philosophy is discussing people here, and not poems or objects of art, the remark could lead to questioning the line between decoration and essential object, surface and meaning, that is present in allegorical interpretations and most moralistic readings of poetry.

So, although Philosophy dispatches the Muses of Poetry and appar-

---

12. Ernst Robert Curtius, "Poetry and Philosophy," *European Literature and the Latin Middle Ages*, trans. Willard R. Trask (Princeton, NJ: Princeton University Press, 1953) 203–5.

ently takes over what acceptable function they may have had, she does so by presuming the existence of a decorative surface of poetry subsidiary to fundamental meaning and value, even as she attacks a similar distinction when it is applied to the appearance and reality of human beings. Of course, one could argue that she is advocating an asceticism that entirely negates decoration. But if this is so, her use of poems in her own discourse contradicts her view.

The earliest and most persistent defenses of poetry, developed in response to the philosophers' attacks on Homer, will prove to be inadequate. The declaration for allegorical and moralistic content, which generated many outlandish readings, made poetry a decorated and diluted form of philosophy. Yet this defense persists, as we shall see in chapter 3, often as the principal one, even into our own time. It is a situation in which both sides accept the same story.

Medieval and Renaissance Attacks

There is no question that throughout the Middle Ages, the Church often stood in the way of poetry, though not without ambivalence. Saint Augustine had echoed the Platonic Socrates' attack on poetic impiety, and there was suspicion of drama, exemplified by the anonymous *Treatise against Miracle Plays* (fourteenth century). The attack here is against desecration of the sacred subjects the plays took up, the plays' alleged tendency to give the audience only pleasure, and mimesis, judged as falsity. These suspicions can be traced back to Tertullian and Saint Jerome. But as damaging and equally long-lived was the view of poetry as belonging to rhetoric. Ancient rhetorical theory, as exemplified by Aristotle's two treatises *Poetics* and *Rhetoric*, drew a fairly clear line between poetry and rhetoric, but *Poetics* mentions poetic metaphor mainly as a rhetorical device, and classical rhetoricians generally gave as examples rhetorical devices from poems. The Aristotelian distinction did not hold up in medieval thought. Many of those who mixed the two or did not grasp the difference can be described as enemies of poetry even as they may have in their own minds been friendly to it. The reason is that under rhetoric poetry becomes identified with persuasion, and all its formal characteristics are regarded as decorations designed to induce the reader to accept an argument. The submission of poetry to rhetoric influenced both attack and defense for centuries.

J. W. H. Atkins cited the anonymous poem "The Owl and the Nightingale," probably written in the thirteenth century, as the first English critical document.[13] He read the nightingale as a defender of secular love poetry and promoter of pleasure and the owl as a proponent of moralistic didacticism. If the author takes a side, it seems to be with the nightingale, but not without fairness to the owl. Though there have been dissenters to this view of the poem as an allegory of a literary quarrel, the opposition dramatized is characteristic of medieval thought, with the attacks on poetry being owlish and moralistic.

Renaissance attacks continued along the lines set out in Plato's *Republic* and were extended in medieval thought with the Church's anxiety about immoral content added. These complaints became more acute in England with the rise of Puritanism. Even some vigorous defenders of poetry (Ascham, Sidney, Harington, Vaughan), as G. Gregory Smith points out, had "latent sympathy" for the Puritan view.[14] Even among literary theorists of cinquecento Italy, of whom there were many, the requirement of Christian teaching and utility prevailed, with delight added, adapted from Plato and made a catchword by repetition of the Horatian phrase *dulce et utile*. Resistance to this remained. We see it in the humanist Pico della Mirandola, who, citing Isidore of Seville, asserted that poets taught falsity and, as perpetrators of lies, were unacceptable to Christians. But Pico himself wrote poems and received praise for them, albeit for their wit and propriety. Hardly ambivalent were the views of Cornelius Agrippa, who in his *On the Uncertainty and Vanity of the Sciences* (1526) repeated Socrates' complaints.

In his monumental *A History of Literary Criticism in the Italian Renaissance*, Bernard Weinberg discusses Francesco Berni's *Dialogo con-*

13. J. W. H. Atkins, *English Literary Criticism: The Medieval Phase* (New York: Peter Smith, 1952), 142–44. Also Atkins, ed. and trans., "The Owl and the Nightingale," *Aberystwyth Studies* 4 (1922): 49–58.

14. G. Gregory Smith, Introduction, *Elizabethan Critical Essays*, ed. Smith (Oxford: Clarendon Press, 1904) 1: xix.

tra i poeti (1526), acknowledging Berni's "jocular tone" and "satirical intent":

> Berni proceeds, at least in part, by upholding the contrary of the arguments usually used in the [Platonic] defense; perhaps this might be called reverse-Platonism. [So widespread was the Renaissance use of Plato to defend poetry that Weinberg identifies him with the defense.] The interlocutors make fun of the self-styled madness of the poets, of their overbearing claim to divine inspiration. They should rather be charged with heresy, uselessness, complete lack of substance and solidity; they are venal and obsequious, malicious and immoral, unashamed plagiarists; they are worthy of punishment rather than of praise.[15]

Even taking into account the jocularity, Weinberg is able to point to a serious animus against poets, it being proposed by one of Berni's interlocutors that poets should be tolerated as people if, as people, they are good for something other than writing poems.

Weinberg cites two Italian critics from the 1560s, one of whom, Benedetto Grassi, mounts a moralistic attack on Terence and claims that poetry has become decadent since the time of the sage ancients and should be banned, at least most of it (1: 283). The other, Frosino Lapini, worries over the possibility that the pleasure generated by a particular sonnet of Petrarch might be dangerous (1: 290–92).[16]

Weinberg's summary of the attack on poetry in Renaissance Italy is on target: Poetry is dangerous because of its rhetorical power to affect the reader or audience for the worse. It is particularly dangerous to the young and ignorant, though critics often admitted that more experienced readers can probe the sensuous surface to glean intellectual meaning, presumably allegorical. The attack remains based on Plato, and the attitude is that poetry

---

15. Bernard Weinberg, *A History of Literary Criticism in the Italian Renaissance* (Chicago: University of Chicago Press, 1961), 1: 261.

16. Benedetto Grassi, *Oratione contra gli Terentiani* (1566); Frosino Lapini, *Letione nella quate si regione in universale del fine della poetica* (1567).

is decorated discourse disguised to seduce and/or persuade. It should be subject to censorship or perhaps banishment.

These views, as Weinberg has demonstrated, are revealed in the prolonged sixteenth-century quarrel over Dante's *Commedia*. It was initiated by a writer with the pseudonym Ridolfo (or Anselmo) Castravilla, author of *Discorso nel quate si nostra l'imperfectione della Commedia de Dante* (1572), which circulated for years in manuscript copies. Castravilla's criticisms are based principally on Aristotle and are not generally moralistic except for the complaint that Dante's narrator is an immoral and impious character. (Giacopo Mazzoni's answer to a critic who takes up where Castravilla left off I shall deal with in chapter 3.) The successor to Castravilla was the ill-tempered poet and academician Bellisaro Bulgarini, who followed Castravilla in his Aristotelian criticisms and added a severe Christian point of view, attacking Dante's use of pagan mythology and the invention of anything he deemed inappropriate to Christian thought and morality.

A strain of thought influenced by Puritan and English middle-class attitudes condemned poetry on moralistic grounds. Perhaps the best known of these attacks is Stephen Gosson's *The Schoole of Abuse, Conteining pleasaunt invective against Poets, Pipers, Plaiers, Jesters, and such like Caterpillars of a Commonwealth.*[17] Its notoriety is earned mainly (and perhaps only) because Sidney wrote his well-known *Apology for Poetry* in response to it. It is likely that this occurred only because Gosson dedicated his work to Sidney, probably unaware that Sidney was a poet, for Sidney's poetry was not published in his lifetime, though it was circulated in manuscript. Nor was Gosson himself actually a Puritan. His Euphuistic prose style hardly suggests what we usually think of as Puritanical, and it is known that he

---

17. Stephen Gosson, *The Schoole of Abuse, Conteining pleasaunt invective against Poets, Pipers, Plaiers, Jesters, and such like Caterpillars of a Commonwealth* (London: Thomas Woodcocke, 1579). Gosson's attack is only one of several published in England in the 1570s and 1580s, usually against the theater. For example, John Northbrooke, *Treatise wherein Dicing, Dauncing, vaine Playes or Enterluds with other idle Pastimes, &c., commonly used on the Saboath Day are reproved by the Authoritie of the Word of God and auntient Writers* (1577), the anonymous *A Treatise of Daunses, wherein it is showed, that they are as it were accessories and dependants (or things annexed) to whoredom: where also by the way is touched and proved, that Playes are ioyned and knit together in a ranck, or rowe with them* (1581), and a series of tracts against the immoral influence of the theater.

actually opposed the Puritans.[18] William Ringler has shown that Gosson and Sidney shared some attitudes toward poetry (124). Gosson held that because poetry included both the good and the bad, it was dangerous: "I must confesse that Poets are whetstones of wit, notwithstanding that wit is dearly bought: where honey and gall are mixt, it will be hard to sever one from the other" (20). Sidney argued that poetry could be a mixture, but he argued also that the good could outweigh the bad.

Gosson had been a student at Oxford of John Rainolds, who had written in praise of poetry,[19] and it can hardly be said that Gosson himself had always been the enemy of poetry. He had, in fact, been a poet, though only four of his poems had been published. He was also the author of plays, none of which have survived. Indeed, even after he had published *The Schoole of Abuse* and another attack called *Playes Confuted* (1582), two of his plays were still being performed in London, though probably against his wishes. At about the time of *The Schoole*, he published another Euphuistic work, *The Ephemerides of Phaelo* (1579).

It seems that even for Gosson, there was once a time when poetry warranted admiration. But that was long ago among the robust Ancient Britons, when poetry was properly moralistic: "The right use of auncient Poetrie was to have the notable exploytes of woorthy Captaines, the holesome councels of good fathers, and vertuous lines of predecessors set down in numbers and song to the Instrument at solemne feastes, that the sound of the one might draw the hearers from kissing the cupp too often; the sense of the other put them in minde of things past, and chaulk the way to do the like" (25). But now, poetry, piping, and playing are "chayned in linkes of abuse," and the bringing of musical instruments into the theaters was "the first cup that poisoned the common wealth" (28–29).

18. See William Ringler, *Stephen Gosson: A Biographical and Critical Study* (Princeton, NJ: Princeton University Press, 1942), 80. For a brief discussion of the many attacks on the stage in this period, see 52–82.

19. John Rainolds, *Oratio in Laudem Artes Poeticae* (c. 1572), introduction and commentary by William Ringler; trans. Walter Allen, Jr. (Princeton, NJ: Princeton University Press, 1940). But Rainolds also published a savage attack on the theater, *Overthrow of Stage-Playes* (1592).

The main charge, like the whole attack, is made with energy and no lack of rhetorical devices:

> . . . pull off the visard that Poets maske in, you shall disclose their reproch, Bewray their vanities, loth their wantonnesse, lament their follie, and perceive their sharpe sayings to be placed as Pearles in Dunghils, fresh pictures on rotten walles, chaste Matrons apparel on common Courtesans. These are the Cuppes of *Circes*, that turn reasonable Creatures into brute Beastes, the balles of Hippomanes, that hinder the course of Atalanta; and the blocks of the Divel that are cast in our wayes, to cut off the rase of toward wittes. No marveyle though Plato shut them out of his Schoole, and banished them quite from his common wealth, as effeminate writers, unprofitable members, and utter enimies to virtue. (20)

There may be no ambivalence on the face of this, but it appears from observation of Gosson's career that there is at least opportunism and perhaps hypocrisy. Though *The Schoole of Abuse* has been called a piece of hackwork (Gosson seems almost always to have written strictly for money), it is a literary *tour de force*, or at least a rhetorical one. In his exuberance he extends his attack to "Fencers, Dyars, Dauncers, Tumblers, Carders, and Bowlers" (45). Plays, however, remain the principal subject of attack, though he does acknowledge the possibility of plays with moral purposes.

Gosson's attack calls on the precedent of Plato and of the Spartans, who banished Tirius, presumably a Spartan poet, though I can find no reference to him. He cites Cicero's claim that poets were liars. He argues that Pindar dwelt longest on "those pointes that profite least" (19) and that the moralistic allegorical readings of Homer were absurd exaggerations (written presumably to save Homer from attack). Wanton poets have led emperors to vanity. Poems are full of lust, incest, and other poisons, and they are particularly dangerous because these poisons are covered over by rhetorical beauties. Gosson expresses many of the lasting complaints about poetry that defenders have felt compelled to answer.

Empiricist Attacks

The movement in philosophy toward epistemology and subsequently language caused a shift in negative attitudes toward poetry and constitutes the second major ground for attack. There were still the earlier grave reservations, particularly with respect to the theater. However, the new emphasis was on questions of empirical truth and use. In these circumstances, the attackers showed little ambivalence or guilt. Rather, they condescendingly relegated poetry to the superficial or the obsolete. The shift can be seen in Thomas Sprat's *History of the Royal Society*.[20] The Society was devoted to the advancement of science, and it is not surprising that Sprat should refer everything to reason and express deep suspicion of linguistic ornamentation. Sprat praises the members of the Society for "the manner of their *Discourse*: which unless they been very watchful to keep in due temper, the whole spirit and vigour of their *Design*, had been soon eaten out, by the luxury and redundance of *speech*. The ill effects of this superfluity of talking have already overwhelmed most other *Arts* and *Professions*" (111). Eloquence, he says, should be banished from all civil societies, for it can as easily be used for the bad as for the good. Tropes, once used with propriety by the wise to promote Reason, are now in league with the passions: "They give the mind a motion too changeable and bewitching, to consist with right practice" (112). He speaks of "specious *Tropes* and *Figures*" and the "vicious abundance of *Phrase*, this trick of *Metaphors*, this volubility of *Tongue*, which makes so great a noise in the World" (112).

Like Gosson, Sprat refers to the wisdom of the Ancients but declares the days in which we should take their views seriously to be nearly over. His argument, unlike Gosson's against the poets' decadence and immorality, is that their stories are exhausted and they are obsolete in the face of new scientific truths: "The *Wit* of the *Fables* and *Religions* of the *Ancient World* is well nigh consum'd: they have already serv'd the *Poets* long enough; and it is now high time to dismiss them; especially seeing they have

---

20. Thomas Sprat, *History of the Royal Society*, ed. Jackson I. Cope and Harold Whitmore Jones (Saint Louis, MO: Washington University Studies, 1958).

this peculiar *imperfection*, that they were only *Fictions* at first" (414). The attack on lies about the gods is here replaced by an attack on ignorance of nature. The obsolescence of poetic fictions, regarded as false, comes about as a result of scientific progress. Then comes adoption of a model for language that eschews all tropes and is identified with mathematics. It is not a return to Plato's recommendation to the young to study mathematics, for the arena of truth is nature, not the ideas or forms.

John Locke's *An Essay Concerning Human Understanding* (1690) sought to give to this scientific attitude a philosophical ground.[21] In his theory of primary and secondary qualities of experience, he sought to systematize a distinction between subjectivity and objectivity, which plays an important role in the history of attitudes toward poetry.

Locke begins by declaring against the existence of innate ideas. Each of us is a *tabula rasa*, or blank tablet, and learns everything from experience. Locke employs "idea" in several senses, but for the present purpose, the important Lockean meaning is sense datum. Ideas are of two sorts: simple and complex. Simple ideas are those of sheer immediate perception coming from one sense only, as in the case of color; from more than one sense, as in the intuition of space, rest, and motion; from reflection, as in the experience of thinking; and from sensation and reflection, as in pleasure and uneasiness. Complex ideas are combinations of simple ones, piled up like building blocks into patterns, though these combinations may also be merely the setting of two ideas in relation or opposition. Experiences, which produce these ideas, possess two kinds of qualities, primary and secondary. The primary refers to all those aspects of a natural object that actually belong to it. These are the measurable qualities: for example, solidity, extension, figure, and mobility. The secondary qualities are those which, though caused by the object, inhere as such in the subjective response of the perceiver: color, sound, taste, and so forth.

As a result of this distinction, empirical truth lies with the object, reduced to its quantitative properties. All the rest is subjective and insub-

21. John Locke, *An Essay Concerning Human Understanding*, ed. Alexander Campbell Fraser, 2 vols. (Oxford: Clarendon Press, 1894).

stantial. Blake called divisions of this sort "cloven,"[22] and a century later, Alfred North Whitehead remarked that this "bifurcation" of nature rendered the reality of nature, bereft of the secondary qualities, "a dull affair, soundless, scentless, colorless, merely the hurrying of material, endlessly, meaninglessly."[23] Poetry is relegated to the secondary, to subjectivity, alienated from the real, which becomes available only to quantitative analysis, or mathematics. This inspired Blake to declare (in his annotations to Berkeley's *Siris*), against Locke and also against the Platonic valorization of mathematics, that God was not a mathematical diagram (664). The identification of poetry with subjectivity has been, as we shall see, accepted to this day by many attackers and defenders, to the detriment of the defense.

The third book of Locke's *Essay* is devoted to a discussion of language and his discontent with its limits. In a chapter titled "The Imperfection of Words," he acknowledges their importance:

> I must confess . . . that when I first began this Discourse of the Understanding, and a good while after, I had not the least thought that any consideration of words was at all necessary to it. But when, having passed over the original and composition of our ideas, I began to examine the extent and certainty of our knowledge, I found it had so near a connexion with words, that, unless their force and manner of signification were first well observed, there could be very little said clearly and pertinently concerning knowledge. (2: 118–19)

The next chapter in Locke's *Essay* is titled "The Abuse of Words." It is possible to recognize an ambiguity in its title, because the abuse is *by* language even as it is declared that words can be abused by their users. In short, words are rather like all that belongs to the secondary qualities of experience; they are subjective in use and unstable in meaning. It is seldom that

22. "Two Horn'd Reasoning Cloven Fiction," *For the Sexes: The Gates of Paradise*, *The Complete Poetry and Prose of William Blake*, ed. David V. Erdman, rev. ed. (Garden City, NY: Anchor Press/Doubleday, 1982), 268.

23. Alfred North Whitehead, *Science and the Modern World* (New York: Macmillan, 1941), 80.

the meaning a speaker assumes his words to have is the same as the meaning a listener gives them. Furthermore, words "interpose themselves so much between our understandings, and the truth which it would contemplate and apprehend, that, like the medium through which visible objects pass, the obscurity and disorder do not seldom cast a mist before our eyes, and impose upon our understandings" (119).

There is little hope for poetry here, particularly since Locke requires that the only proper purpose of language be the conveyance of knowledge from one person to another and efficiency in accomplishing it. This leads to his argument that people who do not use language efficiently along these lines abuse words. If one does not have a distinct idea in mind, one's discourse is merely noise. Words should be used responsibly with respect to their accepted meanings and without equivocation. Especially ominous for poetry is the following stricture: " . . . he that imagined to himself substances such as never have been, and filled his head with ideas which have not any correspondence with the real nature of things, to which yet he gives settled and defined names, may fill his discourse, and perhaps another man's head, with the fantastical imaginations of his own brain, but will be very far from advancing thereby one jot in real and true knowledge" (2: 144). Knowledge, in Locke's sense, is all that he cares about.

Locke is also suspicious of figurative speech when it is not strictly for pleasure, thus eliminating half of the Horatian directive that poems should teach as well as delight. For Locke, the former is impossible for poetry to accomplish. Rhetorical ornament is tricky and subject to use in promulgating the false:

> I confess, in discourses where we seek rather pleasure and delight than information and improvement, such ornaments as are borrowed from them can scarce pass for faults. But yet if we would speak of things as they are, we must allow that all the art of rhetoric, besides order and clearness; all the artificial application of words eloquence hath invented, are for nothing else but to insinuate wrong ideas, move the passions, and thereby mislead the judgment, and so indeed are perfect cheats. (2: 146)

So, the poets abuse language if their marvelous fictions are created for anything but delight, and poetry is identified with rhetoric as a form of abuse. It is impossible to imagine a poem so purely devoted to entertainment as to escape Locke's censure.

Locke is the precursor of all those attitudes toward language even up to our own time that define it wholly in terms of its communicative utility and regard poetry as "deviation" from so-called normal use.[24] This history can be traced up through the views of Jeremy Bentham and James Mill into the practice of logical positivism and analytical philosophy. It tells us quite a lot about the estrangement of modern Anglo-American philosophy from philosophical developments on the European continent that are friendlier to poetry.

We have noticed in both Gosson and Sprat the idea of decline in the value of poetry from the time of the esteemed and vigorous Ancients to the present. This view appears in the long controversy over who were better, the Ancients or the Moderns, the struggle over literary use of the vernacular rather than Latin, and the dispute over the use of rime. It is tied up with the idea of relentless progress, identified with the growth of the natural sciences and technology.

Attack on the Primitive

If we proceed into the nineteenth century past Bentham, whom I shall discuss in chapter 6, we encounter "The Four Ages of Poetry," a witty essay attacking poets by Thomas Love Peacock, mainly known for his satirical novels.[25] He was apparently on friendly terms with Bentham, James Mill, and John Stuart Mill, and he was a close friend of Shelley, whose "Defence of Poetry" was written in answer to his attack.

Peacock's essay has evoked a variety of responses. Some readers treat it as a tongue-in-cheek exercise, others as a straightforward expression of

24. The notion of deviation has not, for the most part, been used derogatorily in modern literary theory beginning with the Russian formalists and the later structuralist movement. There the term is meant to be simply descriptive.

25. H. B. Brett-Smith and C. E. Jones, eds., *The Works of Thomas Love Peacock* (London: Constable and Co., 1934), 8: 3–25.

a utilitarian view. Still others see it as typical of Peacock's tendency, exhibited in other works, to drive a position to extremes in order to present it satirically. Given the tone and context of the essay, it is easy to agree with Carl Dawson's characterization of Peacock's utilitarianism as a part-time commitment.[26] The attack on poetry may seem strange given that Peacock himself published many poems, not all satirical, though his later poetry was of that sort. But he was apparently by his own estimate a failure as a poet, or rather he came to believe that an audience for serious poetry was fast disappearing. In an unfinished essay written before "The Four Ages," Peacock lamented that the reading public had become consumers of the fashionable and transitory and that criticism in the periodicals was ignorant and incompetent.[27] Writing to Shelley in 1820, the year of "The Four Ages," he deplored the decline of poetry in the eyes of the intelligentsia:

> The truth, I am convinced, is that there is no longer a poetical audience among the higher class of minds; that moral, political, and physical science have entirely withdrawn from poetry the attention of all whose attention is worth having; and that the poetical reading public, being composed of the mere dregs of the intellectual community, the most sufficing passport to their favour must rest on the mixture of a little easily-intelligible portion of mawkish sentiment with an absolute negation of reason and knowledge. (8: 219–20)

We see here a disillusion and nostalgia that lead into "The Four Ages" and constitute probably the main impulse for attack. But Peacock had never been an idolater of poets.[28] He was especially critical of the poetry of his time, even though he defended certain poems attacked by others. He did

26. Carl Dawson, *His Fine Wit: A Study of Thomas Love Peacock* (Berkeley and Los Angeles: University of California Press, 1970), 92.

27. "Essay on Fashionable Literature," in Brett-Smith and Jones, *The Works of Thomas Love Peacock*, 8: 263–91. See Marilyn Butler, *Peacock Displayed: A Satirist in His Context* (London: Routledge and Kegan Paul, 1979), 272–85.

28. See, for example, *Headlong Hall*: " . . . the ordinary effect of love, according to some amatory poets, who seem to have composed their whining ditties for the benevolent purpose of bestowing on others that gentle slumber of which they so pathetically lament the privation . . . " (1: 91).

not tire of satirizing Coleridge as the metaphysically-minded Flosky in *Night-mare Abbey*, Pancope in *Headlong Hall*, and Skionar in *Crotchet Castle*; but he defended both "Kubla Khan" and "Christabel" at some length against hostile reviews. Nevertheless, he detested the expressivist poetry of his age, which he regarded as self-indulgent and anti-intellectual.

"The Four Ages" wittily presents a gloomy cyclical view of the history of poetry that goes beyond a simple disparagement of the contemporary. It calls into question, as Sprat did, any reason for poetry to continue to exist. Poetry has passed, Peacock says, through two cycles. The second one is inferior to that of the ancient classical era. Both cycles exhibit decline in their late stages. The first cycle begins with an age of iron in which bards celebrated the exploits and power of their chieftains. The presumption is that it was human nature to seek as much power and property as possible and for each chieftain to acquire a bard to disseminate accounts of his achievements. The origin of poetry was "panegyrical" (4).[29] Peacock rearranged the traditional order of the ages and caused the golden age to follow the age of iron. The golden age was that of Homer and heroic poetry, in which poetry reached a height never again attained. The age of silver that followed was sophisticated (the example is Virgil) but derivative and repetitious. Meanwhile, "as the sciences of morals and of mind advance towards perfection, as they become more enlarged and comprehensive in their views, as reason gains the ascendancy in them over imagination and feeling, poetry can no longer accompany them in their progress, but drops into the background, and leaves them to advance alone" (11). The subsequent age of brass, associated with the decline of Rome, was one of poetry divorced from reason, a sort of second childhood.

The second and lesser cycle began with the Middle Ages, proceeded to the golden age of the Renaissance, and began to wane after Milton in the silver age of Dryden, Pope, Goldsmith, Collins, and Gray. The decline was then abruptly into the modern age of brass, in which feeling and self-

29. This, in particular, separates Peacock's cyclical history from that of Giambattista Vico, to be discussed later, and that of Northrop Frye, which tends toward the Vichian. Carl Dawson, in *His Fine Wit* (90), overstates Peacock's similarity to Vico with respect to nostalgia about the past.

expression again reign. The main culprits are the so-called Lake Poets, who have succumbed to fashion and "perversion of intellect" (18): "They wrote verses on a new principle; saw rocks and rivers in a new light; and remaining studiously ignorant of history, society and human nature, cultivated the phantasy only at the expense of the memory and the reason; and contrived, though they had retreated from the world for the express purpose of seeing nature as she was, to see her only as she was not" (18). Imitators have followed, bringing the age of brass "prematurely to its dotage" (18).

Poetry's cyclical decline contrasts sharply with utilitarian straight-line progress: "While the historian and the philosopher are advancing in, and accelerating, the progress of knowledge, the poet is wallowing in the rubbish of departed ignorance . . . " (19). The poet is a semi-barbarian, a throwback who cannot keep up with the times, for by its very nature poetry is associated with "barbarous manners, obsolete customs, and exploded superstitions" (20). In this age, it possesses three especially unfortunate ingredients: "the rant of unregulated passion, the whine of exaggerated feeling, and the cant of factitious sentiment" (21). Poetry is simply now a waste of time that would better be spent on useful study. It is not difficult to see here an outgrowth of the separation of subject and object. Feeling becomes regarded as untempered by reason and reason untempered by feeling, with the latter situation regarded as far less dangerous than the former.

Peacock does not inveigh against the idea of progress, as many pessimistic poets and philosophers would a century later. One senses that his utilitarian criticism is actually less an attack on poetry than one against his age and its tastes. These tastes, as he saw them, discouraged him from ever again trying to write any poems other than satirical ones.[30]

No teacher of poetry at any level, except perhaps the primary grades, has not experienced the utilitarian attitude to which Peacock has given voice.

---

30. In *Peacock: The Satirical Novels: A Casebook* (London: Macmillan and Co., 1976), 14–15, Lorna Sage argues that Peacock deliberately satirizes a utilitarian bigot in his narrator and poses him against the equally ridiculous contemporary romantic poets. Perhaps. It seems to me that, in any case, Peacock indicates what he thinks the future holds. I do not think that Sage's interpretation eliminates Peacock's ambivalence toward poetry, perhaps the result of bitter disappointment.

It is an irony of his attack that a poet should offer the one most character-istic of his time (and of every time since). Explicit attacks are now rare, but that may only prove Peacock's depressing point. In his view, poetry would eventually no longer be important enough to warrant the trouble.

The Positivistic Attack

The philosophers of late nineteenth- and early twentieth-century logical positivism showed a nearly complete lack of interest in poetry. They were, however, kinder to poetry than to metaphysics, for which they had absolutely no use. The logical positivist Rudolf Carnap used the phrase "pseudo-statement" to describe both metaphysical and poetical state-ments. Pseudo-statements either "contain a word which is erroneously believed to have meaning" or are "put together in a counter-syntactical way."[31] For Carnap, only the propositions of mathematics and empirical science have "sense."[32] If one cannot verify the truth of a statement, one cannot understand it; no information has been communicated, only "ver-bal sounds devoid of meaning though possibly associated with images" ("Elimination," 73). Thus they may express something, but they have no "theoretical content" (*Philosophy*, 27).

Carnap allows, however, a difference between the meaningless asser-tions of the metaphysicians and those of poets. The metaphysician wrongly believes that he "travels in a territory in which truth and falsehood are at stake" ("Elimination," 79). By contrast, lyrical poets "do not try to refute in the poem the statements in a poem by some other lyrical poet; for they know they are in a domain of art and not in the domain of theory" (79–80). The pseudo-statements by both "serve [only] for the *expression of the gen-eral attitude of a person towards life*" (78). The poet's aim is to "express certain feelings of the poet and to excite similar feelings in us. A lyrical poem has no assertorial sense, no theoretical sense, it does not contain knowl-

31. Rudolf Carnap, "The Elimination of Metaphysics through Logical Analysis of Language" (1932), trans. Arthur Pap, *Logical Positivism*, ed. A.J. Ayer (Glencoe, IL: Free Press, 1959), 61.

32. Rudolf Carnap, *Philosophy and Logical Syntax* (London: Kegan Paul, Trench, Trubner and Co., 1935), 36.

edge" (*Philosophy*, 29). Therefore, it can be neither true nor false.[33]
Clearly, Carnap draws a hard and fast line between assertion and expression and identifies assertion with science, expression with art, and confusion of the two with metaphysics.

Carnap's views and those of other logical positivists appear to be derived mainly from Sir Francis Bacon and David Hume, both friendly, in their ways, to poetry. Yet Hume held that only mathematical and empirical propositions have sense. The rest, he said, should be consigned to the flames. (Carnap refers to Hume's statement [*Philosophy*, 36].)

Although Carnap eschews the notion of universes of discourse, each to be judged by its own internal principles, he does argue that for something to have truth value it must be an element of the system derived from empiricism, fitting together logically with the other elements. This system is the only one with truth, which is always only that which is empirically verifiable. However, the thesis of the reality of the world of things can't be made good in any language belonging to that world (20–21).[34]

Carnap's distinction between science and art is based on one between the measurable and the attitudinal. It can be regarded as a new coming (with a difference) of Plato's attack on the sophists and of Locke's separation of primary from secondary qualities of experience.

Carnap, who perhaps represents the last stages of the attack launched by Locke, does not show any ambivalence toward his own certainty about

---

33. This conclusion had been reached on quite other grounds by Sidney. See chapter 3 of this volume.

34. Here Carnap seems to acknowledge the problem of what is known as Russell's paradox (or antinomy). Indeed, Carnap is indebted to Bertrand Russell, particularly to the *Introduction to Mathematical Philosophy*. There Russell remarks, "The sense of reality is vital in logic, and whoever puzzles with it by pretending that Hamlet has another kind of reality is doing a disservice to thought" (London: George Allen and Unwin, 1919), 170. Also, "In the proposition 'I met a unicorn,' the whole four words together make a significant proposition, and the word 'unicorn' by itself is significant in just the same sense as the word 'man'. But the two words 'a unicorn' do not form a subordinate group having a meaning of its own. Thus if we falsely attribute meaning to these two words, we find ourselves saddled with 'a unicorn', with the problem of how there can be such a thing in a world where there are no unicorns" (170). Russell seems to want all sentences to have at least significance, while Carnap would seem to deny anything to such sentences, though he is not consistent in his use of "meaning."

poetry. He finds a place for poetry, but he is condescending almost to the point of scorn. One senses that he is held back from outright dismissal only by a thought that poetry still has some prestige in intellectual circles. Because of this attitude, it is surprising that a logical positivist view did enter on the side of defense, there to create a massive, often confused debate, principally by way of the early work of I. A. Richards. In his *Science and Poetry* (1926), Richards introduced the term "pseudo-statement" to literary criticism. For Richards, a pseudo-statement is "not necessarily false in any sense,"[35] its scientific truth or falsity being irrelevant to poetry's purposes. Poetry has only an "air of making statements." There is a sense in which a pseudo-statement is "true" (Richards puts the word in quotation marks) if it "suits and serves some attitude or links together attitudes which on other grounds are desirable" (60). It would take too long to unravel here the difficulties in this statement; it must suffice to observe that attitudes, as with Carnap, are subjective and opposed to truth. Richards attempted to give psychological value to poetry as an organizer of subjective impulses. In the view of many previous critics, it is the parts of the poem that are organized, as in Aristotle's conception of unity or Coleridge's unity in diversity. Richards puts the whole of the old unity of the poetic object into the organization of the reader's impulses and subjectivized response.

Richards attacked, through what I think is a misreading of Kant's aesthetic, the notion of the "phantom aesthetic state."[36] The attack might better have been directed at certain of Kant's followers. Kant held that aesthetic judgments must be singular, that is, that criteria cannot be brought in from the outside. Judgments from the outside can be made, of course, but they are not aesthetic ones. This does not, in my view, imply an aesthetic state of mind; rather, it requires that aesthetic judgment be limited to attention to the internal relations of the work. Richards's impulse here was, however (and quite rightly), to oppose an extreme and common appropriation of Kant among critics that led to what A. C. Bradley called

---

35. I. A. Richards, *Poetries and Sciences: A Reissue of Science and Poetry (1926, 1935)* (New York: W. W. Norton and Co., 1970), 60fn.

36. I. A. Richards, *Principles of Literary Criticism* (New York: Harcourt, Brace and Co.; London: Kegan Paul, Trench, Trubner and Co., 1928), 11–18.

"life for art's sake" and which rendered the work of art totally autonomous, without any verbal meaning whatever, or even "significance." But Richards was led into what he admitted was a "turgid uncouthness of . . . terminology" gathered up mainly from behaviorism, in which the old Lockean distinction again prevailed in a disguise designed for literary analysis: "In a full critical statement which states not only that an experience is valuable in certain ways, but also that it is caused by certain features in a contemplated object, the part which describes the value of the experience we shall call the *critical* part. That which describes the objective we shall call the *technical* part" (23). This seems to have led R. P. Blackmur, in his essay "A Critic's Job of Work" (1935), to insist that inquiry into the technical part had to come first in order to arrive at evaluation.[37] I mention this to show how the language of the positivistic tradition invaded the work of people not sympathetic to it. This is a case of the defense being trapped in the enemy's language. Richards wanted a "clear demarcation" between the object's features and their effect. But it is difficult to understand how critical analysis of the object can occur at all if the poetic features of that object *as object* are real only if they are reduced to their measurable aspect, as Hume and Carnap had insisted, or are regarded only as existing in the perceiving subject.

In spite of Richards's odd effort to accommodate poetry to the positivistic attitude (including his quixotic attempt to enlist the idealist Coleridge in the project),[38] it is clear that the logical positivistic bias, along with a substantial dose of behaviorism, puts severe limitations on poetry. But the position is not from its own point of view anti-poetical. It merely regards poetry as unimportant, even dispensable for serious thought, as Peacock predicted. Richards's effort to save poetry from the charge of inconsequentiality by making it the balancer of subjective impulses accepts the subject-object terms of the adversary just as earlier defenders accepted Plato's terms.

---

37. R. P. Blackmur, "A Critic's Job of Work," *Language as Gesture* (New York: Harcourt, Brace and Co., 1952).

38. I. A. Richards, *Coleridge on Imagination* (New York: W. W. Norton and Co., 1950).

Few, if any, of the opponents of poetry I have mentioned have not found some place for poetry, however small or demeaning. In doing this, they have usually expressed ambivalence about it. It is as if their philosophical positions have driven them to assertions too narrow, somewhat embarrassing, and against their own suppressed impulses.

3

Defense

The long history of the defense of poetry does not reveal ambivalence, but different defensive arguments have been offered, most of which have adopted the terms of the attackers and have been trapped in those terms and their implications. An exception is Aristotle, who gives to "imitation" a different meaning from that intended by Plato. After him, however, the word tended to slip back into its previous definition or to lose the precision he attempted to give it.

Classical Defenses

The first extant defense of poetry occurs in Aristotle's *Poetics*, but it is not explicitly a defense. The intent is an analytic description of tragedy (in the part that has survived) and how best to write it. Implicitly, however, it says that tragedy, or poetry generally, is worthy of serious and systematic study. It states at the outset that there are such things as good poems, good being those that conform to Aristotle's general description. The value of tragedy has to do in part with imitation; Aristotle holds on to Plato's word, but he redefines "imitation" in a different ontology. It is no longer servile copying thrice removed from the ideal real. He regards it as a part of human nature and a natural source of delight: ". . . though the objects themselves may be painful to see, we delight to view the most realistic representations of them in art, the forms for example of the lowest animal and of dead bodies. The explanation is to be found in a further fact: to be learning something is the greatest of pleasures not only to the philosopher but also to the rest of mankind, however small their capacity for it."[1] Delight is thus combined with learning in imitation, which has an active rather than passive

1. W. D. Ross, ed., "De Poetica," trans. Ingram Bywater, *The Works of Aristotle* (Oxford: Clarendon Press, 1924), 1 1: 1448b, 1–15.

character. This is in part because of its connection with the making of plots and characters, as well as the use of language, thought, melody, and spectacle. These elements, all belonging to artistic imitation, create an object that has its own being, unlike the poem as insisted on by Socrates in Plato's *Ion*, which is a cloudy transparency with no form or being of its own.

Aristotle does not divorce delight and learning, as later critics tended to do. He does not isolate features supposedly intended to achieve one or the other. He holds together form, identified by later critics as the vehicle of delight, and content, the vehicle of the didactic element. Further, his implied defense offers a psychological interpretation of the beneficial effect of tragedy in his notion of the *catharsis* of pity and fear undergone collectively by the audience. There has been much debate about *catharsis*, but it seems sensible, at least, to conclude that the notion arose out of the historical connection of tragedy to Ancient Greek religious rituals, though this view has recently been challenged. In any case, Aristotle's *catharsis* of pity and fear is an answer to Plato's Socrates, who complained that poetry feeds and waters the passions, including pity and fear, both of which Socrates regarded as inappropriate for guardians of the State.

Northrop Frye declared hyperbolically that very little new and sensible in the literary theory of genres had occurred since Aristotle.[2] And he implied even that not much new in literary theory generally had occurred since then (14). Between Aristotle and the development of the idea of aesthetics in the eighteenth century, not a lot that was new was contributed to the defense of poetry, though many defenses were written and controversies abounded. I say this because almost all defenses in that long stretch of centuries were occupied with efforts to respond to Socrates' challenge to demonstrate that poetry delights and teaches. These were worthy efforts, but they were trapped by having to answer in the terms set forth by the enemy. Aristotle endeavored to change, if not the terms, at least the meaning of the governing term "imitation" that Socrates had employed in his attack on the poets. Also, Aristotle tried to avoid the Socratic charge of poetic irrationality by recourse to a secularization and psychologizing of

2. Northrop Frye, *Anatomy of Criticism* (Princeton, NJ: Princeton University Press, 1957), 13.

ritual catharsis. But *Poetics* was lost for centuries, and even when it became available to European critics, it was often misread or its tendency to lay down rules of composition was emphasized at the expense of the redefinition of imitation and the avoidance of a split between form and content. Criticism was recaptured by the Platonic admonition that poems should delight and teach and critics should show that they can.

There was a significant exception. In spite of Socrates' influential remarks, Platonism generated one defense not designed to answer entirely in the usual terms. This was Plotinus's discussion of beauty in the *Enneads* (c. 260). Rather than criticizing the artist for being an imitator thrice removed from the idea, Plotinus emphasized the artist's visionary and creative powers. For Plotinus, pure matter is absolute darkness, and art is the liberation of form from the darkness of matter. It is a reversal upward of emanation, which is downward from the One (or ultimate idea) toward the world's multiplicity and, finally, the dark, indefinite void of pure matter. Beauty is achieved by the artist's inward grasp of the idea and his shaping it from the material object with which he begins. The example employed is that of a sculptor addressing a block of stone. The Idea is not, as it is in Plato, apart from and foreign to the artist. It is in the artist "before ever it enters the stone," and its appearance (always only partial) occurs " in so far as it has subdued the resistance of the material."[3]

Thus, for Plotinus, the artist's imitation infuses the material darkness of the stone with the light of form rather than producing through imitation of an object a false copy. Plotinus's is a valiant effort to work within the Platonic metaphysics. To those for whom the metaphysics or perhaps any metaphysics is inadequate, Plotinus's defense fails. But in giving art a midway position, between pure matter and Idea, yet always aspiring toward the light of the latter, he would make art a mediation: "Thus Pheidias wrought the Zeus upon no model among things of sense but by apprehending what form Zeus must take if he chose to become manifest to sight" (423).

Horace's example is far closer to the main line of defense. His *Ars Poetica* (c. 20 B.C.) is not an explicit defense, however. It is a poem of advice

3. Plotinus, "On the Intellectual Beauty," *The Enneads*, trans. Stephen MacKenna, 3rd ed., revised by B. S. Page (London: Faber and Faber, 1962), 422.

to prospective writers. He does not answer Socrates' demand. He simply asserts that the young writer must keep in mind that a poem should delight and teach, and the teaching should be of what is useful. Everywhere in Roman and later Greek thought we find the notion that poetry *does* delight and teach. Sometimes the idea is combined with the fear of the poet as liar.

In "How the Young Man Should Study Poetry," Plutarch quotes Gorgias to the effect that tragedy is "a deception wherein he who deceives is more honest than he who does not deceive."[4] Just how honest that would be neither Plutarch nor Gorgias says. At the same time, Plutarch argues that as a precaution the young man should be introduced to poetry with nothing in his mind as powerfully "imprinted" as the saying "Many are the lies that poets tell" (81–82). Furthermore, though there is much in poetry that is "pleasant and nourishing," there is also a lot that is "disturbing and misleading" (77–78).

Plutarch is discussing education and poetry's role in it. When at its best in this role, it is an "introductory exercise in philosophy" (81). Youths are thereby trained to "seek the profitable in what gives pleasure, and to find satisfaction therein" (81). Plutarch compares poetry to a vine. When it grows too riotous and luxuriant in giving unalloyed pleasure, it needs to be pruned back: "But where with its grace it approaches a true kind of culture and the sweet allurement of its language is not fruitless or vacuous, there let us introduce philosophy and blend it with poetry" (81).

Aristotle had kept his treatment of poetry separate from his treatment of rhetoric. In later classical criticism, one senses a subjugation of poetic to rhetoric and emphasis on friendly persuasion as use, particularly where the model for poetry becomes oratory. The Platonic connection between poets and rhetoricians remains, but without the attack on either.

One of the classical texts representative of the merging of poetic with rhetoric, political oratory being the implicit model, is the pseudo-Longinus's fragmented first-century work *Peri Hupsous* (*On the Sublime* or sometimes *On Great Writing*). It is not really a defense of poetry; it is a discourse indicating the quality of style to which poets should aspire. The author says

4. Plutarch, *Moralia* (Loeb Classical Library), trans. Frank Cole Babbitt (London: William Heinemann; Cambridge, MA: Harvard University Press, 1986 [1927]), 1: 79.

that transport, not persuasion, is the effect of elevated language on an audience and that sublimity is "the echo of a great soul."[5] Yet Longinus steps back from any notion that the sublime is irrationally produced. Indeed, according to him, there are many examples of sublimity that are independent of passion. He does not want expression to go its own way. The orator (for this is clearly the model) should *not* be possessed. Oratory should come under the precepts of art, and the result should be that the audience is moved: "Our persuasions we can usually control, but the influences of the sublime bring power and irresistible might to bear, and reign over every hearer" (43). So the audience is to be won over by the design of the poet-orator. Longinus has faith in the great soul of the poet to rise above mere persuasion and convey a grandeur valuable for its transcendence of the petty and mundane. But there is a warning that the use of tropes can lead to excess: "Evil are the swelling, both in the body and in diction" (49).

Allegory as Defense

There is a latent fear of poetry when the poetry is that of the Bible and pious respect is required. This is apparent in Saint Augustine's mention of metaphor in Scripture. He decides that obscure figures were provided by God to "conquer pride by work and to combat disdain in our minds."[6] Referring to a passage in the Song of Songs, he asks, "Does one learn anything else besides that which he learns when he hears the same thought expressed in plain words without the similitude? Nevertheless, in a strange way, I contemplate the saints more pleasantly when I envisage them as the teeth of the Church cutting off men from their errors and transferring them to her body after their hardness has been softened as if by being bitten and chewed" (37). Putting aside contemplation of this bloodthirsty figure, we hear him next telling us that he is unable to say why the similitude is "sweeter" to him than a straightforward statement. He says merely

5. W. Rhys Roberts, ed. and trans., *Longinus on the Sublime* (Cambridge: Cambridge University Press, 1935), 61.

6. Saint Augustine, *On Christian Doctrine* (c. 426), trans. D. W. Robertson, Jr. (Indianapolis, IN: Bobbs-Merrill, 1978), 37.

that it is "a problem for another discussion" (38). It seems that he may sense something offensive about metaphors and similes, even as he is charmed by this one.

The problem that Augustine dodges is faced directly by Saint Thomas Aquinas in the *Summa Theologica* (1256–72), and he comes down in defense of metaphor. He points out three specific objections to the use of metaphor in Scripture. They are that Scripture should not employ the devices of poetry, the lowest of the sciences; that figures in the likeness of corporeal things only obscure the spiritual truth; and that when figures are used they should be representations by means of higher rather than lower things. His general answer is as follows:

> It is befitting Holy Scripture to put forward divine and spiritual truths by means of comparisons with material things. For God provides for everything according to the capacity of its nature. Now it is natural for man to attain to intellectual truths through sensible things, because all our knowledge originates from sense. Hence in Holy Scripture spiritual truths are fittingly taught under the likeness of material things.[7]

Thomas's further answers are that sacred doctrine uses metaphors in a necessary and useful way, obscurity is often useful, for it exercises the mind, and divine truths are more properly expounded in less noble figures because thereby one sees that the descriptions are not literal. That is particularly important with respect to references to God. Finally, obscurity hides truth from the unworthy.

Thomas's views encourage thinking about metaphor as if it were the vehicle of allegories of disembodied spiritual truth. This is the result of his use of the elaborate sixfold scheme of interpretation of Scripture derived from John Cassian. Each of the two main divisions, the literal and the spiritual, contains three parts. These need not detain us except for us to note that Thomas requires the literal level to contain the historical so that the

---

7. Anton C. Pegis, ed., *Introduction to Saint Thomas Aquinas* (New York: Random House, 1948), 16.

historicity of the Bible is not "spirited away"[8] into an allegory not grounded in biblical history.

The secularization of the system attempted by Dante in his *Commedia* followed along Thomas's lines, and the poem seeks to keep spirit and "history" (in this case, a fictive history) together. However, in the longer run, secularized metaphor, separated from a spiritual root, tended to be thought of as allegorical representation of abstract ideas. The literal level became the signifier of the idea, and the relation of the two was arbitrary rather than insured by biblical history. Further, the allegorical interpretation or abstract idea became treated as the significant content at the expense of all the formal elements, which had no role but decoration. Delight (*dulce*) became a purely rhetorical aim, and rhetoric a group of devices of persuasion to seduce the reader, who thereby was persuaded of something of supposed use (*utile*) under pleasant conditions.

Obscurity and mystery became more difficult to defend in a secular work that was supposed to entertain as well as inform. Indeed, obscurity would seem to work against delight except for those who enjoy the challenge of puzzles.

It is not surprising, given the importance of the *Commedia*, that the defense of poetry became for a time the defense of the *Commedia*. In his *Vita di Dante*, written in 1363 but not published until 1477, Giovanni Boccaccio evokes Saint Gregory, who likens poetry to Scripture in that it is allegorical, disclosing at the same time "the text and its underlying mystery," thus reaching both little children and sublime thinkers.[9] Ancient poetry, employing fiction (the pagan gods, for example) and gentle persuasion, revealed "the causes of things, the effects of virtues and of vices, what we ought to flee and what follow; in order that we may attain by virtuous action the end that they, although they did not rightly know the true God, believed to be our supreme salvation" (51).

It is with respect to subject matter that poetry and Scripture diverge,

8. The phrase, to my knowledge, is that of Jean Danielou, in *From Shadows to Reality: Studies in the Biblical Typology of the Fathers*, trans. Wulstan Hibbard (Westminster, MD: Newman Press, 1960).

9. Giovanni Boccaccio, "Dante," *The Earliest Lives of Dante*, trans. J. R. Smith (New York: Holt, Rinehart, and Winston, 1901), 50.

and Boccaccio is compelled to defend poetic fictions against the old charge of falsity. Here he has recourse again to allegory, and also, like Thomas, he argues that something gained by labor is sweeter and better retained than something that comes with little effort. The poets also used fables because they present surface delights that philosophic demonstrations lack.

Beyond the difference in subject matter between poetry and theology, the latter could be called the "poetry of God" (54). In his *Genealogy of the Gentile Gods* (1366), Boccaccio identifies the poetic with "whatever is composed as under a veil, and thus exquisitely wrought [in part by use of fictive imagination and rhetorical devices], is poetry and poetry alone."[10] The veil is "a fair and fitting garment of fiction" (39) and thus not utter nonsense. Boccaccio claims that all the types of fiction he can think of occur in the Bible, including the parables of Jesus. But Boccaccio must sacrifice the literal level of the poem in a way that Thomas does not with Scripture, and we must continually fall back on hidden allegorical meaning as the real value, with the fictive surface present merely for delight. This means that the poet is distinguished from the philosopher, not by his thought, but by the means of presenting it, an "outward semblance of . . . invention" (79) rather than an unadorned prose style. Instead of engaging directly in disputation, the poet sings in solitude.

Renaissance Defense

Giacopo Mazzoni's defense of Dante, *Della Difesa Della Commedia di Dante*, first published in three books in 1587, but reprinted with the addition of three more books in 1688, was conceived as an answer to Castravilla and Bulgarini. His "Introduction and Summary," however, goes well beyond a defense of Dante to offer a general theory of poetry, in the process of which he responds to the complaint that Dante's poem lacks verisimilitude. Mazzoni regarded himself as a philosopher, his most ambitious work being *De Triplici Hominum Vita, Actio, Nempe, Contemplativa, et Religiosa Methodi Tres*, an effort to overcome the differences between Plato and

---

10. Charles G. Osgood, trans., *Boccaccio on Poetry* (Princeton, NJ: Princeton University Press, 1930), 42.

Aristotle. Although the *Difesa* is not explicitly such an effort, it grows out of the earlier work, both Plato and Aristotle being invoked.

Mazzoni's defense turns on the notion of the poet as a maker of "idols" or images. To make an idol is the poet's only concern *as poet*, but, as we shall see, there are different uses to which the product of idol-making can be put, and the poet must be aware of them. An idol is the object (in the sense of a thing to be made) of the imitative arts (not the object to be imitated). It is an image and similitude that comes into being by human artifice. It can be of one or another kind: icastic or phantastic (as Plato said). Poetry's subjects, as a result, can sometimes be true, sometimes false. In both cases, they ought to be credible, whether possible or impossible (as Aristotle said). Indeed, the poet's reliance should be on the credible rather than on the true, the false, the possible, or the impossible. A poet making the credible should employ sensible means.

All of this has to do with the issue of verisimilitude, and Mazzoni asserts, "The verisimilitude which is sought by the poets is of such a nature that it is feigned by poets according to their own will."[11] Elsewhere he speaks of phantastic imitation as that created by the "caprice of the artist."[12]

Mazzoni argues that the same thing can be submitted to different arts by different modes of artifice, of which there are three (see fig. 1). Poetry belongs to the third type of artifice, mode, and example—the idol.

Figure 1

Type of artifice	*Mode*	*Example*
Idea: Object of the ruling or governing arts	Observable	Horsemanship
Work: Object of the fabricating arts	Fabricable	Bridle-making arts
Idol: Object of the imitative arts	Imitable	Idol or image of a bridle

11. Quoted from Book I in Hazard Adams, ed., *Critical Theory Since Plato*, trans. Robert L. Montgomery, rev. ed. (Fort Worth, TX: Harcourt Brace Jovanovich, 1992), 174.

12. Giacopo Mazzoni, *On the Defense of the Comedy of Dante: Introduction and Summary*, trans. Robert L. Montgomery (Tallahassee: Florida State University Press, 1983), 46.

At this stage of his argument, Mazzoni declares that it is not reasonable to ask whether utility or delight is the end of poetry. However, both eventually return in his theory. Poetry *as such* is an imitative art with only the idol as its object, but it also can be seen in two more ways that are by-products, so to speak, of the poet's act (see fig. 2). The civil faculty professes to understand the "justness of human actions" (89) and thus is concerned with politics. Poetry is involved with what Mazzoni calls "cessation of activity": play, amusement, recreation, all of which he refers to as "positive privation" (89). Cessation is a necessary and positive contrary to action.

Figure 2

As an imitative art	*As recreation*	*Under the civil faculty*
The making of idols, verse, number, harmony, the credible marvelous	The making of poetry for purposes of delight	The making of poetry to delight usefully

So Mazzoni would have his Plato and his Aristotle, too: The poetic art as such has its own end, as in Aristotle; it comes under the civil faculty, as Plato wanted it to, but with quite different results, for Plato's Socrates had no place for "cessation" in his severe State. It appears that Mazzoni's theory would allow for three forms of literary criticism addressed to the three categories in figure 2 above. Presumably, to extend Mazzoni, criticism directed to poetry as an imitative art would be the ground for the criticism of the other two kinds. After presenting a progressive series of definitions of poetry, Mazzoni offers four corollaries:

> The first of these is that poetry taken in the first two modes is neither ruled nor governed by the civil faculty. The second is that only poetry in the third mode is that which is ruled and governed by moral philosophy or the civil faculty. The third is that the poetic that considers the idol in the first mode and that which likewise considers the idol in the second mode of poetry should not in any way be called a part of moral philosophy. The fourth and last corollary is that only the poetic that considers the idol in the third mode of poetry is that which really

deserves to be called part of the civil faculty. And each good poet should put together his poems according to the rules of this mode of poetry, as Dante has done better than all the others. (108–9)

It appears that this last is a concession to the prevailing authority and an effort to show that neither he nor Dante gives offense. We may observe that Mazzoni has come a long way around to reassertion of the old Horatian *dulce et utile*, but now under State rule. Yet Mazzoni accomplishes two things in the process. First, he justifies something like what Blackmur called a criticism centered on technique. Second, in spite of what appears to be capitulation, he defends the poet's intent to be, *as poet*, nothing but the creator of idols and the resulting credible marvelous. All imitation, including the icastic, would seem to create a phantasm as a result of the poet's "caprice." Mazzoni's aim was principally to show along Aristotelian lines that Dante's poetry of the credible marvelous had verisimilitude, but he also wanted to make Dante acceptable to a kind of Platonism as well. His introduction of the notion of cessation and play under the civil faculty as something useful to the State may have been designed to lessen the likelihood of State tyranny. In the end, though, Mazzoni concedes the domination of moral philosophy over poetic creativity, and we sense the Church looking over his shoulder.

Some of the Platonic issues that Mazzoni does not address are the poet's alleged lack of knowledge of what he writes about and his irrational possession and madness. These Girolamo Fracastoro had treated earlier in his graceful dialogue *Naugarius* (1540). He takes up the first issue at the expense of limiting what is meant by "poet": "When Plato says that poets do not know the things about which they write so eloquently, if he means that they do not know in so far as they are poets and skilled in writing, certainly he is right. But if he means that they know nothing at all, then, indeed, he is wrong."[13] Strictly as an artisan or a technician, the poet knows how to write a poem, but as a human being educated in philosophy, he should know what he writes about.

---

13. Girolamo Fracastoro, *Naugarius Sive di Poetica Dialogus*, trans. Ruth Kelso, *University of Illinois Studies in Language and Literature* 9 (Urbana, 1924), 72.

As for poetic madness, Fracastoro brings the idea of it down to earth. The poet's madness is not externally caused, and certainly not by God. It is the result of the process, not the cause, of composition. It is the result of the poet's having joined together "all the beauties of language and subject" (65). The poet feels "a certain wonderful and almost divine harmony steal into him" as the result of his accomplishment, and he is "carried out of himself" (65).

Fracastoro does not discuss the making of idols, but in his defense of the poet against the charge of lying, he argues that poets make things "more perfect" (70). He speaks of ornamentation, but he insists that ornament is not extraneous to the object but part of its perfection.[14] Ornament contributes to beauty, but Fracastoro's beauty is not a Platonic idea. Rather, there are different beauties appropriate to different subjects. However, he claims finally that there is only one subject "absolutely beautiful" (64), the heroic. He also says that every subject is proper for the poet as long as he can adorn (perfect) it.

In the end, Fracastoro's poet aims to delight and teach, and the art of perfectibility is but a means to those ends. It is by ornament that the poet teaches more effectively than by the direct presentation of abstract ideas and precepts.

In late sixteenth-century England, defenses of poetry were written in the face of Puritan attacks, especially attacks on the stage and on foreign, usually Italianate, influences. Arguments among poets themselves also generated defenses of particular poetic practices. On the one side were those who revered the quantitative verse of the Ancients, on the other the defenders of the Moderns, who advocated writing in the vulgate and who were not averse to folk poetry. There were those who defended the use of rime.[15] There was

14. What he says here may be compared to what George Puttenham, in *The Arte of English Poesie* (1589) (facsimile, Menston, England: The Scolar Press, 1968), says in his third book, titled "Of Ornament." Puttenham emphasizes at the outset the commendability of "the good proportion of any thing" (114) and defends in particular figurative writing.

15. In about 1603, Samuel Daniel defended rime against those who over decades had opposed it. These included Roger Ascham (1570), who invoked Quintilian in support of his view, Richard Stanyhurst (1582), and Thomas Campion (1598). George Gascoigne (1575) felt impelled to warn against "rime without reason." Rime was thought among some to be primitive and connected with unsophisticated folk poetry and ballads, but Sidney admitted the power of the ballad "Chevy Chase."

also a sense that poetry was in the doldrums. The most famous defense of the time was, of course, Sidney's *Apology for Poetry* (written in 1583, published in two versions in 1595). Sidney begins by describing himself as a defender of "poor poetry, which from almost the highest estimation of learning is fallen to be the laughing-stock of children."[16] He ends with an inquiry into why poetry finds "in our time hard welcome in England" (70). The essay is a compendium of defenses frequently offered. At times, it is a direct answer to Gosson's diatribe. To Gosson's complaint that there are better ways to spend one's time, Sidney responds that poetry teaches and moves one to virtue. To the charge of lying, Sidney responds that poetry, dealing in fictions, affirms nothing. To the challenge that it is the nurse of abuse, Sidney replies that anything can be used badly. Finally, to Gosson's citing Plato's attack, Sidney points out that Plato was himself a poet, that lies about the gods already existed in his time, that Plato's aim, in any case, was only to drive out wrong opinion, and that philosophers were jealous of poets.

These arguments were worth repeating in the face of contemporary attacks. However, as Forrest G. Robinson has shown, Sidney offers a ground for defense not developed by others.[17] It is based on an interpretation of the statement by the Ancient Greek poet Simonides of Chios that poetry is a speaking picture. Robinson emphasizes the visual in Sidney's use of the phrase and in his aesthetics generally. The notion of picture means "a concept made visible to the reader's mind" (99): " . . . the poet allows his reader to see a moral universal in action by submerging it in a specific character" (100). Robinson goes on to argue that in Sidney's time a standard assumption was that ideas could be made visible or "seen" in the mind. An interesting question is whether Sidney's "ideas" are derived from nature and are therefore built up into what later writers would call generalizations from sense data or are derived from a Platonic dialectical process. It seems that what Sidney actually says is ambiguous: "And the metaphysic [the philosopher], though it be in the second and abstract notions, and there-

16. Sir Philip Sidney, *An Apology for Poetry*, ed. Forrest G. Robinson (Indianapolis, IN, and New York: Bobbs-Merrill, 1970), 5.

17. Forrest G. Robinson, *The Shape of Things Known: Sidney's* Apology *and Its Philosophical Tradition* (Cambridge, MA: Harvard University Press, 1972).

fore be counted supernatural, yet doth he build upon the depth of nature"
(14). Sidney seems to say that, whatever ideas are, they can be "seen" in a
poem. But these ideas are in effect "another nature, in making things either
better than nature bringeth forth, or, quite anew forms such as never were
in nature . . . " (14).

Sidney locates the poem between history and philosophy, between
the particular example and the universal precept, and argues that the poet
teaches delightfully and therefore more successfully than either. But despite
emphasis on the visual quality of ideas in poetry, the example, because it
is an example of something, is always going to be dependent on and secondary to the precept, which will always be abstract.

There seem to be two choices here for a poetics: a visionary symbolism
of mystical experience or a turn toward allegory. Sidney's turn is to the latter, with the risk that the allegory will be but an arbitrary sign of the idea
despite his emphasis on visualization. This is complicated by his defense
of the poet as fiction-maker and his declaration that the poet's work is neither true nor false and does not demand belief. But, then, how are we to
know that what the poet presents is an improvement on nature or even "what
should or should not be"?

One can read Sidney's *Apology* as merely an entertaining compendium of Renaissance defensive ideas or, as Robinson does, a complex
effort to ground poetry on a "visual epistemology." To do the latter reveals,
I think, an inner conflict over the source of the idea. But it is possible to
argue that the most interesting literary theories contain an unresolvable contradiction or a paradox.

Sidney's theory holds for the importance of the matter of the poem over
the words, the idea or "fore-conceit" over expression. Here his work raises
all the questions about form's relation to content that have dogged defenses
into our own time. Roger Ascham, in his "Scholemaster" (1570), had warned
against the privileging of matter: "Ye know not what hurt ye do to learning,
that care not for wordes but for matter, and so make a deuorse between the
tong and the hart."[18] But Ascham was speaking out for a rhetorical interest

---

18. Roger Ascham, "The Scholemaster," *Elizabethan Critical Essays*, ed. G. Gregory Smith (Oxford: Clarendon Press, 1906), 1: 6.

concerned with effective and sincere communication. The defense of poetry would not change very much until changes in epistemology and linguistics came along together. Though those changes provided the possibility of new arguments, they also left poetry, as we have seen, more embattled than ever.

Defiance and Shelley's Defense

Identification of poetry with the primitive origins of culture or with the ancient sages was made by both attackers and defenders. Peacock had not been alone in his view that poets were throwbacks to a primitive world-view. Many rationalists and empiricists were agreed on this, and insofar as they identified poetry with ancient mythology, so were the Deists.

The incidence of depression and even madness among poets in the eighteenth century is worth a study; some of it must have been a result of the denigration of poetry, explicit or implied, in intellectual life. A mixture of depression and defiance is given voice in Thomas Gray's poem "The Bard" (1757), in which the last surviving Welsh bard casts a curse on the English king Edward I, who (by legend) had ordered the death of all the bards in Wales. Gray has the last bard prophesy that a line of poets will neverthe-less come forth and Wales will regain its power within the royal line. (The latter part of this prophecy he receives in colloquy with his own dead prede-cessors.) His suicidal leap to death from a cliff on Mount Snowdon is an ironic triumph of defiance in the grand style. The bard addresses the king, who passes below with his troops:

> " . . . with joy I see
> "The different dooms our Fates assign.
> "Be thine despair, and scepter'd care,
> "To triumph, and to die, are mine."
> He spoke, and headlong from the mountain height
> Deep in the roaring tide he plunged to endless night.
>   (lines 139–44)[19]

19. My transcription is from H. W. Starr and J. R. Hendrickson, eds., *The Com-plete Poems of Thomas Gray* (Oxford: Clarendon Press, 1966), 23–24.

Depression and defiance reemerged, as we shall see, in a later period of stress for poets—in the face of late nineteenth- and early twentieth-century positivistic disdain for what poets do.

Peacock was actually a latecomer to the view that poetry was an obsolete primitivism. In certain ways, the arguments he offered had been set aside, if not refuted. In his time, the attitude toward mythology and the interest in the nature of language were both becoming more sophisticated. For virtually all of its history, the study of myth for the most part assumed that myths were to be allegorically interpreted either as religious thought clothed in mystery by a priesthood in order that it not be defiled by the vulgar or as historical accounts (Euhemerism) corrupted over time by linguistic change. Traces of these views remained (and remain today), but not in Shelley's answer to Peacock (1840, though written in 1820). By this time, myth and poetry were beginning to be seen as related forms of thought and expression, and language was to be seen as in its origins mythical and poetic. In his *Defence of Poetry*, Shelley speaks of poetry as "connate with the origin of man" and considers that every original language "near to its source is in itself the chaos of a cyclic poem."[20] Poets remain necessary to culture; their language is

> . . . vitally metaphorical; that is, it marks the before unapprehended relations of things and perpetuates their apprehension, until the words which represent them, become, through time, signs for portions or classes of thoughts instead of pictures of integral thoughts; and then if no new poets should arise to create afresh the associations which have been thus disorganized, language will be dead to all the nobler purposes of human intercourse. (30)

It is the role of poetry not only to invent by creating new syntheses but also to sustain the synthetic impulse of the imagination.

At the same time, Shelley does not abandon the notion that poetry delights and teaches, but he significantly changes the old *dulce et utile*.

---

20. Percy Bysshe Shelley, *A Defence of Poetry, The Four Ages of Poetry* (Peacock), ed. John E. Jordan (Indianapolis, IN, and New York: Bobbs-Merrill, 1965), 26 and 30.

Poetry is "accompanied by pleasure." However, this pleasure is not separate from but part of its usefulness. Shelley holds that the charge of poetic immorality rests on a misconception of the way poetry acts to produce the general moral improvement of man. It does not do so by embodying the concepts of right and wrong of the poet's time. Indeed, the poet should avoid making explicit a morality. Rather, "it awakens and enlarges the mind itself by rendering the receptacle of a thousand unapprehended combinations of thought" (39–40). It lifts the veil of hidden beauty; it performs the identification of us with that beauty; it enlarges the circumferences of our imaginations. All of this is pleasurable even as it is *useful*, for it strengthens and purifies the affections and adds spirit to sense. Of course, Shelley admits it is not useful in the sense in which Peacock used the word. By it, Peacock seems to have meant banishment of "the importunity of the wants of our animal nature, the surrounding men with security of life," and so forth (65). For Shelley, these things are important, but they must come in the "footsteps of poets" (65). Poetry precedes ideas and is the root of system. Shelley thought that in a period of materialism poetry was most needed.

It follows from these views that Shelley had a low opinion of allegory, which to his mind cannot be an important aspect of a poem. For him, poetic meaning is not abstract but elusive to conceptual thought: "Veil after veil may be undrawn, and the inmost naked beauty of the meaning never exposed" (63). This description is Platonically tinged, but it is also a forerunner of twentieth-century attacks on paraphrase. But if one follows it out in the strict terms of Plato's *Republic*, the result would be the abandonment of poetry, presumably in favor of dialectic proceeding to the Idea. Shelley's recourse to an ideal yet poetic beauty not apprehensible in image raises the question of whether poetry can, after all, bridge the gap between image and idea. Shelley's secular and temporal notion of icon preceding idea,[21] poetry before philosophy as its repressed root, seems to sit uneasily with his Platonism. This situation helped to generate early twentieth-century neoclassical complaints against him, as in T. E. Hulme, Robert Penn War-

21. See Herbert Read, *Icon and Idea* (Cambridge, MA: Harvard University Press, 1955).

ren, and John Crowe Ransom, the last unhappy with what he called "Platonic poetry," a poetry of ideas.[22]

Aesthetics and Disinterest

When we consider the attitudes toward poetry among certain Enlightenment rationalists and empiricists, it may be at first surprising that the same age was one of aesthetic speculation. Although there were few defenses of poetry as such, aesthetic speculation can be regarded as an implicit defense, even though it began as an attempt to make a science the object of which was a human activity. The term "aesthetic" was adopted by Alexander Gottlieb Baumgarten in his *Meditationes philosophicae de nonnullis ad poema pertinentibus* (1735) and developed in his later *Aesthetica* (1750, 1758). Baumgarten's first interest was human perception. He wanted to create a "scientia cognitionis sensitivae." Monroe C. Beardsley remarks of him, "Evidently Baumgarten is making the most determined effort thus far made to distinguish between two fundamentally different types of discourse: the clear and distinct [the words are Descartes's], or abstract, discourse of science, and the confused, though more or less clear, discourse of poetry, which exists to render and realize sense experience."[23]

In empirical terms, the former discourse is objective, the latter subjective. Poetry was, for the most part, driven to defend itself *as* subjective expression, which was in turn relegated to the feelings and identified with inherently unstable phantasy. Under these conditions, poetry was to act on the subjective emotions of the reader. This view goes back at least to Thomas Hobbes and remains in a whole series of poets and critics to this day. An extreme example along the way is a group of comments by Edgar

---

22. T. E. Hulme, "Romanticism and Classicism," *Speculations* (1924) (New York: Harcourt, Brace, n. d.), 113–40; Robert Penn Warren, "Pure and Impure Poetry" (1943), *New and Selected Essays* (New York: Random House, 1989), 3–28; John Crowe Ransom, "Poetry: A Note in Ontology," *The World's Body* (New York: Charles Scribner's Sons, 1938), 111–42.

23. Monroe C. Beardsley, *Aesthetics from Classical Greece to the Present* (New York: Macmillan, 1966), 158–59.

Allan Poe, including the following: "I need scarcely observe that a poem deserves its title only inasmuch as it excites. . . . "[24] Subjectivity becomes for some the only experienced reality, as in the well-known and for a time notorious passage by Walter Pater: "Experience, already reduced to a group of impressions, is ringed round for each one of us by that thick wall of personality through which no real voice has ever pierced on its way to us, or from us to that which we can only conjecture to be without. Every one of those impressions is the impression of the individual in his isolation, each mind keeping as a solitary prisoner its own dream of a world."[25] A retreat more than a defense.

A more influential implied defense is the one made in Immanuel Kant's *Critique of Judgment* (1790), in which Kant proposes "subjective universality." This is not the place for an account of Kant's aesthetic, but it played so important a part in what followed that brief comment is necessary. What Kant calls "aesthetic judgments" do not involve consideration of objects with respect to use or any "external purpose." Rather, as aesthetic objects, they have "internal purposiveness" or "purposiveness without purpose."[26] All such judgments are singular. It is an aesthetic judgment to declare a particular rose beautiful, but to say that all or some roses are beautiful is to make a generalization or determinative judgment based on a series of singular aesthetic ones. An aesthetic judgment, furthermore, cannot appeal to any external rule. In finding an object beautiful, we abandon any concept of how it is to be or has been used or approaches some ideal of beauty. Thus the appeal to accuracy of imitation or even verisimilitude as a criterion, or to any neoclassical or other rule, must be dispensed with.

Kant does not abandon the notion of subjectivity but seeks to find a universal form of it. An aesthetic judgment must, as such, claim universality by virtue of its freedom from any presumption of external purpose,

24. "The Poetic Principle," *The Complete Works of Edgar Allan Poe*, ed. James A. Harrison (New York: George D. Sproul, 1902), 14: 266.

25. Walter Pater, *The Renaissance* (1873) (New York: Boni and Liveright, 1919), 196.

26. *Critique of Judgment* [*Kritik der Urteilskraft*], trans. J. H. Bernard (Amherst, NY: Prometheus Books, 2000).

including purposes personal to the viewer. Such judgments must therefore be "disinterested," that is, without involvement of the viewer's self-interest. Thus the judgment is "free." But this also means that an "aesthetical idea," as Kant calls it, cannot be drawn from experience of the object in the form of a concept or in language other than its own:

> . . . by an aesthetical Idea I understand that representation of the imagination which occasions much thought, without, however, any definite thought, *i. e.* any *concept*, being capable of being adequate to it; it consequently cannot be completely compassed and made intelligible by language.—We easily see that it is the counterpart (pendant) of a *rational Idea*; which conversely is a concept to which no *intuition* (or representation of the Imagination) can be adequate. (197)

The notion of expanding the mind by setting the imagination at liberty in aesthetic experience is Kant's contribution to a defense of poetry and art generally. This condition he calls "play": "[Poetry] strengthens the mind by making it feel its faculty—free, spontaneous, and independent of natural determination—of considering and judging nature as a phenomenon in accordance with aspects which it does not present in experience either for Sense or Understanding; . . . it declares its exercise to be mere play, which however can be purposely used by the Understanding" (215). Usefulness is always here a by-product, not involved with internal purpose, but the understanding can build on and profit from this play. In this respect, it is contrasted to rhetoric, which is always externally purposive: "Rhetoric, in so far as this means the art of persuasion, *i. e.* of deceiving by a beautiful show (*ars oratoria*), and not mere elegance of speech (eloquence and style), is a Dialectic which borrows from poetry only so much as is needful to win minds to the side of the orator before they have formed a judgment, and to deprive them of their freedom" (215). Thus, against Plato, who identified poets with rhetoricians and sophists, Kant attempts to separate them, rhetoric borrowing from poetry.

The notions of disinterest, play, and the allegedly resultant freedom appear almost at once in Friedrich Schiller's *Letters on the Aesthetic Edu-*

cation of Man (1793–95).[27] Schiller proposes two fundamental human drives, the sensuous drive (*Stofftrieb*) and the formal drive (*Formtrieb*). In a pure state, the sensuous drive would reduce man to a "unit of quantity, an occupied moment of time" (79). The formal drive would annul time and change, questing for the "abstract, eternal, and absolute" (81). Each drive has an appropriate sphere, and it is culture's task to do justice to both, since both are inevitable. However, someone who only feels cannot know himself, as all feeling is ruled by external force; and if he only thinks, he cannot know his own temporal condition. (The tendency in culture is for the sensuous drive to dominate.) There must be a mediator or conjoiner that obliterates neither. This is the play drive (*Spieltrieb*), which Schiller, well schooled in Kant, identifies with aesthetic experience and art. Play is "everything neither subjectively nor objectively contingent, and yet imposes no kind of constraint, either from within or from without" (104–5). Play is without self-interest and external purpose. In play man combines the greatest fullness of existence with the highest autonomy and freedom. Play heals the division represented by the other two drives. Schiller's notion is both an aesthetic and an ethical one.

Schiller identifies the object of the sensuous drive as "life" and that of the formal drive as "form." The play drive's mediation yields "living form," which is a "concept serving to designate all the aesthetic qualities of phenomena" (101). This Schiller calls beauty and identifies with freedom, "the highest of all bounties, . . . the gift of humanity itself," which is restored to man from the strife of sense and form (147). Thus Schiller's cultural claim for art is enormous.

Disinterest, now an aesthetico-ethical principle, was given a rather more mundane treatment in Matthew Arnold's "The Function of Criticism at the Present Time" (1864). He considered it to be what the criticism of poetry and of culture should possess. He regarded his age as not one of creative strength. It could be, he hoped, an age of criticism. Necessary to this would be a "free disinterested play of mind" ranging over all subjects and

---

27. Friedrich Schiller, *Letters on the Aesthetic Education of Man* [*Briefe über die asthetische Erziehung des Menschen*], ed. and trans. E. M. Wilkinson and L. A. Willoughby (Oxford: Clarendon Press, 1967).

done for its own sake.[28] This meant "keeping aloof from what is called 'the practical view of things'" and from "ulterior, political, practical considerations about ideas" (270). The work of criticism, which in his age would include the writing of poetry, would have to be "slow and obscure" (274).

Arnold judges the poetic impulse of his time weak, and the more grandiose claims of Kant and Schiller are brought to earth. There is, however, another side to Arnold. He regards poetry as a potential substitute for religion, the beliefs of which have been shattered by modern science. There is even a Longinian side in his notion of poetic "touchstones," brief passages drawn from poems for their immediate worth.[29] These touchstones, like Wordsworth's spots of time in the memory, seemed to Arnold to perform a kind of transport, not unlike the sublime in the pseudo-Longinus.

Defiance Again

It is not surprising to find that the end of the nineteenth century produced a group of poets in Britain whose lives and careers were often disastrous. A survivor of this period, W. B. Yeats, wrote a play that we can regard as a counterpart in his time to Gray's "The Bard." In *The King's Threshold*, Yeats, too, tells a story of a poet's defiance and death. King Guaire is imposed on by his bishops, generals, and lawyers to banish the court poet Seanchan from his council, he being "a mere man of words."[30] Seanchan promptly begins a hunger strike on the steps of the castle. The king defends his action:

> . . . when he pleaded for the poet's right,
> Established at the establishment of the world,
> I said that I was King and that all rights
> Had their original fountain in some king,

28. R. H. Super, ed., "The Function of Criticism at the Present Time," *The Complete Works of Matthew Arnold: Lectures and Essays in Criticism* (Ann Arbor: University of Michigan Press, 1962), 271.

29. R. H. Super, ed., "The Study of Poetry," *The Complete Works of Matthew Arnold: English Literature and Irish Politics* (Ann Arbor: University of Michigan Press, 1973), 161–88.

30. *The Collected Plays of W. B. Yeats* (New York: Macmillan, 1963), 71.

And that it was the men who ruled the world,
And not the men who sang to it, who should sit
Where there was the most honour. (71)

With considerable trepidation, the poet's oldest pupil decides that the poet's traditional prerogative is not worth dying for and goes over to the king's side. But the king, for his part, is concerned that he will be victimized by the poet's words:

. . . while he is lying there,
Perishing there, my good name in the world
Is perishing also. (72)

The poet becomes a threat to the state:

. . . . But I that sit a throne,
And take my measure from the needs of the State,
Call his wild thought that overruns the measure,
Making words more than deeds, and his proud will
That would unsettle all, most mischievous,
And he himself a most mischievous man. (72)

The king knows that the poet, now antithetical to the power of the State on the one hand and to powerlessness on the other, has his own sort of authority.

The king, in fact, is captive to his own power:

. . . . I cannot give way,
Because I am King; because if I give way
My nobles would call me a weakling, and, it may be
The very throne be shaken. (72)

Schiller might have said that Guaire's ability to play has been stifled. He cannot do what he would like to do, which by now is to restore the poet to his place.

When Seanchan dies, his youngest pupil cries out,

Yet make triumphant music; sing aloud,
For coming times will bless what he has blessed
And curse what he has cursed. (94)

But the oldest pupil, admonishing him, and wiser now, says,

. . . . No, no, be still,
Or pluck a solemn music from the strings.
You wrong his greatness speaking of triumph. (94)

Triumph is conquest and negation. It repeats the crime. The antithetical poet can have none of that. He could accept neither the king's nor his own surrender.

In Yeats's mythological history, the poet is absent from the halls of political power, only a shade, a tattered coat upon a stick, or perhaps a ghostly presence in moments of State ritual in the person of a poet laureate, immortalized in Byron's ironic address to Robert Southey, who had been appointed to that post:

Bob Southey! You're a poet—Poet laureate,
    And representative of all the race;
Although 't is true that you turned out a Tory at
    Last. . . . [31]

One might argue that poetry was not always antithetical, that the ancient bards and court poets were in the pay of political power. That was Peacock's view. But even then, I think, there was something latent in poetry that antithetically threatened power. If Homer's characters Agamemnon and Priam could read *Iliad* from outside it, would they be very happy about

31. Lord Byron, *Don Juan* (Dedication I), ed. Leslie A. Marchand (Boston: Houghton Mifflin, 1958), 7.

it, or Achilles and Hector, for that matter? Are court jesters not antithetical threats? Do Shakespeare's fools, though not poets exactly, inject their
own threat of antitheticality into his plays?

When and why were poets driven from their positions as advisers
(though often cryptic ones) and entertainers (sometimes ironic ones) at
court? When kings no longer put faith in curses? When poets were recognized as possibly seditious? Or was it when what Yeats, in *A Vision*, called
antithetical culture turned "primary"?[32] In that book, Yeats offered a
notion that with the modern world the object, or the "primary" as in Locke's
epistemology, became the place of the real, favored over the subject, which
was then isolated and shorn of the power of true knowledge.

Yeats's play has its comical moments, unlike Gray's highly rhetorical
and somber poem. One senses in it a certain wit combined with defiance.
The wit and defiance are present in Oscar Wilde's well-known dialogue essay
"The Decay of Lying," which despite its appearance of flippancy and
impertinence (or because of these things) manages to symbolize what the
defense had come to as the nineteenth century ended. The strategy is to
turn against the disdain of the rationalists, empiricists, utilitarians, and real-
ists an even haughtier comic disdain. Specifically, the argument attacks so-
called realistic imitation and usefulness. Going beyond Kant, Wilde's
character Vivian, who poses theatrically throughout, claims that objects of
art have no use whatever, while Kant had held only that an object is not judged
with respect to use when it is judged aesthetically (though his language was
not always consistent with this). Art, for Wilde's Vivian, is superior to nature:

> My own experience is that the more we study Art, the less we care
> for Nature. What Art really reveals to us is Nature's lack of design,
> her curious crudities, her extraordinary monotony, her absolutely
> unfinished condition. Nature has good intentions, of course, but as
> Aristotle once said, she cannot carry them out.[33]

32. W. B. Yeats, *A Vision* (New York: Macmillan, 1938).
33. "The Decay of Lying," *Complete Works of Oscar Wilde* (London and Glasgow:
Collins, 1976), 970.

But though art has no use as such, it is culturally influential:

> At present, people see fogs, not because there are fogs, but because
> poets and painters have taught them the mysterious loveliness of such
> effects. There may have been fogs for centuries in London. I dare say
> there were. But no one saw them, and so we do not know anything
> about them. They did not exist till Art had invented them. (986)

Vivian concludes that art expresses only itself, that bad art comes from copying life and nature, and that life imitates art more than art imitates life. Poetry
is not defended here for its power to teach or accuracy of imitation. The
whole mimetic tradition is turned inside out. This seems to bring to cul-
mination the development of the concept of creative imagination implicit
in Kant's notion of human constitutive power and its movement in various
forms into literary criticism with the German idealists and Coleridge.

In Wilde's essay, we have a touch of Aristotle, a touch of Sidney, a
little Kant, and views common in the so-called Decadence. The more solemn
version of art for art's sake appeared in 1901 with A. C. Bradley's "Poetry
for Poetry's Sake," in which he qualified sternly some of the more extreme
implications of the movement and returned to Kantian internal purposiveness, but without a convincing explanation of poetic value.[34]

Bradley is one of the few academic scholars mentioned so far in this
brief history. This is a sign that spirited defenses like those of Sidney and
Shelley may be things of the past. Historical critics valued poetry for its
reflection of history. The New Critics in the United States, for the most
part, defended poems as aesthetic objects and as expressing cultural value
ignored by science. In their wake and as more and more literary criticism
and theory was written by academics, two different directions were taken:
There was dispute among critics about their own theoretical and interpretive
assumptions, and there were analytical studies in which questions of value
nearly disappeared. There was, one supposes, a tacit assumption that these
studies and their objects had value, though it is often unclear what the writ-

---

34. A. C. Bradley, "Poetry for Poetry's Sake," *Oxford Lectures on Poetry* (Bloomington: Indiana University Press, 1961), 3–34.

ers thought those values were. In many cases, the impulse, as in criticism influenced by the Russian Formalists and structural linguistics, was to be scientific and to eschew value judgments. Even later, poetry and literature generally came to be valued in the academy as social data to be applied either negatively or positively in political and/or moralistically oriented arguments. As a sign of how far that had gone, a well-known critical theorist felt impelled to write not a defense of poetry but rather an apology for poetics.[35]

Phenomenological Defense

The only brief recent and explicit defense of poetry known to me is that of Colin Falck. He offers a neo-romantic, expressivist view influenced by Shelley. His view is not *self*-expressivist, however, since it denies the epistemological notion of a detached subject and situates the human being in the world in the manner of modern phenomenology: " . . . the human mind is situated *in* reality rather than being disembodied or detached from it, and . . . the world, or reality as we are able to apprehend it, is an expressive creation out of our embodied and distinctively human preconsciousness."[36] We are obliged to read "the reality which is to be found in a particular artwork . . . and to test these revelations intuitively against the comprehension of reality which we already possess" (400). Art, for Falck, gives ontological truth. This argument seeks to synthesize the best in the romantic tradition of defense and provides a handy summary expression of the kind of phenomenological argument that later underlies Farrell's *Why Does Literature Matter?*

In a number of essays, Martin Heidegger took a phenomenological approach to poetry that showed the depth to which his own work was rooted in it.[37] Though not explicitly a defense, these essays set forth an important spiritual and cultural function for poetry. Heavily influenced by the poets Hölderlin and Rilke, he makes many points in the act of reading their work

35. Murray Krieger, "An Apology for Poetics" (1982), *Words About Words About Words* (Baltimore, MD: Johns Hopkins University Press, 1988), 107–52.

36. Colin Falck, "A Defence of Poetry," *Journal of Aesthetics and Art Criticism* 44.4 (summer 1986): 398.

37. They are collected in *Poetry, Language, Thought*, trans. Albert Hofstadter (New York: Harper and Row, 1971).

and reflecting on specific words, adopting some of them for his own use. One of these is Rilke's "The Open": "In Rilke's language 'open' means something that does not block off." Neither does it set bounds ("What Are Poets For?" [1926], 106). In Heidegger's view, the world of being is most of the time closed to us, partly as the result of technology, a term that for him denotes a way of thinking that results in objectification: "By building the world up technologically as an object, man deliberately and completely blocks his path, already obstructed, into the Open" (116). The Open is "the nonobjective character of full Nature" (112). The consequence is the isolation of man in subjectivity. Poetry's function is to "unconceal," to "disclose" the "thingly element of things" ("The Origin of the Work of Art" [1950], 36). "Everything that might interpose itself between the thing and us in apprehending and talking about it must first be set aside" (25). But philosophy has not been able to do this, which would involve engagement in a dialogue with poetry. The term "dialogue" is important, for Heidegger neither wants poetry to be philosophy nor wants it not to be:

> Poetry and thinking meet each other in one and the same only when, and only as long as, they remain distinctly in the distinctness of their nature. The same never coincides with the equal, not even in the empty indifferent oneness of what is merely identical. The equal or identical always moves toward the absence of difference, so that everything may be reduced to a common denominator. The same, by contrast, is the belonging together of what differs, through a gathering by way of difference. It is in the carrying out and settling of differences that the gathering nature of sameness comes to light. The same banishes all zeal always to level what is different into the equal or identical. The same gathers what is distinct into an original being-at-one. The equal, on the contrary, disperses them into the dull unity of mere uniformity. (" . . . Poetically Man Dwells . . . ," [1954] 218–19)

This passage would seem to put poetry and philosophy (as thinking) into a metaphorical relationship of a sort that I will have more to say about in chapter 7. Here I note only that Heidegger's and my meanings for "identical" are different.

Heidegger remarks in the same essay that unfortunately either poetry has come to be the subject of "aestheticizing," rendering it phantasy, or it has been called "literature" and "studied entirely in educational and scientific terms" (213–14). Poetry shows us the real, the thing itself, the "unconcealedness" of beings ("What Are Poets For?" [1926], 106). In the end, though, phenomenology has retreated into a concept of "inter-subjectivity," trapped once again in the language of epistemology.

It is not the only theory that has been imprisoned in the terms invented by enemies of poetry, some of them well-intentioned.[38] It is worth asking why this is so. Perhaps we shall learn why if we revisit Socrates' remark that there is an ancient war between philosophy and poetry. All of the oppositions that in Blake's terms are negations and cloven fictions are products, over the ages, of philosophical thought. They have been culturally powerful because they have been at least for a time convincing and useful: oppositions between truth and lies, teaching and delight, content and form, rationality and feeling, object and subject. When these oppositions have dominated, poets and critics have been too often driven to occupy one side or the other. Plato went to content, Aristotle to form. Modern logical positivism, as had Locke, opted for the object, Pater in what seems near to despair for the subject. And so it went. Recent philosophy has suffered something of a crisis over this, in which Heidegger has played an important role. But it is unlikely that the ancient war will cease. Neither is it finally desirable that it should. Blake wrote of a patron who was helping him, "Thy friendship hath made my heart to ake / Do be my enemy for friendship's sake." Philosophy will not give up its position, nor will the views that are popularly assumed to drive science and technology. Poetry must stand in opposition for friendship's sake, but in a third, "antithetical" position not defined by its enemies and oldest friends. Part II of this book includes discussions of four characteristics of poetry, as poetry employs them, that make it offensive, antithetical, and for that reason culturally necessary.

38. An interesting polemical work by the classical scholar W. B. Stanford, *Enemies of Poetry* (London: Routledge and Kegan Paul, 1980), briefly examines historicists, scientists, psychologists, mathematicians, philosophers, politicians, and moralists as enemies of poetry and attributes twenty-six fallacies to criticism of the classics.

II. Theoretical:
Four Offenses

4

Gesture

In offering gesture, drama, fiction, and trope (all often contributing to difficulty) as belonging to poetic offense, I do not claim that these characteristics are the only offenses poetry commits. They are, however, the offenses closest to poetry's fundamental nature. Nor do I claim that they occur only in poems. They occur, of course, in most uses of language. One can argue that they were born with language itself. In poetry as we now think of it, these four function as means to an end different from the ends they seek in the habitual languages of business, politics, journalism, science, and even religion. Drama, fiction, and trope are all important in the ways they behave in poems, but all three are subordinate to and support gesture, which I take up first.

The Oxford English Dictionary (OED) defines "gesture" as "a movement of the body or any part of it. Now only in restricted sense: A movement expressive of thought or feeling." Two other definitions are declared obsolete:

> 1. Manner of placing the body; position, posture, attitude, esp. in acts of prayer or worship. Also a specific posture.
>
> 2. In early use: the employment of bodily movements, attitudes, expression of countenance, etc., as a means of giving effect to oratory.

Under any of these definitions, gestures could be inoffensive or offensive. Roger Ascham (1545), as the OED indicates, emphasizes the value of gesture in connection with words: "No man can wryte a thing so earnestly, as when it is spoken with iesture." James Boswell (1758), on the other hand, refers to Samuel Johnson's "unqualified ridicule of rhetorical gesture, or action" and describes Johnson seizing and holding down the hands of a man who was "giving additional force to what he uttered."

Johnson's complaint seems to have been mainly against gesture's connection to oratorical flourish, though it may express his distaste for all display of excess or absurdity. It is, in any case, consistent with what appears to be the aim of Johnson's own prose style and with the common observation that the English, by contrast to the Italians or the French, are not prone to gesturing when they speak. However, the OED's definitions of obsolete usage indicate that gesture was not always limited to what we think of as rhetorical physical movement. Sir Keith Thomas remarks, "The body can also transmit messages without any movement at all."[1] Indeed, one of the obsolete meanings implies not movement but stillness, as in prayer, or carrying of the body in a certain fixed posture.

Gesture has long, probably always, been identified with language, both as an accompaniment and a predecessor of it. Vico remarked, " . . . the first language in the first mute times of the nations must have begun with signs, whether gestures or physical objects, which had natural relations to the ideas [to be expressed]."[2] For him, hieroglyphics were "written" objects, the results of gesture, prior to language as we know it. Hieroglyphs were emblems, similitudes, metaphors. The relation of gesture to hieroglyph to metaphor was fundamental to Vico's new science of mythology.

Vico presumed the existence of a universal "mental" language that underlay the many verbal ones. We know that the language of gesture, like that of words, is not uniform across cultures and undergoes change over time. Thomas observes, "Gestures tend to be polysemous and their meaning can be determined only by context" (4). But "polysemous" is not quite the best word. It indicates that a gesture can have multiple meanings and implies that each of these can be put into words. But can a gesture be put into sufficient words? What does the thumbing of a nose in a particular situation fully mean? Or the cocking of an ear? A certain grimace?

There is, we frequently say, a language of gesture. But can we claim that there is something in and of language that justifies carrying the word

1. Sir Keith Thomas, Introduction, *A Cultural History of Gesture: From Antiquity to the Present Day*, ed. Jan Bremmer and Herman Rodenberg (Cambridge, UK: Polity Press, 1991), 1.

2. Giambattista Vico, *The New Science of Giambattista Vico*, rev. trans. of 3rd ed. (1744), trans. Thomas Goddard Bergin and Max Harold Fisch (Ithaca, NY: Cornell University Press, 1968), 20. By "natural," Vico seems to mean that the first mute language was the result of spontaneous responses to nature.

metaphorically from the body over into language itself? Is there a gesture of language? In his *Phenomenology of Perception*, Maurice Merleau-Ponty assumes that there is. Interested in the body as expression (speech being one of its forms), he remarks, "I do not see anger or a threatening attitude as a psychic fact hidden behind the gesture. I read anger in it. The gesture *does not make me think* of anger, it is anger itself."[3] There is, for him, a "*gestural meaning*, which is immanent in speech" and "a *thought in speech* the existence of which is unsuspected by intellectualism" (179). The linguistic gesture "delineates its own meaning" (186), that is, it does not refer to a thought behind or prior to it, detachable from it as its source.

Merleau-Ponty's notion of gesture has been taken up by Michael Fried in his treatment of the sculpture of Anthony Caro.[4] He cites Merleau-Ponty's view that the "institution of language arises out of primitive gesture" as did Vico before him. Elsewhere, Fried reminds us that gestures are bodily and calls on Heinrich Wölfflin's remark that we "read our image into all phenomena" and, "Not that we expect to find the appearance of a human being in the forms of inorganic nature: we interpret the physical world through the categories that we share with it," the organization of our bodies being the form by which we apprehend things.[5] This is a little different from Vico's notion of the linguistic projection of the body into nature, since with Vico it is not clear whether there is an "appearance of a human body" in the primitive projection of Jove or Pomona or Flora, unless "appearance" can be extended to senses other than sight. Kant seems to have intervened here with the idea of categories. Fried speaks of "the new awareness of the primacy of bodily experience" (36). But if Vico was right about the primitive projection of the body in words, it is also an old awareness, though we would have to qualify "awareness" as not an objectified one, an awareness of one's awareness. Fried himself speaks of bodily "projection," which suggests two things: something akin to Vico's notion of language being extended into natural objects by means of bodily tropes and

3. Maurice Merleau-Ponty, *Phenomenology of Perception* [Phenomenologie de la perception], trans. Colin Smith (London: Routledge and Kegan Paul, 1962), 184.

4. Michael Fried, *Art and Objecthood* (Chicago: University of Chicago Press, 1998), 28–29, 269–75.

5. Michael Fried, *Menzel's Realism* (New Haven, CT: Yale University Press, 2002), 36.

the notion of empathy and identity implicit in that act. Fried was a student of R. P. Blackmur and mentions Blackmur's "special excruciation . . . to demonstrate, in masterpieces of sympathetic analysis, how language that has been wrought to the uttermost in great poetry may reach the condition of consummate gesture" (*Art*, 270).

Another indication that there is a gesture of language lies in the long connection between poetry and rhetoric that was recognized by poets through at least the eighteenth century. Classical treatises and handbooks on rhetoric long maintained gesture's influence, pointing to the importance of and sometimes codifying appropriate oratorical gestures. Baldassare Castiglione's *Book of the Courtier* (1528) became a favorite,[6] its views being reflected, for example, in John Donne's poetry[7] and taken up centuries later by W. B. Yeats. In Yeats's case, gesture was connected with drama and the theatrical mask, as it was with Oscar Wilde shortly before him. The perfect courtier's gestures are, according to Castiglione, "fashioned and compact . . . with grace," and this grace is a "verie arte that appeareth not to be arte," the result of a studied casualness, nonchalance, or recklessness implicit in the Italian *sprezzatura* with its lack of "curiositie" or apparent affectation. To read Vico is to imagine the movement of gesture into language.

Blackmur is the only literary critic known to me to use the term "gesture" in any sustained way.[8] In his essay "Language as Gesture" (1935), he begins by alluding to the puzzle that is in his essay's title:

> Language is made of words, and gesture is made of motion. There is one half of the puzzle. The other half is equally self-evident if only

6. Baldassare Castiglione, *The Book of the Courtier* [Libro del Cortegiano], trans. Sir Thomas Hoby (1561), (London: J. M. Dent and Sons; New York: E. P. Dutton and Co., 1928), esp. 33, 46.

7. See Peter de Sa Wiggins, *Donne, Castiglione, and the Poetry of Courtliness* (Bloomington: Indiana University Press, 2002).

8. David E. Smith's *Gesture as a Stylistic Device in Kleist's "Michael Kohlhaas" and Kafka's "Der Prozess"* (Bern, Switzerland: Herbert Lang; Frankfurt am Main, Germany: Peter Lang, 1976), one of the few studies of gesture in literature, stresses description and imagistic presentation of gestures made by characters. Blackmur's use of the term includes this but is much broader. The term is used briefly by other writers including Colin Falck in his "A Defence of Poetry," *Journal of Aesthetics and Art Criticism* 44.4 (summer 1986): 393.

because it is an equally familiar part of the baggage of our thought. It is the same statement put the other way round. Words are made of motion, made of action or response, at whatever remove; and gesture is made of language—made of the language beneath or beyond or alongside the language of words. When the language of words fails we resort to the language of gesture. If we stop there, we stop with the puzzle. If we go on, and say that when the language of words most succeeds it *becomes* gesture in its words, we shall have solved the verbal puzzle with which we began by discovering one approach to the central or dead-end mystery of meaningful expression in the language of the arts.[9]

Blackmur turns around Vico's historical view that gesture preceded words and thinks of gesture, at least in our time, as proceeding from language, especially when we feel language, in our usual view of it, is going to fail us. As this point, poetry steps in, gesturing *in* language.

A few pages later, Blackmur writes: "Gesture, in language, is the outward and dramatic play of inward and imaged meaning. It is the play of meaningfulness among words which cannot be defined in the formulas of the dictionary, but which is defined in their use together; gesture is that meaningfulness which is moving in every sense of that word; what moves the words and what moves us" (6). Blackmur's "meaningfulness" appears to be an effort to avoid the straightforward "meaning," severely limited in denotation by the logical positivists. At the same time, it is an effort to rescue for gesture some of the authority of "meaning." Meaningfulness is exactly that quality of language given short shrift by the positivists. It is as

9. R. P. Blackmur, "Language as Gesture," *Language as Gesture: Essays in Poetry* (New York: Harcourt, Brace and Co., 1952), 3. A recent book expressing a philosophy of gesture is David Michael Kleinberg-Levin's passionate *Gestures of Ethical Life: Reading Hölderlin's Question of Measure After Heidegger* (Stanford, CA: Stanford University Press, 2005). The book's concern is with gesture as a mode of expression necessary to ethical life. Writing, a gesture of the hand, which opposes the distinction between body and soul, is "a discipline secretly measured by the reach of its concern for the social redemption of gestures— the intangible potential that still awaits recognition . . . " (56). Except for an important early chapter on Hölderlin, the book is concerned with philosophers and in some cases their philosophical gestures: Heidegger, Adorno, Benjamin, Merleau-Ponty, and Levinas.

if Blackmur is emphasizing fullness, a burgeoning beyond capturable meaning: "surplus" in a later critical jargon. (But Blackmur does not consistently substitute "meaningfulness" for "meaning" in his essay.)

Until he reaches his conclusion, Blackmur's examples of verbal gesture in poems are short passages or phrases. One suspects that Matthew Arnold's touchstones would qualify as gestures.[10] Two of Blackmur's examples of verbal gesture involve repetitions: "Macbeth's 'Tomorrow and tomorrow and tomorrow,' or Lear's 'Never never never never,' would seem good examples of simple repetition metamorphosing the most familiar words into the most engulfing gesture" (13). With respect to another example, he refers to understanding the "fury in the words . . . and not the words themselves" (12). This notion appears implicit in Blackmur's final presentation, Yeats's "I am of Ireland." It achieves "the pure meaningfulness of gesture" (23–24). Anyone who has tried to explain the force of this poem will understand what Blackmur is getting at and why he is not commenting further on it.

Blackmur has provided yet another term for the effect of poetry that is beyond analytic description. Over the centuries, there have been many: the *je ne sais quoi* of Bouhours, Kant's internal purposiveness, Paul Valéry's comparison of dancing to poetry and walking to a destination to other discursive forms, Susanne K. Langer's presentational forms, and so on. Clive Bell's "significant form" is a parallel in art criticism. Each of these differs by virtue of its intellectual context, but all point toward what is, let us say, unspoken but resident in (like Merleau-Ponty's gesture) or, perhaps, projected from the language of the poem.

I would like to give gesture in some of its aspects a little more body than Blackmur does. I begin with the conventions of poetic verbal gesture, both formal and informal.[11] Of course, there are conventional gestures, but the kind of gesture that is the gesture in language of the poem is unique

10. Offered by Arnold in "The Study of Poetry," *The Complete Works of Matthew Arnold, IX: English Literature and Irish Politics*, ed. R. H. Super (Ann Arbor: University of Michigan Press, 1973), 161–88.

11. In his novel *Immortality*, Milan Kundera writes of the inspiration for a character coming from a gesture performed by a woman (a woman gesturing was also the inspiration for Blackmur's essay): "The gesture revealed nothing of that woman's essence, one

even as it brings along convention. There are various forms of gesture in which speakers of poems function. I say "in which" to allow for the possibility that the speaker is put into, say, a sonnet form by an "arranger"[12] who may also be gesturing. The poem's speaker may be formally orating, preaching, meditating, deliberating, addressing, and so forth. The speaker may be performing, among other things, a panegyric, an elegy, or a satirical attack. Each of these may be and is performed uniquely. The relation of the speaker and the speech to the convention is always unique, but we sense something they have in common as well. This relation escapes analytic language and defies a definition that would proceed by indicating only the common characteristics of, say, sonnets. Sometimes rhetorical devices reveal the poem's intent. Often we recognize a convention of gesture, but what we recognize in such a case is abstract, something we have learned elsewhere. Often we are hard put to explain a gesture's force, no matter how conventional we think it to be. Conventions are gestural, but they are never all of the poem's gesture, for the poem itself makes a total gesture.

At an even higher level of abstraction, there are what we call "schools" of poetry: the metaphysicals, the cavaliers, the romantics, the moderns, the

---

could rather say that the woman revealed to me the charm of a gesture. A gesture cannot be regarded as the expression of an individual, as his creation (because no individual is capable of creating a fully original gesture belonging to nobody else) . . . " (trans. Peter Kusi [New York: Grove Weidenfeld, 1991], 7).

I am not convinced of this with respect to Blackmur's notion of gesture in and as the poem, and I am not convinced of it even with respect to life, for every context in which a gesture is made is different and contributes to its meaning. The gestures of a mimic are not exactly those of the person mimicked or of another mimicking the same person. There is always a difference. Any mimicry includes and yet moves beyond what is mimicked, and a poem draws on the real even as it moves beyond it.

12. The term "arranger" is a creation of the criticism of James Joyce's *Ulysses*. To my knowledge, it was first used by David Hayman. See his *Ulysses: The Mechanics of Meaning* (Madison: University of Wisconsin Press, 1982). The arranger is like the director of a play (the speaker of a poem being a character in it). For example, in the "Sirens" chapter of *Ulysses*, the characters are in a fugue, though they do not know it. In a sonnet, the situation is somewhat different. The speaker (or writer) speaks or writes the whole poem. Whether the speaker is in the sonnet form and being written by it (arranged) or is the controller of it (the maker of it) is often undecidable. An arranger is a character at a larger circumference in the work than the narrator. *Ulysses* can be read at various circumferences: arrangement, narration, the actions of Bloom, and so on.

beats, and so on.[13] But when put to it to characterize the work of these schools, we are confronted with difference. Critics have quarreled over these terms or limited themselves to general remarks about subject matter, verse technique, or whatever particularly interests them. We seem able to recognize something we call (inappropriately) metaphysical poetry or something we call (perhaps appropriately) cavalier or romantic. The characterizations of Donne's poems and metaphysical poetry generally by Dryden and Johnson seem off the point and at the same time offer evidence that poetic offense has been committed. Dryden on Donne:

> He affects the metaphysics, not only in his satires, but in his amorous verses, where nature only should reign; and perplexes the minds of the fair sex with nice speculations of philosophy, when he should engage their hearts, and entertain them with the softness of love.[14]

Johnson on the metaphysicals:

> The most heterogeneous ideas are yoked by violence together; nature and art are ransacked for illustrations, comparisons, and allusions; their learning instructs, and their subtlety surprises; but the reader commonly thinks his improvement dearly bought, and, though he sometimes admires, is seldom pleased.[15]

Peacock's treatment of the so-called Lake Poets is an amusing accusation of the offense of silliness, but it seems today not very close to their work. This is perhaps because what they had in common was more gestural and evasive of description than abstractable.

By means of conventions of address or form, poems make gestures claiming kinship, affirming traditions, establishing connections, forcing contrasts, and disrupting expectations. What is one who has read the love

---

13. Merleau-Ponty observes, "Conventions are a late form of relationship between men; they presuppose an earlier means of communication, and language must be put back into this current of intercourse" (187).

14. From *A Discourse Concerning the Origin and Progress of Satire* (1693).

15. From the essay on Abraham Cowley in *Lives of the English Poets* (1779–81).

sonnets of Petrarch, Spenser, Sidney, Daniel, and Shakespeare to make of John Donne's "Holy Sonnet VII"?

> At the round earths imagin'd corners, blow
> Your trumpets, Angells, and arise, arise
> From death, you numberless infinities
> Of soules, and to your scattred bodies goe,
> All whom the flood did, and fire shall o'erthrow,   5
> All whom warre, dearth, age, agues, tyrannies,
> Despaire, law, chance, hath slaine, and you whose eyes,
> Shall behold God, and never taste deaths woe.
> But let them sleepe, Lord, and me mourne a space,
> For, if above all these, my sinnes abound,   10
> 'Tis late to aske abundance of thy grace,
> When we are there; here on this lowly ground
> Teach mee how to repent; for that's as good
> As if thou'hadst seal'd my pardon, with thy blood.[16]

The reminder of cosmic paradox in the convention of the four angels standing at the corners of a sphere and its placement at the poem's beginning contribute to a gesture that intensifies the seeming presumptuousness of direct address to angels, indeed of demand. The corners are there, but they are also not there; they are imagined (from the Bible), tempering our thought of the speaker's belief in their presence even as they are invoked. The vastness of the demand, finally addressed to everyone, risks the charge of hubris. It is enforced by the catalog in lines 6 and 7, forming a shuddering within the iambic pattern. This is presaged by alliteration, the parts of which are separated by a pause in line 5, ruffling the rhythm and turning the machine of meter into a mimesis of speech. All of this seems to intensify by contrast the powerful shift of tone when the sestet begins. Line 9's pauses, placed around the accented "Lord" at the line's very center, signal a change of speed, of tone, as the poem's thought turns inward, away from the gesture of demand

16. My transcription is from Sir Herbert Grierson, ed., *The Poems of John Donne* (London: Oxford University Press, 1933), 296.

and then outward again toward supplication. At that turn, at the hinge of octave to sestet, the speaker undergoes a change of heart or, more nearly, a sudden realization that were his demand to be answered he would have to face the Last Judgment in a state of sin. All of the rhetorical vigor of the octave is dissipated with the realization that for him the time is not yet right.

The sonnet is of Petrarchan form, but it ends in a couplet, and the force of the iambic is challenged by the first three feet of line 13, "Teach me how to repent," where the accents fall on "teach," "how," and "-pent," followed by a caesura before the iambic recovers. This is followed by the slightly elongated line 14 (depending on how "thou'hadst" is pronounced). The couplet as conclusion and its rhythmic variations convey a certain simplicity and matter-of-factness, as if there has been accomplishment. This is in sharp contrast to the octave. We have here a process of gesturing, but of course every gesture is temporal.

The gesture is within and of the sonnet even as it is against the sonnet form, impossible without it. The sonnet convention is a way of forming gesture. Donne helped open up the sonnet to new subject matter, an offense within poetry against convention conventionally received. He forced cacophonies on it. He made his poems move dramatically, even sometimes violently. The first image is offered as both possible and impossible, the forceful introduction of the angels seeming to triumph over the tentativeness of "imagin'd." Johnson seized successfully on the offense, but he could not appreciate its value.

It is often considered that much of late seventeenth- and early eighteenth-century English poetry is highly conventionalized to the point of evoking boredom, in major part because of the use almost everywhere of the heroic couplet; this, if true, would certainly narrow the range of gesture. Certainly any conventionalized gesture can be worked nearly to death (though later it may sometimes be successfully revived). But the heroic couplet had its own liberating possibilities. I would like to treat as gestural a poem in heroic couplets that is completely devoid of the pyrotechnics of Donne or the epigrammatic wit of which the couplet is often a vehicle, as in Pope's verse "essays." It is full of conventional phrases. Except for a few that I shall mention, the variations within the iambic pentameter lines are not unusual and only enough to escape tedium. Yet, as gesture, the poem seems to me certainly a success.

The poem is Dryden's "To the Memory of Mr. Oldham." I quote it
in full:

> FAREWELL, too little and too lately known,
> Whom I began to think and call my own:
> For sure our Souls were near alli'd, and thine
> Cast in the same poetick mold with mine.
> One common Note on either Lyre did strike,   5
> And Knaves and Fools we both abhorr'd alike.
> To the same Goal did both our Studies drive:
> The last set out the soonest did arrive.
> Thus *Nisus* fell upon the slippery place,
> Whilst his young Friend perform'd and won the Race.   10
> O early ripe! To thy abundant Store
> What could advancing Age have added more?
> It might (what Nature never gives the Young)
> Have taught the Numbers of thy Native Tongue.
> But Satire needs not those, and Wit will shine   15
> Through the harsh Cadence of a rugged Line.
> A noble Error, and but seldom made,
> When Poets are by too much force betray'd.
> Thy gen'rous Fruits, though gather'd ere their prime,
> Still shew'd a Quickness; and maturing Time   20
> But mellows what we write to the dull Sweets of Rhyme.
> Once more, hail and farewell! farewell thou young,
> But ah! Too short, *Marcellus* of our Tongue!
> Thy Brows with Ivy and with Laurels bound;
> But Fate and gloomy Night encompass thee around.[17]   25

It is difficult to arrive at an adequate statement of this poem's merit. In 1920,
Mark Van Doren praised it, noting its artificiality and its many classical
echoes, memories from Dryden's store of reading. Van Doren declared,

---

17. My transcription is from John Sargeaunt, ed., *The Poems of John Dryden* (London: Oxford University Press, 1910), 178.

"There is not an original word in the work. It is a classical mosaic. . . . "[18]
There is no point in asking what Van Doren meant by an "original word."
Few poets other than Lewis Carroll coin them, and most of his were port-
manteaus. But it is not difficult to grasp what Van Doren was driving at.
The poem collects verbal conventions familiar to the classical elegy. If any-
thing approaches the unique, it is the very large number of them.

Nevertheless, it is a considerable success, as can be seen by comparing
it to all of Dryden's other elegies and epitaphs, including even the longer,
more ambitious poem about Mrs. Anne Killegrew. How can one defend
this judgment against the offense of its pile of classical clichés? I have
recourse to the notion of a total gesture. The use of conventional details is
not hyperbolic but deliberately, I think, somewhat muted. The poem is by
no means showy or oratorical, though it certainly has rhetorical devices.
The syntax is straightforward. The speaker does not overpraise and even
admits that Oldham's verse (he was a satirical poet) lacks "the Numbers of
[his] Native Tongue," excusing this as a "noble Error" in the case of a satirist.
The onomatopoetic flourish of line 16 seems decorous as a description of
something acceptable if not graceful in Oldham's satirical style. The alexandrines (though without the central pause) of lines 21 and 25 seem especially effective. The verbal content of both is entirely conventional, but the
lengthened lines compel lingering and remembering.

Northrop Frye said of Milton that he must not have asked what he
should say about Edward King when he sat down to write "Lycidas."
Instead, he must have asked, "How does poetry require that such a subject should be treated?"[19] The inevitable answer is: by employing certain
conventions and striking a certain tone. Dryden chooses not to make his
moan, not to overstate, but rather to face his subject directly with a certain simplicity. It is the evenness of tone, ruffled at the moments of the
alexandrines, that sustains the gesture. What Dryden did here he never
again accomplished in the genre of the elegy. Perhaps with the materials

18. Mark Van Doren, *John Dryden: A Study of His Poetry* (1920) (Bloomington:
Indiana University Press, 1960), 125.
19. Northrop Frye, *Anatomy of Criticism* (Princeton, NJ: Princeton University Press,
1957), 97.

at hand, only one such accomplishment was likely. Total gesture is not easy to sustain.

Is there something offensive here? I think an offense lies in the attitude projected. For some, the poem is not emotive enough for its subject. For others, the rhetorical movement is so tied to oratorical convention that the gesture may seem false or insincere. But beyond this, gesture itself is here offensive because it frustrates the desire for a summary interpretation.

By contrast to Dryden's poem, the gesturing of Lord Byron's narrator in *Don Juan* is theatrical, impertinent, and thus outrageous; but as the poem proceeds, the mood changes. Late in the poem, there is an actor on a darkening stage. Byron's poem is more than terms such as "narrative" and "satire" can contain. The principal reason is that we are very quickly removed to a position from which we are watching not just the story told but also the self-dramatization of the narrator.[20] This behavior, extreme in the earlier cantos, is gesture, and without gesture the narrator, whom we suspect of deliberate offense, disappears as a person of interest. It is perhaps unsettling to recognize that the narrator may be in competition with his characters.

Gesture in *Don Juan* begins with the introductory materials and proceeds with the offhand way in which the hero is introduced.[21] Juan has been a character in a pantomime, "sent to the devil somewhat ere his time," and he is chosen by the narrator because there is no true hero to be found "in the present age."

20. There is a parallel with this removal to observation of the narrator's and then the arranger's behavior in Joyce's *Ulysses*. With respect to *Don Juan*, see my "Byron, Yeats, and Joyce: Heroism and Technic," *Antithetical Essays in Literary Criticism and Liberal Education* (Tallahassee: Florida State University Press, 1990), esp. 77–81. Byron's narrator is not Byron but Byron's creation. First-person poems can always be treated as spoken (or written) by a created fictional character. Even third-person narrations can. To declare this to be so is often regarded as offensive on the critic's part, especially when romantic poetry or love poetry is the subject and sincerity becomes an issue. The matter extends to prose fiction, with, for example, Joyce Cary's trilogies being criticized because his own voice is never heard, only those of his narrators. Plato was apparently the first to make this sort of complaint.

21. I include here Byron's prose preface to Cantos 1 and 2, suppressed by Byron and not published until the edition of 1898–1901.

The narrator offends against appropriate poetic behavior; he recognizes that most poets begin *in medias res*:

That is the usual method, but not mine—
My way is to begin with the beginning;
The regularity of my design
Forbids all wandering as the worst of sinning,
And therefore I shall open with a line
(Although it cost me half an hour in spinning),
Narrating somewhat of Don Juan's father,
And also of his mother, if you'd rather.[22]

But the poem wanders constantly (poets are liars?), and the last line's "if you'd rather" is an impertinent offense against the reader. The narrator interferes with his story throughout, calling attention to himself with lengthy digressions, confessing to this fault (6: xcvi) and proceeding immediately to digress even further. At certain points, the reader begins to wonder whether it is the story that is in fact the digression.

In describing a love scene, the narrator declares out of mock propriety that he cannot go on (1: cxv), then goes on, declares a canto to be ended, and then proceeds through thirty-four more stanzas. He lies when he says that the reader can expect certain events to occur (1: cc), equivocates over how long his poem will be, threatening at one point a hundred cantos (12: lv), says late in his poem that he has only begun,[23] plays insolently with the notion of the Muse, coldly describes an act of cannibalism (2: lxxvii), is lured from his story by personal associations that his narrative calls up (2: clxxviii–clxxxi), lapses into seriousness, brings down to earth the traditional poetical idea of the hero's return (3: xxiii), and confesses he has nothing planned "unless it were to be a moment merry" (4: v). Occasionally, however, the narrator has to make an effort to maintain the impertinent comic gesture, for

22. My transcription is from Lord Byron, *Don Juan*, ed. Leslie A. Marchand (Boston: Houghton Mifflin, 1958), 11 (1: vii).

23. Byron died with the poem unfinished, only part of Canto 17 having been completed.

. . . if I laugh at any mortal thing,
'Tis that I may not weep, and if I weep,
'Tis that our nature cannot always bring
Itself to apathy. (4: iv)

This immensely complicates the gesture. It is a gesture that John Keats seems
to have missed, for he complained in disgust that Byron tried to be new
and different by making solemn things gay and gay things solemn. We discover beneath the narrator's comedy a somber vision, darkening into the
last cantos, a gesture rousing the faculties to act. In Canto 9, the narrator
declares, " . . . being of no party / I shall offend all parties" (9: xxvi). He
is talking about war and politics at the time, but the statement could serve
as the poem's epigraph. Even the reader he addresses as "grim" instead of
the conventional "dear" (15: xcv), and late in the poem he continues to
promise to reform himself. He does not.

Satires always affront someone, but Byron's is one of the few that from
time to time affront the reader for reasons not political. At the same time,
there is an implicit assumption of a pact between narrator and reader after
all. But some readers will resist being drawn into the pact. The removals,
digressions, and cavalier play with the story are deliberate affronts to readerly expectations. Everything in *Don Juan* is contained in a gesture.

My last example, of an entirely different sort, is brief enough to quote
in full. Indeed, it must be quoted in full if at all. It is by William Carlos
Williams:

THIS IS JUST TO SAY
I have eaten
the plums
that were in
the icebox

and which   5
you were probably
saving
for breakfast

Forgive me

they were delicious   10

so sweet

and so cold[24]

Almost seventy years since the poem was written, we are accustomed to free, unrimed, unpunctuated, and uncapitalized verse. Nevertheless, we continue to expect poetry in some way to be distinguishable from prose. To this point in this book, we have been concerned with the kind of offense that has been easily recognizable as such. But what about a poem people might well say isn't really a poem at all? Would the following be a poem? "This is just to say I have eaten the plums that were in the icebox and which you were probably saving for breakfast. Forgive me; they were delicious, so sweet and so cold." It has become something else.

One of the complaints about Joyce's *Ulysses* has been (and we still hear it) that if we didn't have the title no one would have the least idea that the book is connected with *Odyssey*. But we do have the title, and a title is every bit as much a part of the work as any other part. Indeed, it has a privileged position. Joyce's title tells us to be on the lookout. With Williams's poem, the division into lines and stanzas tells us how to read it. Stanzas 1 and 2 each have twelve syllables; the concluding stanza has thirteen. Each stanza is what we used to call a complete thought or sentence. Each line has one accent or stressed syllable. All of this creates a subtle tension between the devices of verse and what might in its straightforward syntax be prose. The title, very different from Joyce's in function, forces itself syntactically into the body of the verse, even as it remains separate as a title. But its function is not to point to subject matter or make an allusion but to declare a gesture that it is probably best not to attempt to describe. Nevertheless, I shall try to say a little. The poem as note comes out of a domestic situation in which the reader and intended receiver know and are comfortable with each other. It is a love poem.

It departs from poetic conventions only to return to them by means

24. A. Walton Litz and Christopher McGowan, eds., *The Collected Poems of William Carlos Williams, Volume I: 1909–1939* (New York: New Directions Press, 1986), 372.

of suggestion, and its language is that of common speech. Its presumption and offense is partly this commonness, yet the verse is controlled. As T. S. Eliot remarked, "No *vers* is *libre* for the man who wants to do a good job."[25]

Do we have the right to say that poetry is gesture or gestures, even poetry we judge to be bad (see chapter 12)? No, in that such a statement is but a trope inviting us to compare what happens in poetry to a physical movement or a certain immobility. Locke would call that way of talking a "perfect cheat." It is, at best, an instructive analogy. Yes, in that the trope rightly points to something in or of the poem that is not capturable by our usual words, though its presence is evident as we read. Still, it is adequate, and that is the poem's ultimate offense: its refusal to reveal itself fully to reason and interpretation, angering those who want the poem to behave as they believe language properly should. They want it to be decipherable, preferably monosemously, but if not, polysemously, the meanings all at attention in their respective places, ready for inspection by the guardians of the State. The tradition of allegorical interpretation provided such readings in response to poems of clearly allegorical intent, but even such poems— Spenser's *Faerie Queene*, Dante's *Commedia*—gesture beyond and transgress the boundaries of their allegorical content. One could argue that the more rigidly and narrowly allegorical a poem is the less interesting it is, because the freedom of gesture is suppressed in a system of meaning. But such purity of meaning is never achieved. If purity is the standard, the poem will inevitably give offense.

The gesture of poetry is not like that of everyday discourse, even if poetry uses the same words and syntax. The difference lies in what seems to be its intent (not necessarily the poet's) and the way the poem achieves it. In everyday life, gesture, when it is not simply reflexive, usually has a conscious external purpose that can be extractable in other words. Poets can certainly write poems and have such purposes in mind, but the poem's value as a poem, if it has any, will be in the gesture that transcends that pur-

25. This statement, made more than once by Eliot, is quoted by Charles O. Hartman in his *Free Verse: An Essay on Prosody* (Princeton, NJ: Princeton University Press, 1986), 10. This excellent book has enlightening discussions of some of Williams's poems; see 93–103.

pose and may even seem to contradict it. In the other arts, museums contain many objects constructed for some external purpose, but they are not there for that reason. Keats wrote of his dislike of "poetry that has a palpable design upon us,"[26] a design that I take to be like the external purpose of an entertaining advertisement or a moral lesson. In poetic gesture, words remain, in a sense, mute, yet capable of releasing what Keats called "a momentous depth of speculation."[27]

26. John Keats, letter to John Hamilton Reynolds, 3 February 1818. 26.
27. John Keats, letter to George and Thomas Keats, 28 December 1817.

5

Drama

Gesture is the stuff of drama where drama employs means beyond words. Yet I have offered the notion of a verbal gesture both in and as the poem. There has, of course, been a long identification of poetry with drama. As we know, the first extant poetics, that of Aristotle, was, at least in its surviving state, concerned mainly with drama. The mode of presenting Homer was originally dramatic performance by a bard, and Greek drama in its origins seems to have had only one actor. Plato's Ion is a late version of a bardic reciter of Homer. Socrates argues that Ion is not himself when he speaks of Homer, claiming that he is possessed. Denis Diderot argued more than two thousand years later that the actor, if successful, has "a disinterested onlooker inside him."[1] One might claim that Ion's allegedly irrational possession was the ultimate in successful acting.

In his *Narrative Discourse*, Gerard Genette subsumed drama under narrative,[2] but I reverse that order, holding that every narrative is an act by a fictive character, therefore dramatic. That is the reason there is no chapter in this book on the offense of narrative as such, since I subsume it under drama, though it is clear that many performances take narrative form, as in the parables performed by Jesus. There is nothing new about the notion of every poem being dramatic. Cleanth Brooks offered it in one of the influential works of the New Criticism, *The Well Wrought Urn*, where he declared, " . . . the structure of poetry is that of the drama."[3] It is something "'acted out'—something which arrives at its conclusion through conflict— something which builds conflict into its very being" (187). It is *"an action*

1. Denis Diderot, *The Paradox of Acting* [*Paradoxe sur le comedien*], trans. Walter Herries Pollack (New York: Hill and Wang, 1957), 14.

2. Gerard Genette, *Narrative Discourse: An Essay in Method* [*Discours du recit*, 1972], trans. Jane E. Lewin (Ithaca, NY: Cornell University Press, 1980).

3. Cleanth Brooks, *The Well Wrought Urn* (New York: Reynal and Hitchcock, 1947), 187.

rather than . . . a formula for action" (187). In a later essay, he repeated this idea, the poem there being like a "little drama."[4] The emphasis in the latter was on the poetic effect's dependence on all of the poem's elements. Thus poems "never contain abstract statements" (731), or, rather, they may contain them, but they must be read as "speeches in a drama" (731), and they cannot necessarily be connected to the author's views. Thus, Keats's "beauty is truth, truth beauty" must be read in the dramatic context of the poem as a whole and not as the author's personal statement. This position differs from that set forth by Socrates in Plato's *Republic*, even though both separate author and statement. Socrates argued that dramatic imitation is bad because we cannot tell what the poet's own thought is. Brooks did not care about that.

Although Brooks used, in addition to drama, a metaphor of organic growth, probably drawn from Coleridge, to describe a poem, his conception of the poem's unity tended toward spatialization. His use of the notion of drama seems to be present principally to support his view of the poem as a unified structure rather than to emphasize the poem as always a spoken or written acted part. For Brooks, the poem had an "inner core," a "pattern," "a structure of meanings, evaluations, and interpretations." The structure was one of "balancing and harmonizing connotations, attitudes, and meanings" (*Urn*, 178). My reason for citing Brooks here is not to invoke his notion of unity but rather to note that he thought of poems, even when written in the first person, as dramas.

The offense of drama in poetry is closely related to these matters. Poetry may contain assertions but is not itself assertion. A poem is a dramatic presentation, even a lyric, for even in the lyric the poet has put a fictive creation on the stage to speak, write, or think. The result is offense, especially to those who think of language as principally for communication. How are we to know what the poet really thinks? Why is the poet always masked? Why is the poet apparently imitating someone else, someone else who is not real? We cannot count on the poet's sincerity. Beyond this is

4. Cleanth Brooks, "Irony as a Principle of Structure" (1949), *Literary Opinion in America*, ed. Morton Dauwen Zabel, 3rd ed. rev. (New York: Harper and Row, 1962), 2: 730.

the offense of the whole situation: The poet cannot escape this dramatic making of the fiction of a speaker. It is in the nature of poetry. It follows, if we are to attribute meaning to a poem, that the meaning is of a sort different from what people usually think meaning to be.

I extend the notion of drama to narrative poems (and novels), even those written strictly in the third person without what is sometimes called authorial intrusion. One must assume the potentiality and thus the possibility of a third-person narrator as "present" and acting at the circumference of narration. This clearly occurs in the narrative high jinks of Joyce's *Ulysses* and, more disconcertingly, in his *Finnegans Wake*. The act of narration is thus fictionalized and not attributable directly to an author, who must be regarded as the maker of the narrator's action. Of course, in most third-person narrations, the narrative act as dramatic act yields a minimum of characterization of the narrator and may not require much critical discussion, but it remains important to recognize this characterization and to distinguish speaker (or writer) from author.[5]

Certain theoretical issues follow from all this. Brooks used the notion of drama to emphasize conflict and development, and in the process he distinguished the author from the poem's speaker. In an essay of 1946, W. K. Wimsatt and Monroe C. Beardsley attacked any effort to interpret a poem by reference to the author's intent. They, too, argued that the poem is dramatic: "We ought to impute the thoughts and attitudes of the poem immediately to the dramatic *speaker*, and if to the author at all, only by an act of biographical inference."[6] A decade earlier, Kenneth Burke had proposed language as a mode of action, as "dramatistic," and noted in any situation the elements of act, scene, agent, agency, and purpose.[7] All of these views were offered in opposition to the allegedly romantic and still popular view

5. In making drama surround any act of narration, I disagree not only with Genette but also with most narrative theorists known to me. For an excellent account of narrative theories, see Wallace Martin, *Recent Theories of Narrative* (Ithaca, NY: Cornell University Press, 1986).

6. W. K. Wimsatt, Jr., "The Intentional Fallacy," *The Verbal Icon: Studies in the Meaning of Poetry* (New York: Noonday Press, 1964), 5. Beardsley was coauthor of this essay. In chapter 10, I dispute this last point with respect to the trilogies of Joyce Cary.

7. Developed later in Burke's *A Grammar of Motives* (New York: Prentice-Hall, 1945), xv–xxiii.

that the poem is a self-expression—in Wordsworth's words, a "spontaneous overflow of powerful feeling," "recollected in tranquility."[8] They challenged also Shelley's declaration that the original impulse of the poem is fading by the time of composition and that every poem is but a weak copy of what the poet desired to express.[9] Particularly with Wimsatt and Beardsley, the argument was that, in any case, we cannot know the poet's intention. Though they did not explicitly go so far, one could argue that poets might forget, lie about intent, or just prove themselves bad interpreters of their own work. The argument was extended later by Northrop Frye, who did not identify himself with the New Critics: "If we had the privilege of Gulliver in Glubdubdrib to call up the ghost of, say, Shakespeare, to ask him what he meant by such a passage, we could only get, with maddening iteration, the same answer: 'I meant it to form a part of the play'."[10]

These arguments drive us back to a view of the poem as pointing toward its own internality, its Kantian "internal purposiveness," rather than outward toward the author as origin of a meaning that can be discursively pronounced. But these critics did not go so far as to dismiss the author altogether. The author still did compose the work. The author as an individual did exist. Inquiry into the author's relation to the text was regarded as a biographical and psychological, not a critical one. Poetry was a use of language different from that with the intent only of communicating information from one person to others.

For other reasons, the French structuralists and poststructuralists dismissed the author, though not to identify the poem with drama or to distinguish it from other uses of language. Their notions were more radical. Writing in 1968, and apparently unaware of the New Criticism in North America, Roland Barthes claimed that all writing is "the destruction of every voice, every origin."[11] For him, the whole idea of an author was a creation of the post-medieval world, and he complained that the modern "image of litera-

---

8. In his preface to the second edition of *Lyrical Ballads* (1800).

9. In his *Defence of Poetry*.

10. Northrop Frye, *Anatomy of Criticism* (Princeton, NJ: Princeton University Press, 1957), 86.

11. Roland Barthes, "The Death of the Author" (1968), *The Rustle of Language* [*Le Bruissement de la langue*] (New York: Hill and Wang, 1986), 49.

ture . . . is tyrannically centered on the author, his person, his history, his tastes, his passions" (50). Following Mallarmé, he argued that it is "language which speaks, not the author" (50). Extending Saussure's structuralist notion of language as radically differential and seeing that in a differential system the search for more and more meaning is without end, Barthes spoke of language as the origin that paradoxically calls all origins into question. No so-called author can halt the infinite regress of meaning. The reader, not the author, becomes the "site" of a "multiplicity" of forces collected in a text (54).

Shortly (1969) after Barthes's essay appeared, Michel Foucault also considered the author a creation of the modern world and noted that contemporary writing in particular accepts the author's disappearance. For him, the term "author" was functional only, serving as a means of classification. He opted for "author-function," a term to be employed to "characterize the existence, circulation, and operation of certain discourses within a society."[12] Barthes's program was political and anti-theological, an attack on all notions of origin. Foucault's was political and historical.[13] Both saw European humanism as the culprit and began with language, not man. They projected from there a highly abstracted, subjectless notion of "author," treated strictly as a word and then as a convergence of social forces. The interest of neither was principally literary, and neither viewed a literary work as a "whole," either Aristotelian or Coleridgean. Quite the opposite. They identified wholes with a fundamental interpreted meaning and then denied the possibility of it. (But Aristotle's whole was not one of meaning but of form.) They dismissed the author as a source of the denied meaning. Because they had no notion of a poetic text as different from other forms of writing, they did not proceed to any idea of the dramatic.

Indeed, all writing was viewed as the same. Foucault wrote, "Criticism has been concerned for some time now with aspects of a text not fully dependent on the notion of an individual writer; studies of genre or the

---

12. Michel Foucault, "What Is an Author?" [Qu'est-ce qu-un auteur?], *Language, Counter-Memory, Practice*, trans. Donald F. Bouchard and Sherry Simon (Ithaca, NY: Cornell University Press, 1977), 125.

13. Foucault tried to separate himself from structuralism, attacking the structuralist (and poststructuralist) linguistic model and adopting the idea of power relations, still modeled, however, on the structuralists' system of linguistic differences.

analysis of recurring textual motifs and their variations from a norm other than the author" (126). Foucault here was less provincial in his sense of what had been going on in criticism than was Barthes.[14] But the questions that he posed at the end of his essay as the right ones to ask show as they proceed that his inquiry belonged to history and the social sciences, with the ends of these disciplines in mind. Any piece of writing, not just poetry, was grist to this mill:

> What are the modes of existence of this discourse?
> Where does it come from; how is it circulated; who controlled it?
> What placements are determined for possible subjects?
> Who can fulfill these diverse functions of the subject? (138)

The political aspect of the attack was on the liberal and humanistic concept of the human individual.[15] It ignored the notion of the poem as such.

It may be concluded that we need not indulge with a vengeance a drive toward abstraction, which has always been the tendency at the higher reaches of critical theory in the social sciences. We need not abstract away the author or reject all notions of the author for the sake of a theory. *Someone* has written the poem (though sometimes it is a collaboration). The question, properly to be approached, is not whether or not authors exist but rather what their relation to the reading of a poem is.

The reason for my having considered these various treatments of the author is that they raise the possibility, even when they have different intentions and interests, of always treating poems as dramatic. In this connection, it is difficult to determine which is likely to give more offense, the rejection of the human subject by Foucault or the rejection of an ultimate, attainable discursive meaning, as implied in the work of Brooks and

14. It is interesting to speculate on what the condition of literary criticism would be today had the Europeans and North Americans known each other's work earlier.

15. Foucault himself said, "The subject [including the author] should not be entirely abandoned." But then he went on simply to restate his conception of the author, which was abstracted into a pure function after all: "It should be reconsidered, not to restore the theme of an originating subject, but to seize its functions, its intervention in discourse, and its system of dependencies . . . " (137).

Barthes. We need not tarry longer with the question of the author except
to recognize that it was tied in these discourses to the question of poetic
meaning. However, we recognize that the question of poetic meaning is in
itself a field for offense. Those offended are likely to accuse such critics of
denying all meaning, but it can be argued (presuming the term "meaning"
is even relevant to what we are considering) that the drama of poetry frees
the poem from a restrictive meaning or interpretation and helps generate
an accumulation of meaning as time passes. Thus poetry, as Blake said,
"rouzes the faculties [of the reader] to act"[16] by opening an area for speculation. This is an offense to those who want their truth neat, and we saw
many who thought new developments in theory were an attack on the possibility of any meaning at all, when the conclusion to be reached should
have been that more and ever more meaning was being insisted on.

The identification of poetry with drama was most decisively acknowledged in the English dramatic monologues of the nineteenth century, particularly those of Robert Browning. In them it is quite clear to the reader
that the speaker is not the poet, that one can understand from the words
as much as necessary about the place and time of the event, that the speaker
is sufficiently identifiable, that one can infer who the person addressed is
(if this is necessary). As a result, one can speculate with some success about
the characters' motivations.

Of course, the drama becomes silent in our reading. Murray Krieger
distinguished between the drama and the silently read poem:

> In brief, the apparent presence—the tangible presence—in the drama
> of the objects of representation gave it an immediacy denied to words
> alone. No matter how forceful the conjuring power of verbal images,
> only drama could claim to produce a *sensible* illusion of reality. For
> words, strictly speaking, must always, at the source of our experi-
> encing them, be intelligible only—transmitting their images and
> objects only through the medium of mind—and not sensible, with

16. Letter to Dr. Trusler, 23 August 1799, *The Complete Poetry and Prose of William
Blake*, ed. David V. Erdman, rev. ed. (Garden City, NY: Anchor Press/Doubleday, 1982),
702.

their images and objects, as with pictures, grasped immediately as they are read.[17]

It is not clear to me that the eye is not also a mediator in the matter of sight, but we may put this aside. Poems, Krieger argued, have not depended on performance to the extent that drama does. This is true enough, but reading is itself a constitutive act, an interior performance, especially the reading of poetry. In Burke's terms, the reader, presented with the act and the agent, infers the scene and the characters' purposes.

In reading Browning's "My Last Duchess" what happens? We infer from the subtitle and what is said that the place is Ferrara and the speaker is its duke, that he has taken the emissary of a count upstairs in his palace to view a portrait, kept concealed behind a curtain, of his deceased wife. We know that the emissary speaks, and we infer the substance of what he says. We infer that the emissary turns to depart. Indeed, we are more certain of the accuracy of these inferences than we are of the meaning and intent of some of the duke's words, which we realize are vague and ambiguous: Did the duke order the murder of his duchess? Is his talk a threat meant to be conveyed to his prospective bride, the count's daughter?

The duke's words perform gestures. His whole monologue is itself a gesture appearing to have a malicious intent, though it is presented with enough ambiguity to make outright accusation difficult. The duke plays with the emissary, Browning with the reader. Krieger was right to say that the poem cannot present a sensible illusion, but the reader's mind can perform an adequate substitute.[18]

The ambiguities of the duke's speech are, of course, offensive. He comes across as evil. But there is another offense: the fact that readerly inferences are required, unsettling a popular view of what a poem should do.

---

17. *Ekphrasis: The Illusion of the Natural Sign* (Baltimore: Johns Hopkins University Press, 1992), 34.

18. In his *Practical Criticism* (1929) (New York: Harcourt, Brace and Co.; London: Routledge and Kegan Paul, 1949), 235, I. A. Richards pointed out that in his experiments with readers, those who did not respond by producing images or visualizing were, in his view, as good readers as those who did.

What is the author's judgment? The offense is that the poem challenges the reader to judge; it does not close itself by surrounding its action with a judgment. Many will claim that Browning's judgment is in the very fabric of the poem, but even if that is so, the reader must think it out.

Dramatic dialogues and monologues are the most obvious examples of the relation of poem to drama. Next are interior monologues such as T. S. Eliot's "The Love Song of J. Alfred Prufrock." Then there are those that stand somewhere between exterior and interior, where the distinction seems not quite relevant, as in Tennyson's "Ulysses" and "The Lotus-Eaters." In many such works, the reader would be mistaken to specify place and time. I am reminded of a student who, after hearing me discourse on poems being like dramas, began a paper on Keats's "Ode on a Grecian Urn" with the arresting sentence "John Keats went up to his attic and found this old shape." A valiant or perhaps desperate effort, seizing on the phrase "Attic shape," to follow instructions. It is enough to say that Keats's speaker, who does not need literally to be speaking but thinking, is either viewing or remembering a Grecian urn and that, as an ode, the poem has a certain rhetorical nature that formalizes the drama. The conventions of rhetorical address need to be understood in order to read most poetry. Neither is the poem a piece of naturalistic language. No one, to my knowledge, ever spoke in real life to an urn in this way. All drama and all acting have their artifice. If we have gone to a film or a play and complained that it wasn't "real," we have almost certainly not said what was bothering us. Yet it is probably offensive for someone to reply, "Of course it wasn't real; it never is."

But if that is so, and it certainly is, the question arises: Why should we spend our time on fictions, things that are not, and statements that do not come out and say what they mean? Or the conclusion is that poetry's value lies in allowing us momentarily to escape from the real.

The employment of masks in Ancient Greek drama was probably an effort to abstract toward the presentation of some pure form of emotion or perhaps to improve on nature. We can extend the notion of the mask of drama in certain ways to apply it to poetry, though we risk offense to do so. In his dialogue "The Critic as Artist" (1890), Wilde has one of his characters say, "Man is least himself when he talks in his own person. Give him a mask, and he will tell you the truth."[19] Perhaps with this paradox, offensive on the face of it, we can restore the banished author, albeit disguised. Is the author's play as a whole a mask? Can the metaphor of the dramatic mask, unsettling and possibly offensive since it may suggest deception or even crime, be of use to the notion of the poem as drama?

The drama as a mask of the author may be more acceptable than Barthes's "death of the author" or Foucault's abstract "author-function." Yeats, influenced by Wilde, made much of the mask. In 1909, he mused on the possibility of human nature copying drama: "I think that all happiness depends on the energy to assume the mask of some other self."[20]

At about the same time, he had remarked, "There is a relation between discipline and the theatrical sense. If we cannot imagine ourselves as different from what we are and assume that second self, we cannot impose a discipline upon ourselves, though we may accept one from others. Active virtue as distinguished from the passive acceptance of a current code is therefore, theatrical, consciously dramatic, the wearing of a mask."[21] The mask is "style, personality—deliberately adopted" (279). By contrast, character, in Yeats's language, is something imposed on us or accepted from others. Yeats's "active virtue" is his antithetical response to the passive "primary." These notions lead into lines from one of Yeats's last poems, "Lapis Lazuli":

> All perform their tragic play,
> There struts Hamlet, there is Lear,
> That's Ophelia, that Cordelia;
> Yet they, should the last scene be there,
> The great stage curtain about to drop,
> If worthy their prominent part in the play,
> Do not break up their lines to weep.

19. *Complete Works of Oscar Wilde* (London and Glasgow, 1948), 1045. Lon L. Fuller reminds us in his *Legal Fictions* (Stanford, CA: Stanford University Press, 1967), 19, that the word for "person" originally meant "mask."

20. "The Death of Synge: Extracts from a Diary Kept in 1909," *The Autobiography of William Butler Yeats* (New York: Macmillan, 1953), 306.

21. "Estrangement: Extracts from a Diary kept in 1909," *The Autobiography of William Butler Yeats*, 285.

They know that Hamlet and Lear are gay;
Gaiety transfiguring all that dread.[22]

The offense of these lines lies in part in their causing the reader to be uncertain whether the poem refers to life or to art, whether these Hamlets and Lears are characters presented by actors or are the actors acting, whether the gaiety is that of the characters or of the actors. Or is it somehow both?

In *The Paradox of Acting*, Diderot went so far as to say that he did not think much of players who "play from the heart" (15). He considered feeble the playing of an actress bounded by the feelings of which she herself was capable (16). He claimed that the greatest actors are "the least sensitive of all creatures" (18). The reason is that they are too concerned with "observing, considering, and reproducing" (18). What is truth in the drama? "Reflect a little as to what, in the language of the theatre, is *being true*. Is it showing as they are in nature? Certainly not. . . . It is the conforming of the action, diction, face, voice, movement, gesture, to an ideal type invented by the poet, and frequently enhanced by the player" (23). Yeats's interest in Castiglione's courtier figure is related to this, for the courtier is an actor so adept that one does not think of him as acting even as one admires the act. But Yeats went further than his remarks of 1909 indicate. He implied that the mask is not just some desirable "other self" but the real achieved self, nature matured into art.

A comparison with Keats's view is instructive. Keats's poet is like Diderot's actor and to some extent Yeats's mask: "As to the poetical Character . . . it is not itself—it has no self—it is every thing and nothing—It has no character . . . no identity."[23]

We have noticed that the idea of the poem as drama runs the risk that the reader will impose an inappropriate specificity on the scene. A few examples, all sonnets, should reveal the variety of scenic possibilities. I choose

22. W. B. Yeats, *The Poems: A New Edition*, ed. Richard J. Finneran (New York: Macmillan, 1983), 294.

23. John Keats, letter to Richard Woodhouse, 27 October 1818. Keats's complaint about what he called the "egotistical sublime" in Wordsworth is connected to this. It appears that Keats thought Wordsworth insufficiently masked in his poems. See the letter to John Hamilton Reynolds, 3 February 1818.

sonnets because they are of a fairly fixed verse form, and form always affects to some extent how we construe scene. I have mentioned already two scenes: one as if on a stage ("My Last Duchess") and one performed on the stage of the mind, an interior monologue. These are fairly straightforward compared to the gradations we find in sonnets.

John Stuart Mill observed, "Eloquence is *heard*, poetry is *over-heard*," and he went on to claim, "All poetry is of the nature of soliloquy. It may be said that poetry, which is printed on hot-pressed paper and sold at a bookseller's shop, is a soliloquy in full dress, and on the stage."[24] Soliloquies in plays are odd in that sometimes we think the character is talking to us even as we are overhearing, this "us" being perhaps a version of the fictive "dear reader" of some novels and narrative poems. I am thinking of poems that in their formality are like dramatized moments of oratory, what Yeats called "high talk" (343). The notion can be exemplified by poems clearly designed for a certain occasion, making a certain formal gesture, as in a funeral elegy or Dryden's epitaph poems or in the deliberate, admiring, though distanced parody of Yeats's "Under Ben Bulben" in W. H. Auden's elegy on Yeats's death.[25]

I choose the sonnet also as an example that clearly embodies dramatically a formal gesture. In sonnets, the scene of drama is seldom a specific physical one. Scene is subordinated to the occasion and is replaced by attitude. That requires a certain acting, a certain masking. In Spenser's "One day I wrote her name upon the strand," the speaker (or writer) narrates. We can imagine the narration addressed to a general audience, as in conventional story-telling, but by implication it is obliquely addressed to one person, the beloved. This doubled address is not unusual in love sonnets. In Shakespeare's sonnets, the beloved is frequently addressed directly, but sometimes obliquely, as in "Let me not to the marriage of true minds admit impediments," in which the speaker (or writer) declares his constancy but

24. John Stuart Mill, "What Is Poetry?" ("Thoughts on Poetry and Its Varieties," 1833), *Autobiography and Literary Essays*, ed. John M. Robson and Jack Stillinger (Toronto: University of Toronto Press, 1981), 348–49.

25. This poem declares that Yeats "became his admirers" and is now "scattered among a hundred cities," as if in death he abandoned a self to become what he created, his poems, which in turn became those who read them.

also seems to admonish the beloved. In "Poor soul, the center of my sinful earth," the self is divided and addressed, but the poem seems meant to be overheard or read by the beloved.

In "Batter my heart, three-personed God," Donne, taking the convention of the love sonnet, shocks by dramatizing an act of prayer as a request for violence to be done him by God.[26] Part of the poem's violence is the paradox in the prayer itself as well as the bold gesture of the speaker's direct address to God and the suggestion of masochism, bondage, adultery, divorce, and rape. There is a deliberate charging up of the energy of the address itself. The poem is an odd prayer, hardly a meditation.

In another way, Milton's *tour de force* of sound "On the Late Massacre in Piemont" is a prayer that dramatizes an entirely different relation to deity. It is spoken as if it were an oration, a command, a spell against evil, in which rhetorical devices and sound structure convey a solemn formality. Finally, there is Yeats's "Leda and the Swan," often not immediately recognized as a sonnet. It expresses an imaginative vision, occurring as the words are spoken or in vivid remembrance, leading to a series of questions. In all of these cases the speaker, writer, or thinker is in a dramatic situation, although the vision is an internal one. He is a character on the poem's stage.

Of course, close attention to a dramatic situation is more important in some poems than in others. It may yield much or not much. Attention to Byron's narrator yields much. Attention to Virgil's yields less, though, of course, a criticism of Virgil's narrator's politics will yield a lot. This last seems to me in a different, broader, and more abstract, historical context, where the offense is not one of poetry, but possibly one of ideology, if the ideology does not please you.

Drama's offense is well documented in the attacks on it as feigning. In Joyce Cary's novel *Except the Lord*, the narrator Chester Nimmo, politician son of an itinerant preacher and taught to regard plays as sinful, tells of going to a carnival as a child and being enticed to enter a tent where a

26. The allusion to the Trinity here seems oddly gratuitous unless the reader is supposed to be impressed by the awesomeness of the fact that there are three batterers invoked even as One is addressed, increasing the amount of violence the speaker desires to be perpetrated against/for him.

play was being performed. It was a typical melodrama of the time, based on a famous murder. The effect was electric and seductive. Nimmo asserts that it changed his life. In the experience, he was "beyond reflection . . . all exposed surface," and he remarks, "I have heard it said that a man's first experience in the theatre opens a new world to him—it would be better to say that it destroys the old one."[27] Further, "Believe me, art, and especially the drama, above all the popular drama, has a fearful power and responsibility in the world—it acts directly upon the very centre of feeling and passion" (93). Nimmo notes here its prime offense. As we shall see in chapter 10, Cary was himself criticized because in his trilogies, it was thought, his own voice is never directly heard and we don't know what he thinks. It is always someone acting out a narration. He was accused of creating a morally indeterminate world.

The offense of drama has an interesting parallel in the offense of writing, as described by Socrates to Phaedrus:

> The painter's products stand before us as though they were alive, but if you question them they maintain a most majestic silence. It is the same with written words; they seem to talk to you as though they were intelligent, but if you ask them anything about what they say, from a desire to be instructed, they go on telling you just the same thing forever. And once a thing is put in writing, the composition, whatever it may be, drifts all over the place, getting into the hands not only of those who understand it but equally of those who have no business; it doesn't know how to address the right people, and not to address the wrong.[28]

Writing uproots the words from their origin in a speaker, much as drama distances the work from the author.

I cannot end this chapter without observing that there is a sense in which all writing and even speaking are masks of drama. The difference

---

27. Joyce Cary, *Except the Lord* (London: Michael Joseph, 1953), 89, 93.
28. "Phaedrus," *The Collected Dialogues of Plato*, ed. Edith Hamilton and Huntington Cairns (Princeton, NJ: Princeton University Press, 1961), 521.

here between poetry and other uses of words does not lie only in the degree of elaboration, as in style as mask, but rather more in this: With the poem, the difference is that you are invited, or, if not invited, you are free, to assume that the poem *is* a mask. Indeed, the poet probably prefers that you do so, since it allows for his or her privacy. For the writer of a business letter, if the reader were to make that assumption, it would be a disastrous failure of rhetoric.

6

Fiction

"Temple of lies, where men and women practiced feigning as an art, to deceive and confuse honest souls." This is the complaint Chester Nimmo had heard from his preacher father.[1] Versions of it have persisted since Plato's treatment of imitative poets. From very early, "fiction" seems to have had a twofold meaning, expressing a certain ambivalence. There was the Greek *poiesis*, poem or thing made or created, and the Latin *fingere*, meaning to shape, form, mold, or model. But at the same time, words related to it, such as *fictum*, denoted falsehood or pretense; and *fictio*, though it meant forming or formation, carried also the idea of disguise.

The ambivalence was present in Aristotle: "Any impossibilities there may be in his [the poet's] description of things are faults. But from another point of view they are justifiable, if they serve the end of poetry itself. . . . "[2] Aristotle also argues that it is better to make the mistake of painting the hind with horns than to paint it inartistically so that it is unrecognizable (1460b, 31–33) and that, for the purposes of poetry, a "likely impossibility is always preferable to an unconvincing possibility" (1460a, 26–27). The emphasis is clearly on *poiesis* in the sense of a making or shaping of something. But later defenses emphasized Aristotle's allowance that the poet could properly represent things as they ought to be or men as better than they are.[3] A cap was put on all of this by Wilde's dialogue "The Decay of Lying," where, as we saw, Vivian argues that nature fails to accomplish what art does and invokes Aristotle in his support.[4] Vivian goes on to condemn "careless habits of accuracy" (973). His conclusion is that "Lying, the telling of beautiful untrue things, is the proper aim of Art" (992).

1. Joyce Cary, *Except the Lord* (London: Michael Joseph, 1953), 87.
2. W. D. Ross, "De Poetica," in *The Works of Aristotle*, trans. Ingram Bywater (Oxford: Clarendon Press, 1924), 11: 1460b.
3. For example, Sir Philip Sidney in his *Apology for Poetry*.
4. *Complete Works of Oscar Wilde* (London and Glasgow: Collins, 1948), 970.

Wilde's witty dialogue reflects a change in the notion of fictions that began in the late eighteenth century. The impetus for that change was epistemological and empiricist. Until then, fictions, as we have seen, were either attacked as lies or defended as idealized improvements on nature, allegories hidden from the vulgar, or sheer entertainment with no serious purpose or use. By the late eighteenth century, the situation was changing radically. Fictions were, for some philosophers, no longer necessarily lies or a façade for deliberately hidden wisdom. At the same time, fictions came to be seen as stretching far beyond the realm of the poetic or literary, finally to encompass virtually everything regarded as knowledge. It came to be seen that fictions were necessary and, in fact, ubiquitous in discourse. Locke's division of experience into primary and secondary qualities played an early preparatory role in this, though he had no theory of fictions and certainly a narrow view of language. Berkeley's *reductio* of Locke's division may strike us today as part of the process toward a theory of fictions, though Berkeley would be astounded to recognize this. David Hume's skeptical critique of causality led him to think of causality and other things as necessary fictions, but the real turning point came later with Kant's proposal that the understanding is constitutive of knowledge, operating through the categories of quantity, quality, relation, and modality, and that things in themselves were unknowable as such.

Necessary or at least useful nonliterary fictions had been recognized prior to this, particularly in the law. Vico, arguing in *The New Science* that what he called poetic logic preceded all later thought, called Ancient Roman law a "serious poem" and ancient jurisprudence "a severe kind of poetry."[5] The sources of such logic lay in the imaginative universals that the founders of Roman law, incapable of making abstract universals, created. These were, for example, signs of ownership, coats of arms, and other feignings, in contrast to abstract terms without images. Vico speaks of masks in connection with this: " . . . under the person ['person' originally meaning 'mask'] or mask of the father of a family were concealed all his children and servants,

5. Giambattista Vico, *The New Science of Giambattista Vico*, rev. trans. of 3rd ed. (1744), trans. Thomas Goddard Bergin and Max Harold Fisch (Ithaca, NY: Cornell University Press, 1968), 386.

and under the real name or emblem of a house were concealed all its agnates [relatives] and gentiles [clansmen]. Thus we saw Ajax the tower of the Greeks and Horatius at the bridge withstanding the whole of Tuscany . . . " (389). Masks were brought into the forum much as the poets brought masks on the stage. Thus Vico argued that ancient jurisprudence was poetic, and the connection to poetry was the fiction.[6] "By its [the law's] fictions what had happened was taken as not having happened, and what had not happened as having happened; those not yet born as already born; the living as dead, and the dead as still living in their estates pending acceptance. It introduced so many empty masks without subjects, *iura imaginaria*, rights invented by imagination" (390). The formulae in which laws were expressed were even called *carmina*, or songs.

In later law, fictions remain, but generally with recognition of their falsity and utility. The difference between a fiction and a lie, as Sidney said about poems, is that a fiction is not intended to deceive. Lon L. Fuller observes, as did Vico, that fictions are often metaphorical expressions in which the criterion is adequacy, not truth or falsity.[7] Indeed, when legal fictions are believed as truth, they lose their use and become dangerous (9). Likewise, any effort to eliminate fictions from the law would be only to substitute "dead metaphors for live ones" (17), because of the ineradicability of metaphor in language.[8] Pierre de Tourtoulon remarks, "Judicial theory is all the more objective when it presents itself as fictitious and all the more delusive when it claims to do without fictions."[9]

Yet Fuller says, "The fiction has generally been regarded as something of which the law ought to be ashamed, and yet without which the law cannot, as yet, dispense" (2), and Fuller's own discourse, meant to explain

---

6. And the trope of synecdoche, discussed in chapter 7.

7. Lon L. Fuller, *Legal Fictions* (Stanford, CA: Stanford University Press, 1967), 10.

8. Bentham remarks: "the words *rights* and *obligations* have raised those thick vapours which have intercepted the light; their origin has been unknown; they have been lost in abstractions. These words have been the foundations of reasoning as if they had been eternal entities which did not derive their birth from the law, but which, on the contrary, had given birth to it." C. K. Ogden, ed., *Bentham's Theory of Fictions* (New York: Harcourt Brace and Co.; London: Kegan Paul, Trench, Trubner and Co., 1932), cxxx.

9. Pierre de Tourtoulon, *Philosophy in the Development of the Law* (New York: Macmillan, 1922), 295.

the necessity and function of fictions, seems to express some regret when he says, "A metaphorical element taints all our concepts" (115).

Pierre J. J. Olivier speaks of legal fictions as false assumptions, always unverifiable, that are consciously made "in order to create, extend, or explain a legal rule," and he observes that all abstract thoughts are fictions.[10] In this he echoes Jeremy Bentham, who, in the group of excerpts from his works collected by C. K. Ogden, developed a general theory of fictions, classifying what he calls "entities" into types. There are "real entities," those things that have physical existence and are available to sense. There are "inferential entities," things that we feel are real but are imperceptible. There are "collective entities," the result of abstraction and generalization (152). But then Bentham collapses together some part of inferential entities and all of fictitious entities:

> A fictitious entity is an entity to which, though by the grammatical form of the Discourse employed in speaking of it, existence be ascribed, yet in truth and reality existence is not meant to be ascribed.
>
> Every noun-substantive which is not the name of a real entity, perceptible or inferential, is the name of a fictitious entity.
>
> Every fictitious entity bears some relation to some real entity, and can no otherwise be understood than in so far as that relation is perceived—a conception of that relation is obtained. (12)

Examples are motion, relation, faculty, power. Fictive terms such as these produce no image, though often metaphor is involved. We can, for example, speak of a real entity as being *in* motion or *at* rest.[11] We cannot do without such fictions. As Ogden remarks, explaining Bentham's view, "To say that, in discourse fictitious language ought never, on any occasion, to be employed, would be as much as to say that no discourse on the subject, of which the operations, or affectations, or other phenomena of the mind

10. Pierre J. J. Oliver, *Legal Fictions in Practice and Legal Science* (Rotterdam: Rotterdam University Press, 1975), 12.

11. These are what Bentham calls fictions of the first remove (from a real entity). With respect to motion, fictions of the second remove would, for example, be slowness and quickness.

are included, ought ever to be held" (xliii). But at times Bentham treats fictitious entities and their names as unfortunate necessities, and he would like
to limit figurative discourse to situations where it is absolutely necessary
to the ends of conceptualization and communication. The deader the
metaphor the better, for dead metaphors, he thinks, have lost their false
character. Whenever fictions are employed, their fictive nature should be
made known. This would be a large order, since almost all discourse is, for
Bentham, fictive.

The suspicion of fictions used for any but pragmatic purposes is connected to Bentham's division between the fictive entities already mentioned
and "fabulous entities." In Ogden's account, "Fabulous entities, whether
persons or things, are supposed material objects, of which the separate existence is capable of becoming a subject of belief, and of which, accordingly,
the same sort of picture is capable of being drawn in and preserved in the
mind, as of any really existent object" (xxxvi). Examples are gods, fabulous kings and animals, El Dorado, and so on.

One might think that a theory of fictions would raise up poetry or at
least give it serious attention. Bentham's does not.[12] Indeed, it relegates
poetry to the same area as that of superstition and false belief:

> Between poetry and truth there is a natural opposition: false morals,
> fictitious nature. The poet always stands in need of something false.
> When he pretends to lay his foundations in truth, the ornaments of his
> superstructure are fictions; his business consists in stimulating our
> passions, and exciting our prejudices. Truth, exactitude of every kind,

12. Serious treatment had to wait for Frank Kermode's *The Sense of an Ending: Studies in the Theory of Fiction* (New York: Oxford University Press, 1970) and Wolfgang Iser's
The Fictive and the Imaginary (Baltimore: Johns Hopkins University Press, 1993), the latter of which contains helpful accounts of Bentham's and Hans Vaihinger's theories. See
also my *Philosophy of the Literary Symbolic* (Tallahassee: Florida State University Press,
1983), esp. chapter 7, "Symbol, Fiction, and Figment." C. G. Prado, in his *Making Believe:
Philosophical Reflections on Fiction* (Westport, CT: Greenwood Press, 1984), emphasizes
a pragmatic view of fictions derived principally from the work of Richard Rorty and proposes that "the explanatory and organizational power of myth and the role and power of
stories are intrinsically related in that what underlies both is an elemental conceptual phenomenon: the organizational role of narrative" (136).

is fatal to poetry. The poet must see everything through coloured media, and strive to make everyone else do the same. It is true, there have been noble spirits, to whom poetry and philosophy have been equally indebted; but these exceptions do not counteract the mischiefs which have resulted from this magic art.[13]

However, Bentham does allow that poets are at least not insincere, and he thinks that in any case they want only to amuse.

Though not quite as dismissive as Bentham of poetic fictions and names for fabulous entities, Hans Vaihinger's Kantian-derived "idealistic" or "critical" positivism has no place of importance for poetry in his theory of fictions. Vaihinger stepped beyond Kant's view that most "ideational constructs" are subjective to conclude that they are all simply fictions. Kant's categories, for example, are fictions, as is Kant's thing-in-itself. In Vaihinger, virtually everything becomes fictive, though he endeavors to distinguish hypotheses from fictions.[14] Fictions have pragmatic use, but they do not connect, as they do with Bentham, to real entities, for Vaihinger's Kantianism and pragmatism tend to dismiss the questions that surround the reality and knowability of real entities. When Vaihinger speaks of "aesthetic fictions," he has almost nothing to say. He relegates them to "figments." The term reveals a certain disdain, though Vaihinger tries to avoid that implication by resorting to a vaguely classical, rhetorical notion of aesthetic value: "Aesthetic fictions serve the purpose of awakening within us certain uplifting or otherwise important feelings" (82). He also speaks of the abuse of fictions in some poetry, rather as Locke does about the abuse of language.

So the theory of fictions begins from the assumption of epistemological subjectivity and proceeds to a radical pragmatism in which poetry is relegated to a lower caste or outcast position as fable or figment. The ground

---

13. Quoted by Ogden, *Bentham's Theory of Fictions*, footnote 2, xciii; from Bentham's *Works*, 2: 253–54.

14. Hans Vaihinger, *The Philosophy of 'As If': A System of the Theoretical, Practical, and Religious Fictions of Mankind* [*Philosophie des Als Ob* (1924)], trans. C. K. Ogden (New York: Harcourt, Brace and Co.; London: Kegan Paul, Trench, Trubner and Co., 1925), 82. In what he called the "Law of Ideational Shifts," Vaihinger proposed an historical movement from fiction to hypothesis to the decadence of dogma, or the reverse.

for this relegation is, with Bentham, the old charge of the lie. In Vaihinger's case, the situation is somewhat different since legitimate fictions are those that are clearly useful. If figments could be proved useful, they would recover some of the dignity lost by the stigma of the term.

In the Kantian tradition, to which Vaihinger in his way belonged, Ernst Cassirer's study of cultural "symbolic forms" can be considered a presentation of kinds of human fiction-making. For Cassirer, art (including literary art) is one of these. The others are language, myth, religion, history, and science. In his *An Essay on Man*, Cassirer does not consider art to be of a lower caste.[15] His aim is to establish a definition of man that is not substantive but functional. Man must be defined by what he does, by his work (68). There can be no single reductive, foundational assumption about man's nature, as, for example, Nietzsche's will to power, Freud's sexual instinct, or Marx's economic instinct.[16]

Cassirer's symbolic forms have a certain parallel to the constitutive and regulative forms of understanding and reason in Kant: "Man cannot escape from his own achievement. He cannot but adopt the conditions of his own life. No longer in a merely physical universe, man lives in a symbolic universe" (25). Human experience is a "tangled web," woven by the symbolic forms that are its threads. Man mediates between the "receptor system" and the "effector system" by constituting a symbolic universe, but this universe is not seamless.[17] It is composed of forms with differing and

15. Ernst Cassirer, *An Essay on Man* (New Haven, CT: Yale University Press, 1944). This book followed on Cassirer's three-volume *Philosophy of Symbolic Forms* [*Philosophie der Symbolischen Formen*], 1923–1929. There are important differences. In the latter work, Cassirer had been better acquainted with structural linguistics. He also devoted a chapter entirely to art.

16. "All human works arise under particular historical and sociological conditions. But we could never understand these special conditions unless we were able to grasp the genera; structural principles underlying these works" (69). These principles are the symbolic forms of human work. Such activities are not separate from historical existence but "have nevertheless a purport and a value of their own" (64).

17. The receptor system alone would be like Locke's passive receptor of sense data. It receives signals and belongs to the physical world. The effector system alone would be the maker from reception of only a Pavlovian response, also of the physical world. The symbolic system is the humanly constructed world of "meaning" beyond the reach of other animals. This world is "ideal" in that it is not "actual." It constitutes, for example, a past and a future.

conflicting purposes. The task of philosophy is to grasp the general structural principles that underlie these creative functions, not to discover a substance. It is to find some unity in the "perpetual strife of diverse conflicting forces," those functions or "constitutive conditions" of human society. In the symbolic forms, there is a "ceaseless struggle between tradition and innovation," some forms seeming to emphasize one more than another, though the emphasis may change over time.

Cassirer's dialectic is one of permanence and change in the forms, but there is also conflict between the forms. He sees this as necessary and productive, a Heraclitan dissonant harmony: "'Men do not understand,' said Heraclitus, 'how that which is torn in different directions comes into accord with itself—harmony in contrariety, as in the case of the bow and the lyre'" (222–23). Cassirer gives attention, therefore, to the function of art as a form of human work. Myth and language are interwoven with the others, myth being a primitive form that "defies and challenges our fundamental categories of thought" (73). Cassirer's "myth" owes much to Vico's "poetic logic." Myth is akin to poetry, but it hardens into dogmatic belief, while poetry does not make the demand of belief. This anticipates Frank Kermode's distinction between myth and fiction; for Kermode, a fiction believed in becomes a myth. It ceases to be of any use to the search for knowledge because it is fixed.

Cassirer's major contrast is between art and science, as is that of most of the modernist defenders of poetry. Language, as it proceeds to higher and higher levels of abstraction, and science are " . . . abbreviations of reality; art is an intensification of reality. Language and science depend on one and the same process of abstraction; art may be described as a continuous process of concretion" (143). This view leads to the notion that art, as well as myth, opposes the separation of subject and object and, like myth, emphasizes in its constitutive work the "sympathy of the whole," the solidity of life.[18] Thus, presumably, art has its own logic, a "logic of the imagination" (153).[19]

---

18. In this, Cassirer is influenced by Emil Durkheim's *Elementary Forms of Religious Life* (1912).

19. This phrase is Vico's, as Cassirer indicates. Vico influenced Cassirer more than Cassirer's references to him show.

Clearly Cassirer's forms make fictions (and are themselves fictions), though he does not employ this term. One of his references to Galileo describes what we can call a fiction. Galileo refers to " . . . an entirely isolated body which moves without the influence of any external force. Such a body has never been observed and could never be observed" (59). But Galileo's science of dynamics grew out of that fiction.

The functional unity Cassirer finds in the symbolic forms is expression. Man must express his life. But this expression is one of polarities, which create and sustain "tensions and frictions." His view is that art contributes its form of human expression in cooperative opposition to other forms. This is not very far from declaring it antithetical and offensive, though Cassirer would not, I think, want to use these terms, as they may be too strong to express the overall or transcending harmony of opposites that he desires.

Let us ask what offenses we can attribute to poetic fictions. First of all, a fiction is never "pure" any more than poetry is ever pure.[20] As Wolfgang Iser properly reminds us, poetic fictions, indeed all fictions, "overstep" or "outstrip" reality but bring the reality overstepped with them (xv, 13). Otherwise they would be pure nonsense. So the fiction is offensive because it feigns truth; a pure poetic fiction would be offensive for its triviality and uselessness, except perhaps for impertinence that might cause action. Among fictive structures, mathematics could be called pure in that its symbols have no reference in nature, no images. Its offense would be its capacity, nevertheless, to constitute realities.

Because, as Cassirer argues, poetry concentrates on particularity, it often offends against morality, usually conceived as abstract law of thought and behavior. This is clearest in works that, according to Frye, belong to the phases of "low mimetic" realism and modernist irony. Common examples of the former are Balzac and Zola. Zola was offensive to groups normally opposed to each other. This indicates in him an antitheticality opposed even to his own theorizing.[21] He was disliked by aesthetes for his

20. See Robert Penn Warren, "Pure and Impure Poetry" (1943), *New and Selected Essays* (New York: Random House, 1989), 3–28.

21. I refer here to *The Experimental Novel* (1880), where Zola declares that he appropriates the methods of experimental medicine as set forth by Claude Bernard in his *Introduction à l'étude de la médecine expérimentale.*

"scientific" approach and by moralists for his subject matter. This occasioned the ironic remarks of Vivian in Wilde's *The Decay of Lying*: "The author [Zola] is perfectly truthful and describes things exactly as they happen. What more can any moralist desire? We have no sympathy at all with the moral indignation of our time against M. Zola. It is simply the indignation of Tartuffe on being exposed" (601).[22] Yet the great symbolist aesthete Mallarmé acknowledged Zola's greatness, his "marvelous sense of organization" and "tremendous feeling for life." He admitted that Zola's works were "in a sense, poems."[23] Cassirer comments on Zola's having imaginative power in spite of his inadequate aesthetics (157), leading us to think that it is the art itself that is offensive, not necessarily the theory that somehow led to it.

The identification of the fictive, and in some cases all art, with play, suggested in Kant and developed in Schiller, carries with it a certain irony in that, except for Mazzoni, play is generally viewed as trivial (unless professionalized) and, by many, offensive. Figments, fabulous fictions, and the like are commonly relegated to play, though in Schiller, play became the highest form of human activity.[24]

Cassirer defends art for its expression of the fullness of experienced reality in contrast to the "impoverishment" of reality in symbolic forms that move to greater and greater removes of abstraction. Yet this expression of fullness has given offense. As noted in one of T. S. Eliot's works, man cannot stand too much reality. On the other hand, poetry, or at least roman-

22. Vivian admits, "There is something almost epic in his work." He also declares, "But his work is entirely wrong from beginning to end, and wrong not on the ground of morals but on the ground of art" (601).

23. Bradford Cook, trans., "The Evolution of Literature" (interview of Mallarmé conducted by Jules Huret, 14 March 1891), *Mallarmé: Selected Prose Poems, Essays, and Letters* (Baltimore: Johns Hopkins Press, 1956), 23–24. But Mallarmé wants literature to be "more of an intellectual thing than that."

24. The best-known treatise on play is J. Huizinga, *Homo Ludens: A Study of the Play-Element in Culture* (1944) (Boston: Beacon Press, 1955). In my view it is marred by its lack of attention to Kant and its misreading of Schiller in the one place where he is mentioned. A recent treatment of play that is far more sophisticated is Iser's, in *The Fictive and the Imaginary*, esp. 270–80.

tic poetry, has been accused of flying off into the "circumambient gas,"[25] taking leave of the real for ideal realms. Either way lies offense.

That poetic fictions are sometimes regarded as offensive on both sides of a divide suggests that their cultural role may be more disturbing than Cassirer allows. He treats them as part of the unity of human activities, though a unity of tensions. It appears that they may be further on the side of active dissent and that this condition has become more extreme over time. Poets have often come to dramatize this antitheticality by wild overstatement:

> Bose: "Can you give me a message for India?"
>
> Yeats: "Let 100,000 men of one side meet the other. That is my message to India, insistence on the antinomy." He strode swiftly across the room, took up Sato's sword, and unsheathed it dramatically and shouted, "Conflict, more conflict."[26]

Poetry is not very often this overtly offensive. But it seems to give offense when we discover that the poem's speaker (or poet as speaker), like Yeats acting a role above, is himself a fictive creation and that the poem is not necessarily an outpouring of the poet's own self or feelings. It offends against sincerity. It is a mask.

The question that poetic fictions leave with us is whether the movement into them takes us ever further from the real than we go when we create a historic past or a scientific fiction, its fictive nature blotted out, at least in the public mind.

The paradoxes of fictions—even, and maybe even principally, scientific fictions when put into everyday terms—are in some eyes offensive and beyond the criterion of belief. Paradox is unsettling, whether in poetry or in physics, but scientific paradoxes are often the result of try-

25. The phrase is T. E. Hulme's in his *Speculations: Essays on Humanism and the Philosophy of Art* (posthumously published in 1924), ed. Herbert Read (New York: Harcourt, Brace, and Co., n.d.), 120. The main recipient of the attack is probably Shelley.

26. Quoted in Joseph Hone, *W. B. Yeats: 1865–1939* (New York: Macmillan, 1943), 491. Bose was a professor visiting from India.

ing to put into words something adequately expressed mathematically. Poetic fictions renew over and over the distrust that Sidney attempted to combat. If fictions are "as if" constructions, to use Vaihinger's phrase, they appear to be gigantic tropes, again offenses against truth and straight-forward talk.

7

Trope

A brief summary may be helpful here before discussing the trope, which is interrelated with the three preceding sources of offense: The principal offense of gesture, as with metaphor, is its carrying of the poem beyond what is available to the language of reason and interpretation. It challenges the notion that the poem has what Sidney called a "fore-conceit." It evades capture by any external theory.[1] The principal offense of drama is the mask that hides the author and seems to displace meaning from its source. The result has been the accusation of falsehood and that the poem is illusion acting on the feelings. Fictions are offensive because they have appeared to be unrealities, deceptions, at best requiring some suspension not only of one's disbelief but also of one's beliefs. Indulgence in them has often been thought a poor way to spend one's time. Let me observe once again that gesture, drama, fiction, and trope do not define poetry. They all occur both inside and outside poetry and occasionally all together outside it, as, for example, in television commercials, where their purpose is persuasion and where they are frequently offensive, though not entirely for reasons discussed in this book.

1. On this point, see Leroy F. Searle, "The Conscience of the King: Oedipus, Hamlet, and the Problem of Reading," *Comparative Literature* 44.4 (Fall 1997). He objects to the idea that "what we find in texts are . . . examples of other concepts, other truths, prior to the imaginative work and presumably explanatory of it. It is the mode by which critics, in selecting some theory or 'approach,' read the text by way of the presumed authority of the independently articulated theory, which then seems to sanction an indifference to the integrity of the text in question" (298). See also Northrop Frye, "It looks now as though Freud's view of the Oedipus complex were a psychological conception that throws some light on literary criticism. Perhaps we shall eventually decide that we have got it the wrong way round: that what happened was that the myth of Oedipus informed and gave structure to some psychological investigations at this point." *Anatomy of Criticism* (Princeton: Princeton University Press, 1957), 353. I need not remark how offensive this might be to Freudians.

Unfortunately, because over time tropes have been treated simply as rhetorical devices, they have frequently been considered mainly in their relation to such external usages, even when poetry is the subject. The most often discussed trope is, of course, metaphor, which in most definitions is tacitly described as a comparison—a simile with "like" or "as" deleted. *Webster's Ninth Collegiate Dictionary* is typical: "A figure of speech in which a word or phrase literally denoting one kind of object or idea is used in place of another to suggest a likeness or analogy between them." This is metaphor in its rhetorical or external use, and that sense goes back even to the Greek *metapherein*, to transfer, to carry over. In rhetorical tradition, metaphor is regarded as making a comparison for the purpose of informing, heightening effect, persuading, moving to action, and so forth. It is mainly a decoration, useful to some external purpose, although Aristotle had early made a distinction between metaphor and ornament.

In poetry, a metaphor expresses an identity internal to the poem. It has ethical implications reaching outward. It does not claim absolute sameness at the expense of difference. Totemic people who identified themselves with crocodiles did not go into the water to swim around with their brothers and sisters.[2] Presumably neither would Vico's primitive giants have done so. By identity I mean sameness and difference at the same time, coexisting. The sameness here is not merely a sameness indicating two like aspects of two objects while difference exists in the other aspects. It is a total oneness *and* a total individuality. For what happens inside poetry the dictionary's definition is inadequate, for it privileges difference. Only in a mathematical formula would there be sameness alone.

Most poets are sane and do not give up the difference in their metaphors, but they do insist on the same as well. When Edmund Spenser's speaker refers to the "huge massacres" that his beloved's eyes cause, she is not likely to be charged with murder or war crimes. When the speaker of William Blake's poem addresses a sick rose, we do not conclude that Blake is concerned with a certain type of plant disease, as a student of agriculture once tried to convince me. Even Geoffrey, the famous cat of

2. See Bronislaw Malinowski, *Magic, Science and Religion and Other Essays* (Boston: Beacon Press, 1948), 3ff.

Christopher Smart, becomes in his poem a metaphorical cat, a "Cherub Cat," who "knows that God is his saviour," though he can hardly be that in, as we say, "real life."[3] Two things the same in metaphor are still also different. While being identical, they retain their identities.

What, then, is the point of these phantasies, long defended and attacked? It cannot be scientific, though scientists do employ metaphor in their discussions, writings, provisional fictions, and even conceptualizations. It cannot be metaphysical. The logical positivist Carnap at least got that right about poetry (though little else). If we are going to characterize tropes of identity in the language of "real life," we can claim that such tropes are ethical; identity is not sameness but *relation*, in which sameness and difference coexist. Identity accounts for the great use in poetry of the trope of apostrophe:

> Sweet Thames! Run softly, till I end my song.

> Leave me, O love which reachest but to dust.

> Fair daffodils, we weep to see
> You haste away so soon.

> Yet, once more, O ye Laurels.[4]

Even

> Let us go then, you and I,

where, in T. S. Eliot's "The Love Song of J. Alfred Prufrock," the apostrophe indicates ironically an unfortunate alienation, but in that very act it declares ethically for identity.

John Donne's well-known passage from his *Devotions* defines identity ethically: "No man is an island, entire of itself, every man is a piece of

---

3. From the sonnet "One day I wrote her name upon the strand," 'The Sick Rose," and "Jubilate Agno" respectively.

4. From Edmund Spenser's "Prothalamion," Sir Philip Sidney's sonnet, Robert Herrick's "To Daffodils," and John Milton's "Lycidas" respectively.

the continent, a part of the main. If a clod be washed away by the sea, Europe is the less, as well as if a promontory were, as well as if a manor of thy friend's or of thine were: any man's death diminishes me, because I am involved in mankind, and therefor never send to know for whom the bell tolls; it tolls for thee" (17: "Meditation"). The plight of pathetic Urizen in Blake's *The Four Zoas* expresses the alienation of total difference: " . . . no one answerd every one wrapped up / In his own sorrow" (6: 42–43), and the poem as a whole rejects it as an illusion generated in great part by Locke's notion of epistemological subjectivity. Indeed, I don't think it possible for poetry to avoid the expression of identity as defined above and still be poetry. It would mean abandonment of metaphor.

Tropes of identity are offensive both to a Platonic philosophy of the same and to recent philosophies of difference. The four principal tropes spoken of as such by the Roman rhetorician Quintilian, and later Vico, are all tropes of identity: metaphor, synecdoche, metonymy, and irony. Irony is in a certain way the most radical of these in that it begins with difference. The ironic statement does not seem to say what it apparently means. But as gesture, it makes its opposite the same while maintaining the assertion of difference, all the time meaning what it does not appear to say. A simple translation to the opposite is not adequate, as it loses the gesture, which is one of identity with the implied reader.

The four tropes of Quintilian were adopted by Vico as those to which all the others could be reduced. The first three Vico emphasized in his presentation of the "poetic logic" of primitive man. The fourth, irony, had, for Vico, to be a later human invention because it involved a "lie" on the surface of the statement. He thought lies beyond the power of his primitive poetic logicians because they could not invent anything that was based on reflection wearing only the mask of truth. Metaphor, on the other hand, was for them the vehicle of truth, and the earliest fables were, to these people, true narrations. To translate them into other terms by way of interpretation was literally unthinkable. Metaphor was literal. Vico's view was that language originated in fable and trope because primitive man was incapable of creating abstract universals with no imagistic content. Primitive man was able to think only in concrete ("imaginative") class concepts, or universals, which were originally created out of words representing all or part of his own immediately present body projected outward. Thus the thunder and lightning of the sky were produced by an angry gigantic human body, Jove, whom Vico called the first fable. Homer was an imaginative class concept embodying an image of Ancient Greek society. Our present languages retain vestiges of these early identifications of the human body with the world. (One of them is the imagistic and synecdochic identification of macrocosm with microcosm to be discussed later.) Vico specifically refers to the following (the translators have substituted some English examples for Italian words that have no English parallels of this sort): " . . . head for top or beginning; the brow and shoulders of a hill; the eyes of needles and potatoes; mouth for any opening; the lip of a cup or pitcher; the teeth of a rake, a saw, a comb; the beard of wheat; the tongue of a shoe. . . . Heaven or the sea smiles; the wind whistles."[5]

The trope began as what we today would call, as did Vico, "a fantastic speech making use of physical substances endowed with life" (127–28). Thus arose divinities embodying and giving images to whole classes of things. By these, primitive man "explained everything appertaining to the sky, the earth, and the sea" (125).[6] For example, all flowers were Flora, all fruits Pomona. Modern culture would no longer think only in this way, and Vico speaks of his own and anyone's great difficulty conceiving of the linguistic condition of the earliest people:

> . . . the nature of our civilized minds is so detached from the senses, even in the vulgar, by abstractions corresponding to all the abstract terms our languages abound in, and so refined by the art of writing, and as it were spiritualized by the use of numbers, because even the vulgar know how to count and reckon, that it is naturally beyond our power to form the vast image of this mistress called "Sympathetic Nature." . . . It is equally beyond our power to enter into the vast imaginations of those first men, whose minds were not in the least

5. Giambattista Vico, *The New Science of Giambattista Vico*, rev. trans. of 3rd ed. (1744), trans. Thomas Goddard Bergin and Max Harold Fisch (Ithaca, NY: Cornell University Press, 1968), 129 (sn. 405).

6. This explains, for Vico, the origin of poetry and of Aristotle's (and, later, Mazzoni's) notion of the credible impossibility. See Vico, *The New Science of Giambattista Vico*, 120.

abstract, refined, or spiritualized, because they were entirely immersed in the senses, buffeted by the passions, buried in the body. (118)

It appears that for Vico the main problem for modern understanding of this is the trope. Our misunderstanding of it has corrupted our sense of the development of language, what is deviant in language and what is not. All the tropes, which "have hitherto been considered ingenious inventions of writers, were necessary modes of expression of all the first poetic nations" (131). Now they are merely "figurative." For the poetic "theologians," the figure was literal; modern culture puts the abstract idea first:

We nowadays reverse this practice in respect of spiritual things, such as the faculties of the human mind, the passions, virtues, vices, sciences, and arts; for the most part the ideas we form of them are so many feminine personifications, to which we refer all the causes, properties, and effects that severally appertain to them. For when we wish to give utterance to our understanding of spiritual things, we must seek aid from our imagination to explain them and, like painters, form human images of them. (128)

Pomona and Flora, now merely figures, are stand-ins for abstract ideas. For Vico, "spiritual" refers to anything abstract and without image. Therefore, mathematics is spiritual. What he has described here is allegory in the sense of personified abstractions—allegory in the sense that many romantic period poets and critics attacked. "But these theological poets, unable to make use of the understanding, did the opposite and more sublime thing: they attributed senses and passions . . . to bodies, and to bodies as vast as sky, sea, and earth. Later, as these vast imaginations shrank and the power of abstraction grew, the personifications were reduced to diminutive signs . . . " (128).

Though it would appear impossible for modern poets to achieve this sublimity, Vico does speak of it when he describes the "threefold labor of great poetry": "To invent sublime fables suited to the popular understanding, 2) to perturb to excess, with a view to the end proposed: 3) to

teach the vulgar to act virtuously, as the poets have taught themselves"
(117). Perturbing to excess must mean incitement to think the literality
of metaphor, and sublimity must mean the poet's achievement of tropological identity between the human body and the world as human body
or bodies. But this, it appears to me, must transcend the fear that motivated the original poets. Their first fable was Jove, created out of fear of
the sky and its anger in thunder and lightning, eventually transmuted into
the moral law of modern societies. In the modern poet's and reader's
return, as it were, to poetic logic (never fully accomplishable, of course,
and undesirable in any case), fear is not the motivation. The value lies in
the contemplation of human ethical possibility concretely embodied in
tropes of identity.

At times Vico comes close to explicit expression of this view, especially in his respect for the primitive sublime. He recognizes that something
has been lost that poetry can to an extent make up for. But poetry should
not and in any case cannot return to the primitive state. It must exercise
and appeal to the understanding, which has liberated man from the fear
that founded human society. It does so by supplying what is lacking: the
Vichian sublimity that is antithetical to the very understanding to which it
must appeal. No longer can we know immediately a physical identity with
earth, sky, and sea. Identity must occur at the ethical level of metaphor, recognized as such, as a vision of human desire.

Of course, metaphors and other tropes occur in all uses of language.
Lakoff and Johnson (and others) have asserted that our conceptual system
is "fundamentally metaphorical."[7] But many commentators on metaphor
think that metaphor's only function is to lead to the production of conceptual
systems and that metaphor is for that reason itself conceptual in nature. It
is odd, then, that there has grown up the notion that metaphors (and other
tropes) are "deviant." But deviant from what? Deviant from the view that
language ought ahistorically and ideally to be modeled on mathematics (as
in Plato and, later, the assumptions of symbolic logic). This idea of deviance

---

7. George Lakoff and Mark Johnson, *Metaphors We Live By* (Chicago: University of
Chicago Press, 1980), 3.

is congruent with that of the metaphor as merely a figure or device of rhetorical embellishment.[8] It has frequently muddled discourse about tropes.[9] The notion of deviance is at the bottom of many attitudes toward poetry, most attacks, and many defenses. Mark Turner, on the other hand, argues that story is fundamental to the mind and that a basic cognitive principle is the parable, which is "the projection of one story on another."[10] We see here that story is, as in Vico, connected to metaphor. Further, story is a "constant mental activity, essential to human thought" (12), and the origin of language is the projection of story. Turner objects to the commonly held view "that language is built up from the sober to the exotic; that out of syntactic phrase structures, one builds up language; that out of language one builds up narrative; that out of narrative, literary narrative is born as a special [deviant?] performance; and that out of literary narrative comes parable" (168). For him, the reverse of all this is true.

A parable is metaphorical, and there has grown up around metaphor a number of misconceptions that are named and succinctly described by Israel Scheffler.[11] These he calls myths, and there are ten of them. I would put some of his objections to these myths differently, particularly his dis-

---

8. There are other notions of deviation that would still be regarded as such if language were viewed as fundamentally or even thoroughly metaphorical: for example, the several devices disrupting the story in Laurence Sterne's *Tristram Shandy*. On the other hand, one could argue that story-telling, grounded in Vichian fable, which certainly always deviates to some degree from strict chronology, was and is the fundamental form of language. On ordinary language and deviation, see Mary Louise Pratt, *Toward a Speech Act Theory of Literary Discourse* (Bloomington: Indiana University Press, 1977), esp. 199ff., where *Tristram Shandy* is an example.

9. Samuel R. Levin, in *Metaphoric Worlds: Conceptions of a Romantic Nature* (New Haven, CT, and London: Yale University Press, 1988), 22, writes, "The interpretation of metaphor is a conceptual exercise induced by challenging (because deviant) linguistic form." However, in his interesting discussion of Vico, he observes, "To [early man] his poetry was 'factual'; the need to construe was unimaginable, there being no conceivable basis for him to do so (a corollary being that in the context of early poetry the notion of linguistic deviance makes no sense)" (120). If we look at the matter historically, deviance seems to be the reverse of what we generally think it is.

10. Mark Turner, *The Literary Mind* (New York and Oxford: Oxford University Press, 1996), i.

11. Israel Scheffler, *Symbolic Worlds: Art, Science, Language, Ritual* (Cambridge and New York: Cambridge University Press, 1997), 67–73.

cussion of the myth of suggestiveness; however, his discussions are always valuable—and suggestive! His myths of falsehood and embellishment are, as we have seen, the ones most often employed in attacks on poetry: the rejection of all but empirically verifiable statements and the view that metaphors are without cognitive content and are therefore purely decorative.

The books I have cited indicate a change in attitude toward metaphor or at least the rise of one that opposes deviation theories and declares against viewing metaphor and other tropes merely as devices of rhetoric. But these efforts have been concerned to show that metaphor functions creatively in all thought, not merely in poetry. In addition to being present as what Turner calls the "root" (i) of human thought, they are part, and a very important part, of poetic antitheticality, which is both offensive and potentially ethical.

In short poems, identity is frequently expressed as ecstatic moments; often such poems employ apostrophe. One of the most interesting and complicated in this respect is Keats's "Ode to a Nightingale." I do not propose yet another detailed reading of this much discussed poem. I note, nevertheless, a number of things: It dramatizes a fleeting identity. The speaker expresses regret at the loss and at fancy's inability to cheat him into a sustained condition of oneness with the bird, surely a world of illusion. The speaker cannot decide whether he has had a vision or a waking dream, and then he wonders whether he is even now awake or asleep. The first question asked is whether what happened occurred in the real world of physical experience or was a hallucination. The second question asks whether he was then asleep and is now awake or then awake and now asleep. The implied question is: What is real? Is it the moment of identity or the condition of loss at the poem's end? Can both be real but in different senses, at different levels, one physical and one we may call ethical? I suggest that this latter is the case.

People cannot fly with birds or as birds, but they can express a desire to do so in metaphorical identity and achieve a moment of sympathetic identification, fleeting as it may be, in the act. It is in poetry—on poetry's "viewless wings"—that this can occur. But there is something offensive about this for those who regard such flights as silly sentimental stuff and perhaps even fear it, and for those who want their poems, if they want them at all,

to be of real life and their poets not to fly off into T. E. Hulme's "circumambient gas."

Identity, however, need not be ecstatic. The poetic subject may be
one of deep solemnity, even grief, and the theme one of loss, yet still one
of relation, as in Tennyson's *In Memoriam*:

> And gazing on thee, sullen tree,
>> Sick for thy stubborn hardihood,
>> I seem to fail from out my blood
> And grow incorporate into thee.

Or, in the same poem:

> Calm on the seas, and silver sleep,
>> And waves that sway themselves in rest,
>> And dead calm in that noble breast
> That heaves but with the heaving deep.

The expression of identity may be one that challenges convention and
propriety, as more than one person thought the so-called metaphysical
poets had done. In Donne's "The Canonization," the speaker recklessly
invites anyone to describe him and his lover even as two flies, two tapers,
or eagle and dove, as long as they are described as one; and he goes on
to claim,

> The Phoenix riddle hath more wit
> By us, we two being one, are it.

In one of the Holy Sonnets of Donne, there is the assertion, "I am a little
world made cunningly." One of the fundamental tropes of poetry is synecdoche, and of all synecdoches the greatest is that of the identity of microcosm and macrocosm, and specifically that of man and world. In Vico's
history, this synecdoche is fundamental to primitive poetic logic and what
he sometimes calls "poetic metaphysics." For his primitive giants, poetry
and metaphysics were one: " . . . poetic wisdom, the first wisdom of the

gentile world, must have begun with a metaphysics not rational and abstract like that of learned men now, but felt and imagined as that of these first men must have been, who, without power of ratiocination, were all robust sense and vigorous imagination. This metaphysics was their poetry, a faculty born with them . . . " (116). Even after poetry and metaphysics seemed to part company, the synecdoche of microcosm and macrocosm frequently occurred in both. But the function in each was different. Metaphysical systems claimed a truth of correspondence to the world, though the expressions of many of them now appear to be more like poems. Leonard Barkan points out that the more scientifically out-of-date the metaphysical synecdoche became, the richer it became as a poetic convention.[12] Today expressions of those systems, no longer believed in as truth, remain of more than historical interest, though it may require a special taste to appreciate them as poems. Is Giordano Bruno read today as a philosopher or a poet? The question is somewhat like asking whether a Grecian urn is a utilitarian object or a work of art. Modern poetic expression of microcosm and macrocosm does not require that the trope express verifiable fact, even if it may have once seemed to.

George Perrigo Conger holds that microcosmic theories were always more ethical and religious than physical.[13] They have always been present in occultism. However, it may be better to say that until the rise of empiricism, distinctions between ethical, religious, and physical theories were far less clear. One can call, among many possible exhibits, Plotinus, Proclus, and the fabulous Hermes Trismegistus, once alleged to be the author of the Smaragdine Tablets. The tendency, as Conger points out, was "toward concrete, as distinguished from abstract speculation." The former emphasized "mutual interaction between the universe and man" (134). He observes that in the Middle Ages such theories reconciled religion and natural science (52). Even in the later, occult writings of the Renaissance, the aim seems to have been reconciliation of science (med-

12. Leonard Barkan, *Nature's Work of Art: The Human Body as an Image of the World* (New Haven and London: Yale University Press, 1975), 48.

13. George Perrigo Conger, *Theories of Microcosms and Macrocosms in the History of Philosophy* (1922) (New York: Russell and Russell, 1967), 16.

icine in Paracelsus, for example) with magic and astrology. Paracelsus's aim was to know the great world and thereby by synecdoche to know man. For Jacob Boehme, the world was the body of God. Similar microcosmic notions turned up in certain German romantic philosophers, in whose work philosophy seemed not at odds with poetry. The late nineteenth-century interest of many poets in the occult suggests nostalgia for affinity with a Vichian poetic metaphysics.

It is permissible, I hope, to observe cautiously, since I am about as far from being an expert in these matters as possible, that synecdoche has had a revival, not in the occult, where it has never slept, but in mathematics and physical science. This has occurred in set theory and the subsequent idea of the fractal. Late in the nineteenth century, Georg Cantor, the creator of set theory and the theory of transfinite numbers, stated as an axiom that "the whole of something can be numerically equal to one of its parts."[14] Martin Davis puts it as follows:

> Cantor reasoned much as Leibniz had and faced the same dilemma: *either* it makes no sense to speak of the *number* of elements in an infinite set *or* some infinite sets will have the same number of elements as one of its subsets. However, while Leibniz had chosen one horn of the dilemma, Cantor chose the other. He went on to develop a theory of number that would apply to infinite sets and just accepted the consequence that an infinite set could have the same number of elements as one of its parts.[15]

Or, as Rudy Rucker puts it,

> If infinite sets do not behave like finite sets, this does not mean that infinity is an inconsistent notion. It means, rather, that infinite numbers obey a different "arithmetic" from finite numbers. If using the ordinary notions of "equal" and "less than" on infinite sets leads to

14. Edna Kramer, *The Nature and Growth of Modern Mathematics* (New York: Hawthorne Books, 1970), 580.
15. Martin Davis, *Engines of Logic* (New York: W. W. Norton and Co, 2001), 65.

contradictions, this is not a sign that infinite sets cannot exist, but, rather, that these notions do not apply without modifications to infinite sets.[16]

The problem is put in two ways in the quotations above, both with recourse to tropes, whether the authors know it or not. In the first, recourse is to synecdoche, in the second to paradox. It is interesting to notice that this synecdoche was for a long time a stumbling block, an offense, to mathematicians, who resisted the notions that a set could be, in a sense, the same size as a subset, a line could have as many points as a line half as long, and "endless processes [could be] treated as finished things" (8).[17]

Conger observes that philosophers can be divided into two groups throughout history (134). There are philosophers and philosophies favoring microcosmic theories (I offer Conger's list): hylozoism, Pythagoreanism, probably stoicism, Philo Judaeus, neo-Platonism, medieval Jewish philosophy, encyclopedia of the Arabian Brotherhood of Sincerity, Paracelsus, Boehme, Leibniz, Schelling, Schleiermacher, Schopenhauer, Fechner, and absolute idealism. Opposed are the Eleatics, sophists, Epicureans, skeptics, Aristotle, medieval theologians, critical philosophy, empiricism, and humanism.

Poets may have shown sporadic friendliness to the occult in times of crisis, when they turned to create some form of mythology to substitute for lost belief. One finds this imaginative venture in Blake's so-called prophetic books, though he explicitly eschewed the occult. The venture

---

16. Rudy Rucker, *Infinity and the Mind* (1982) (Princeton, NJ: Princeton University Press, 1995), 6.

17. I am not competent to take the discussion to the question of whether this endless process is treated as "closed" or "open" in Cantor's notion of "absolute infinity," though I think it implies both. Elsewhere, I have argued with respect to Blake that there is such a thing as an open synecdoche ("Synecdoche and Method," *Antithetical Essays in Literary Criticism and Liberal Education* [Tallahassee: Florida State University Press, 1990], esp. 21–28). I am indebted to Brad Zukovic for alerting me to the books referred to above and for reminding me of Blake's statement about the line " . . . a Line or Lineament is not formed by Chance a line is a Line in its Minutest Subdivision Straight or Crooked It is Itself & Not Intermeasurable with or by any Thing Else." Letter to George Cumberland, 12 April 1827.

seems to have enabled him to avoid the intellectual despair of some of his early contemporaries.

Blake insisted on the visionary existence of his "giant forms." Later poets came to identify their poems not with truth in the empirical sense but with providing what science could not and religion no longer could. Two passages in Wallace Stevens's *Adagia* are summary ones:

> The relation of art to life is of the first importance especially in a skeptical age since, in the absence of a belief in God, the mind turns to its own creations and examines them, not alone from the aesthetic point of view, but for what they reveal, for what they validate and invalidate, for the support that they give.[18]

The second is especially significant for its play on the words "fiction" and "belief":

> The final belief is to believe in a fiction, which you know to be a fiction, there being nothing else. The exquisite truth is to know that it is a fiction and that you believe in it willingly. (163)

The movement from uncritical belief, or the yearning for it, to acknowledgment of the synecdoche's role as an ethical form is dramatized in Yeats's remarkable work *A Vision*, in which he describes his search for a system of thought based on astrology, a form of microcosm philosophy, only to discover that it had no power to explain externality or to predict events. In the end, it provided "metaphors for poetry": " . . . now that the system stands out in my imagination I regard them [its symbols] as stylistic arrangements of experience comparable to the cubes in the drawings of Wyndham Lewis or the ovoids in the sculpture of Brancusi. They have helped me to hold in a single thought reality and justice."[19]

---

18. Wallace Stevens, *Opus Posthumous* (New York: Alfred A. Knopf, 1957), 159.

19. W. B. Yeats, *A Vision* (New York: Macmillan and Co., 1938), 25. I have discussed this passage and the whole book in *The Book of Yeats's Vision* (Ann Arbor: University of Michigan Press, 1995); see esp. 33–34.

Microcosm and macrocosm compose the largest conceivable trope of identity, being the ultimate containing form that Frye thought of as total metaphor, "in which everything is potentially identical with everything else" (124), the ultimate poetic aim, the expression of ultimate human desire. Mythology, apart from occult philosophy, is full of images of the world as a gigantic human body. The synecdoche's persistence beyond literal belief in it attests to its continued significance on another level where it expresses ethical desire.

In concluding Part II of this book, I want to say something about the difficulty of reading in relation to offense. When someone reads a poem and cannot understand it, that person may or may not be offended; for many people, poems they say they do not understand are pleasant and moving. "Understanding" implies interpretation. The word indicates that underneath the poem, there is something recoverable that is the poem's meaning, its solid ground, so to speak. This notion is a stumbling block, for there is no such ground; at least it can never be reached by interpretation, which is always reductive and subject, if not to revision, at least to addendum. Difficulty, then, can be the result of readerly frustration if one assumes that there is a reachable and terminal interpretation.

In writings about literary education there has been much discussion of teachers who provide interpretations of poems and ask questions of students that imply interpretive finality.[20] This, of course, is hard to avoid, because teaching will inevitably have something categorical about it that threatens to put the poem fully into support of the teacher's approach. Further, there are among readers always simple misconstructions of words, inaccurate descriptions, lack of knowledge about things a poem mentions, and so forth. There is even a considerable history of interpretation in which elaborate theories of allegory have been offered to provide keys to meaning, some of these, as we have seen in chapter 3, in defense of poetry.[21]

20. See Susan Hynds, "Questions of Difficulty in Literary Reading," *The Idea of Difficulty in Literature*, ed. Alan C. Purves (Albany: State University of New York Press, 1991), 118–39.

21. On this point, see my "The Difficulty of Difficulty," *The Idea of Difficulty in Literature*, esp. 23–36.

This was an outgrowth of a tradition in which Scripture was held to hold mysterious meaning, kept sacrosanct by a priesthood of interpreters. In some times and places, difficulty under the name of obscurity has been positively valued, as for example in Mallarmé's advocacy of mystery in literature.

One kind of difficulty involves a reader's simple misunderstanding. Another has its source in the assumption, which leads to the charge of offense, of a terminal meaning that runs counter to the role of gesture. Susan Hynds calls this the "myth of the best response."[22] It does not follow that one response cannot be better than another. It does involve anxious refusal to let the poem stand free of translation into other words. Keats was trying to get at something like this when he observed in as sophisticated a poet and critic as Coleridge a sort of failure, though Keats was not talking only about literary interpretation: "Coleridge . . . would let go by a fine isolated verisimilitude caught from the Penetralium of mystery, from being incapable of remaining content with half-knowledge."[23] He was, in my view, suggesting that Coleridge was anxious about being content with gesture. Keats's remark concludes with his well-known characterization of Shakespeare as possessing "negative capability," which he regarded as the ability to be in "uncertainties, mysteries, doubts, without any irritable reaching after fact and reason," this being terminal understanding.

Other than gesture, my three offenses are not involved so much with the difficulty of interpretation as with irritated recognition. Drama, fiction, and trope have not been mystifying to those on the attack but instead generally have been understood as present and offensive to good sense and proper communication. The attackers have known about drama but have resented its distancing of the author and the difficulty of determining a point of view or attitude. They have known about fictions but may not have recognized their ubiquity. They have recognized tropes but may have wanted to admit them only as having rhetorical use. Although Vico and others regarded tropes as fundamental to language, full recognition of their presence virtually everywhere had to await Jacques Derrida's observation that

22. Hynds, "Questions of Difficulty," 120.
23. John Keats, letter to George and Thomas Keats, 28 December 1817.

any philosophical analysis of metaphor cannot escape the presence of metaphor in its own text.[24]

For the most part, difficulty remains less a feature of a text than the result of "disparity between dimensions of the text and the socially embedded and motivated interpretive process of particular readers."[25] It has been argued that institutional pressures seem to require simple answers to complex questions. Helen Rugueiro Elam has identified this with a typical American desire for efficiency.[26] Carried into reading, the result is a desire to declare a sufficient meaning the communication of which is not frustrated by gestural offense. The four offenses are potential in all use of language, but poems think *in* them, while other uses claim to communicate *with* them.

If all of this is true and terminal meaning cannot be reached by interpretation, is there a purpose for criticism other than repeating this as a valuable truism? Yes, at its best, criticism carries on a continuing conversation about poetry. Its conversation is a challenge to future critics to improve on it, point out something it has missed, and look into the possibility of the significance of the poem for a new time. Criticism needs renewal in every age in order to free poetry from the prejudices of that age and the unintended prejudices of even the best critics of the past, to free poetry to perform its provocative, antithetical cultural role.

24. Jacques Derrida, "White Mythology: Metaphor in the Text of Philosophy," *Margins of Philosophy* (1972), trans. Alan Bass (Chicago: University of Chicago Press, 1982), 207–72.

25. Hynds, "Questions of Difficulty," 117.

26. Helen Rugueiro Elam, "The Difficulty of Reading," *The Idea of Difficulty in Literature*, 73.

III. Critical:
Studies in Antithetical Offense

8

Vico and Blake: Poetic Logic as Offense

To this point, my concern has been mainly offense in shorter poetic forms. In Part III, I intend to explore a variety of works that are friendly to antithetical offense or commit it. I begin with more remarks about a friend, Giambattista Vico, the philosopher who, being not at war with poetry, most radically lays out the ground for a poetic logic, and Blake, who also offers it. I proceed to long works by Blake and Joyce, emphasizing connections among the three. I then turn to the prose fiction of Joyce Cary, emphasizing the role of the dramatic in his work, how this offense is extended to include the politics of antitheticality, and the problem that some readers have had with both. Following that, I discuss the critical writing of Seamus Heaney, as an example of a criticism, friendly to offense, that acknowledges what I call an antithetical stance for poets. Last, I discuss the offense against poetry itself of what I call great bad poetry.

Though Blake may never have heard of Vico, Vico's history and theory of language would certainly have interested him. We know that Joyce read both Vico and Blake and acknowledged this in his writings. Vico endorses a major poetic offense when he finds the source of language in gesture and poetic trope. He also grounds his whole theory of history and culture on a fiction of his own invention.

Blake and Joyce in *Jerusalem* and *Finnegans Wake* respectively have made of their practices exemplary offenses. In my view, their two works come close to the center of the poetic, laying out a range of poetic possibilities and making that range open to view to a rarely paralleled extent. The primary offense of *Jerusalem* and *Finnegans Wake* is that they are tropological *tours de force*, requiring us to pass into what Vico calls poetic logic. More than that, they take stances that oppose the common binary oppositions that have pervaded our culture. These stances, embodying the offenses to which I have devoted chapters, characterize poetic antitheticality.

Vico

Vico's *New Science* offers a view antithetical to the usual distinction between poetry and prose, art and discourse, and other such oppositions. It is, if not itself a poem, at least a friend to offense. Benedetto Croce correctly saw that Vico had denied "the dualism between poetry and language" and with it the notion that poetry was originally either allegorical expression of prior esoteric wisdom or merely language decorated by rhetorical figures for the purpose of giving pleasure.[1]

Vico conceived of what he called poetic logic as dominant in the barbaric age of gods and heroes but enduring as the foundation for abstract logic in the age of men. Poetic logic began when language began in mute gestures, which eventuated in words. In the fiction Vico creates to imagine the beginnings of human culture, the first word, spoken in fear of the sky's thunder, was the imaginative universal Jove (Giove), with its counterparts in other languages, there being, in his view, a universal mental language prior to words. After the myth of Jove was invented, there came the panoply of other gods. Vico offers no story of ancient wise men capable of creating abstract universals and then developing a secret wisdom language that hid abstract truth under allegory. That notion of secret wisdom came with the stultification of language in a later age. As a result, a new and different barbarism then arose. Vico goes so far as to assert that mute gesture must have occurred a second time when the barbaric nations invading Europe could not understand or make themselves understood by the conquered. Thus gesture and hieroglyphics again came into use.

This seems far-fetched. In any case, the barbarism of the new cycle, beginning with the so-called Dark Ages, was not the barbarism of a returned poetic logic but instead the barbarism of reflection. This suggests that each

---

1. Benedetto Croce, *The Philosophy of Giambattista Vico* (1911), trans. R. G. Collingwood (1913) (New York: Russell and Russell, 1964), esp. 48ff. Nevertheless, Croce thought Vico had relegated poetry (in the sense of the poetic as a form of thought) entirely to the area of ancient primitivism, Vico's age of gods and heroes. For the idealist Croce, poetry was "an ideal category, not a historic fact" (59), and he thought Vico had confused " the philosophical concept of the poetic form of the mind and the empirical concept of the barbaric form of civilisation" (56).

cycle reverses the previous one and that abstract thought, divorced from the poetic, has its own barbaric form. Language becomes deadened in custom, and abstraction and figuration become dominant. By figuration I mean the reduction of tropes to personified abstractions and the classification of figures into rhetorical devices.

Vico does not say that in the Dark Ages there was a complete reversion to the poetic logic of the primitive giants. That would have been impossible. Through all of the historical cycles, the labor of great poetry continued: the making of fables and the perturbation of readers to excess, the latter of which seems to mean the creation of the sublime in something like the Longinian sense—transport, but no longer generated by fear, as it was in the earliest poetical people. What Vico identifies with a return to something near to muteness Shelley in his *Defense of Poetry* sees as a deadening of language in custom, similar to Vico's notion of the movement from poetic logic to figurative abstraction. For Shelley, answering Peacock's notion of the obsolescence of poetry, it became cyclically necessary for poets to reinvigorate metaphor. Vico did contrast modern poetry to that of the earliest poets; he was well aware of the reversal that created allegorical rather than mythological personification in the moderns. But he never denied the presence, latent in modern poetry, of a poetic tropologic of metaphors, which are "fable[s] in brief" and are the origin and ground of language.[2] All human sciences and arts arise out of and are renewed in poetic apprehension.[3]

Vico's fondness for the imaginations of his gross giants and for poetry is congruent with his concept of the proper process of education. In *On the Study Methods of Our Time* (1709), Vico takes care to warn against the intro-

---

2. Giambattista Vico, *The New Science of Giambattista Vico*, rev. trans. of 3rd ed. (1744), trans. Thomas Goddard Bergin and Max Harold Fisch (Ithaca, NY: Cornell University Press, 1968), 117.

3. Croce argued that Vico thought poetic logic had been entirely overcome by abstract logic, but Donald Phillip Verene, *Vico's Science of Imagination* (Ithaca, NY: Cornell University Press, 1981), disagrees with Croce: "The reflective mind is not the support of itself . . . , but develops from and always has beneath its activity the imaginative forms of early life" (93). Some may say Verene makes more of a modern of Vico than is warranted, but he is right to observe that Vico's imaginative universal "gives way" to the intelligible (abstract) universal but does not suffer obliteration. Verene argues that those things first felt as imaginative universals can proceed to take the form of a logical judgment (173) and continue to do so.

duction of abstraction in the form of philosophical criticism into the education of youth. Moreover, "Youth's natural inclination to the arts in which imagination or memory (or a combination of both) is prevalent (such as painting, poetry, oratory, jurisprudence) should by no means be blunted."[4]

The imaginative universal was Vico's most radical notion. Among the three principal tropes of identity that Vico emphasizes as fundamental—metaphor, metonymy, and synecdoche (irony was to come later in history)—the imaginative universal belongs to synecdoche. It is a serious or "severe" trope, and it is the fundamental trope of both Blake and Joyce. It is of course true, as we have seen, that Vico declares the impossibility of modern people being able really to think in poetic logic, but he claims that he has managed at least to understand poetic logic from its own point of view.[5] Thinking in tropes implies a tropologic that functions to purposes different from those of a logic producing abstract universals. It is here that irony enters, for any literary critic. Criticism is not the negation of poetry, although more than one poet has thought it so. Rather, it is a necessary reasoning contrary to poetry and must know itself well enough to appreciate the irony of its situation. Even the best criticism cannot avoid being in some sense what it opposes. Northrop Frye said that all literary commentary is allegorical in some sense, and R. P. Blackmur remarked in this connection that literary criticism was an unfortunate necessity in any case.

Some readers see as preposterous the story of origin that Vico tells— the story of the first fable, Jove. But it is best to see the story as itself an attempt at fiction and poetic logic at a point where history and reason fail us. His fable can be viewed as a bridge toward that logic; an irony is involved in that we are to believe it even as we do not. One is reminded of Socrates' recourse to fable at crucial moments when dialectical search fails to deliver.

4. Giambattista Vico, *On the Study Methods of Our Time* [*De nostri temporis studiorum ratione*], trans. Elio Gianturco (Indianapolis: The Bobbs-Merrill Co, 1965), 14. The whole of section 1–2, 3–20, is relevant to this point. For my own discussion of educational process, see my *Antithetical Essays in Literary Criticism and Liberal Education* (Tallahassee: Florida State University Press), 1990, esp. 238–39, 253–54.

5. " . . . we can scarcely understand, still less imagine, how those men thought who founded gentile humanity" (118). "[We had] to descend from these human and refined natures of ours to those quite wild and savage natures, which we cannot at all imagine and can comprehend only with great effort" (Vico, *New Science*, 100).

Not to have invented his fable as a fable would have forced Vico to fall back into the mode of figurative abstraction, characteristic of the historical reversal that made the grasp of poetic logic so difficult.

Among Vico's principles are these two, translated as follows: "Men of limited ideas take for law what the words expressly say" (*New Science*, 93), and "Intelligent men take for law whatever impartial utility dictates in each case" (*New Science*, 94). The first of these seems to describe an attitude tied only to poetic logic and culturally deficient. The second seems to describe an attitude with the capacity for abstract logic. Vico is talking here about interpretation of the law and advocating with respect to it a necessary pragmatism. But if a poetic text, not a legal document, is the subject, perhaps a reversal would be necessary. Otherwise one would lapse into what Vico calls "esoteric" interpretation, seeking the hidden meaning behind the words and probably putting the poem to ideological use. Vico could not have been aware that his remarks anticipate the modern dissatisfaction with paraphrase of poems and fixed interpretation or what is now sometimes called interpretive "closure."

Vico is usually and rightly seen as an opponent of Cartesianism, and that opposition has been well documented.[6] Critics cite his opposition to Descartes's method, his favoring of Euclidean geometry over analytical, his insistence on man's historical nature, and his emphasis on common sense and the verisimilar, in contrast to Descartes's valorization of geometrical clarity. But Vico's imaginative universal may be better understood by contrasting his linguistic views to those of Locke. Vico always sees language in a historical way. For him, it exhibits change and dynamic development. Locke's view of language, as we saw in chapter 2, is based on a never explicitly acknowledged model to which all of its phenomenal appearances ought to aspire. It is an ideal language purified of tropes. Although he is an empiricist, Locke has a Platonizing view of language similar to that which would wish language to be mathematical and thus "spiritualized" of tropes and images. Words are imperfect exactly as they exhibit figuration. I repeat the

---

6. See Mark Lilla, *G. B. Vico: The Making of an Anti-Modern* (Cambridge, MA: Harvard University Press, 1993). Also Linda Gardiner Janek, "A Renaissance Quarrel: The Origin of Vico's Anti-Cartesianism," *New Vico Studies*, 1983, 39–50.

following passage: " . . . all the artificial and figurative application of words eloquence hath invented, are for nothing else but to insinuate wrong ideas, move the passions, and thereby mislead the judgment, and so indeed are perfect cheats."[7] One has little trouble determining what the professor of rhetoric at Naples would have thought of that. In his remarks on the abuse of words, Locke has by implication radically detemporalized man and language, erasing poetic logic as a ground for linguistic and intellectual development. If Locke had thought historically, he might even have regarded tropes as having become attached to language through a process of corruption or fall. For him, poetry is a trivial pastime. It is at best entertainment without substance, or it is allegorical expression of coded information, as in what Vico called "esoteric wisdom," which he separated explicitly from poetry.

Vico's notion of poetic logic clearly opposes these views. Poetry was never purely allegorical in this sense; it was always about something, but in a different key.[8]

Vico and Blake

Blake and Vico agree on a number of things and disagree on others. The agreements are far more important to an offense of poetry than are the disagreements. Blake is anti-Lockean (and anti-Cartesian, though he does not mention Descartes in his extant writings). He specifically mentions having read Locke. He concludes in his annotations to the *Discourses* of Sir Joshua Reynolds that Reynolds's opinions are similar to Locke's and that they both "mock Inspiration and Vision."[9] Blake is especially opposed to Locke's distinction between primary and secondary qualities of perception, which is one of the things that he calls a "cloven fiction," that is, a

7. John Locke, *An Essay Concerning Human Understanding*, ed. Alexander Campbell Fraser (Oxford: Clarendon Press, 1924), 2: 246.
8. I borrow the phrase from Susanne K. Langer, *Philosophy in a New Key: A Study of the Symbolism of Reason, Rite, and Art* (Cambridge, MA: Harvard University Press, 1942). But for Vico, it was an old key. Langer makes no mention of Vico.
9. David V. Erdman, ed., *The Complete Poetry and Prose of William Blake* (Garden City, NY: Anchor Books/Doubleday, 1982), 660.

negation that brings things to a halt rather than fostering a prolific contrariety. By extending his views expressed in the annotations and elsewhere, we can see that he would attack Locke's conception of words, and his attitude leads to a notion similar to that of the imaginative universal of Vico.

Blake makes no reference in his poems or prose to the biblical story of Adam correctly naming the beasts. He seems to attribute the naming of everything to the "ancient Poets" and identifies it with a creative or imaginative act in which the poets "animated all sensible objects with Gods or Geniuses" (38). In Blake, no god threatens or comes down from the sky to deliver the key to language. It is humanly made, and there is no other.[10] The act of Blake's ancient poets is what Vico calls "allegory" (*New Science*, 128) and Blake "vision" (554) or "allegory addressd to the Intellectual powers" (730). Neither of these is allegory in the denigrated romantic sense in which I have been using the term.[11] By that definition, it is merely the translation of abstract ideas into an imagistic code. Indeed, the key to Vichian and Blakean allegory is to be found in Blake's notion of animation and Vico's "sympathetic nature" (*New Science*, 118), a piece of poetic wisdom that

10. There is a nostalgic notion that poetry goes back to primordial innocence prior to the Fall. I distinguish this notion from Blake's, which in this respect is more like Vico's. In his novel *City of Glass*, Paul Auster tells a story that illustrates this nostalgia. In *City of Glass*, the mad professor Stillman (who, I take it, is fixed in his views but still a man) would return us to the stillness of the divine language before the Fall. Working from Genesis and *Paradise Lost*, he concocts a theory that human life as we know it came into being only with the eating of the apple in Paradise. Prior to that, there was neither good nor evil. God had given to Adam onomathesia (Vico's word), and words revealed the essence of things: "names became detached from things; words devolved into a collection of arbitrary signs; language had been severed from god. The story of the Garden, therefore, records not only the Fall of man, but the Fall of language" (*The New York Trilogy* [New York: Penguin Books, 1990], 52). Stillman goes on to claim that the Tower of Babel episode in the Bible is "an exact recapitulation of what happened in the Garden—only expanded, made general in its significance to all mankind" (53). I take Stillman's story as expressive of desire for a language that supposedly existed prior to the birth of the arbitrary sign and the infinite chain of signification that has been the recent obsession of American literary theory.

11. Paul de Man, following Walter Benjamin, attempted to rehabilitate allegory from the attacks on it by Goethe, the English Romantics, and the American New Critics. Blake and Vico both meant by "allegory" something different from what de Man meant. De Man's attack was really a negation of the sameness with pure spirit allegedly claimed for the literary symbol in favor of a universal difference based in part on the Saussurean notion of language as radically differential. De Man attacked the symbol as an illusion modeled on the

Vico declares we have extreme difficulty grasping. In Blake's terms, too many modern men lack "vision," which is a mental, creative power. Vico's "sympathetic nature" is identifiable with tropes of identity, in which sameness and difference coexist. As Vico attributes this sublime power to the childhood of the race (and to children), so Blake in his *Songs of Innocence* attributes it to children, though there it is tilted toward sameness, and therefore the strife introduced in *Songs of Experience* is required as a contrary. From a reading of *Songs of Experience*, we look back at *Songs of Innocence* and are able to see that some of them can be given a reading under Vico's fourth trope, irony, restoring difference to sameness. Or, as Blake says, "Without Contraries is no progression" (34). So, for Blake, innocence is alone insufficient to poetry, as is experience without the vision of innocence. Together they are antithetical to their separation and mutual negation. Together they are offensive to those who would have only one in isolated form—sentimentality or cynicism.

The historical story Blake tells in a section of *The Marriage of Heaven and Hell* is one of decline from the visionary acts of the ancient poets to the assumption of power by a "priesthood" of abstractionists or what Vico would

---

Christian concept of miraculous incarnation, a mystical oneness of pure spirit in and as body. De Man regarded the literary symbol as a delusion brought about by a secularization of this concept. Vico's allegory, not de Man's, is an imaginative projection from the human body. In a number of places, Blake attacks allegory, though he uses the phrase "allegory addressed to the intellectual powers" favorably, contrasting it to that addressed to the "corporeal understanding." What Blake calls "vision" is contrary to the allegory-symbolism negation that privileges either one or the other. "Symbol" and "symbolism" do not appear anywhere in Blake's writings. Vico employed the former, meaning usually the emblematic; and it is fairly clear that he would have opposed it if it were to be defined as a secularization of a miraculous incarnation of pure spirit (with the reservation that as a Catholic he would have accepted the Incarnation as a historical fact). The Jesus of Blake's poem is not such an incarnation but rather an imaginative universal of a humanity exercising divine imaginative power, a universal man. Nor is this man constructed out of fear, as was Vico's Jove. The relevant texts are Paul de Man, "The Rhetoric of Temporality" (1969), *Blindness and Insight*, 2nd ed. (Minneapolis: University of Minnesota Press, 1983), 187–228; and Walter Benjamin, *The Origin of German Tragic Drama* [*Ursprung des deutschen Trauerspiels*] (1925), trans. John Osborne (London: NLB, 1977), esp. 159–235. For discussion of the allegory-symbolism distinction, see my *Philosophy of the Literary Symbolic* (Tallahassee: Florida State University Press, 1983) and works cited therein.

likely have called practitioners and guardians of esoteric wisdom. For Blake's history, the primordial act of reasoning was a projection of the name into the object rather than the assignment of correct names that had a prior divine determination, presumably in the mind of an exterior, distant god. The collapse occurred, according to Blake, when human beings abstracted the gods created by the poets' animation of objects from those objects, thus destroying sympathetic identification and rendering words, in Vico's terms, "spiritual." What began in Vichian "fable" ultimately became Blake's "forms of worship" of an alien unfathomable deity. It was forgotten that deities were projections of human imagination. Here, then, is Blake's compressed history:

> The ancient Poets animated all sensible objects with Gods or Geniuses, calling them by the names and adorning them with the properties of woods, rivers, mountains, lakes, cities, nations, and whatever their enlarged & numerous senses could percieve [*sic*].
>
> And particularly they studied the genius of each city & country. Placing it under its mental deity.
>
> Till a system was formed, which some took advantage of & enslav'd the vulgar by attempting to realize or abstract the mental deities from their objects: thus began Priesthood.
>
> Choosing forms of worship from poetic tales.
>
> And at length they pronounced that the Gods had orderd such things.
>
> Thus men forgot that All deities reside in the human breast. (38)

Vico would have agreed with this with respect to the gentes, as he called them, and probably with respect to all people: What is in Vico's term "certain" is what man makes. It is important to note that Vico related fact to fiction etymologically, opposing another negation: fact as truth, fiction as lie.

Vico had also a theory of what seems to be, from Blake's point of view, a decline, but for Vico the decline is part of a cyclical process. According to Vico, the ancient poets (he calls them "theological poets") made their gods substances of the sky, earth, and sea. What Blake might have called Vico's version of the Fall is a fall of these deities to the status of decorative and diminutive signs, allegorical images in the derogatory romantic sense of allegory. In contrast to Vico, Blake offers no theory of fear in his view of the origin of language. Rather, he sees a primordial sense of identity with the world in the earliest times and among children.

Blake is attracted to single-origin theories of language, following biblical history. In this he differs from Vico, who, in contrast to most syncretic mythographers of his time, steers away from a single historical origin that then broke up into the Babel of tongues. Vico imagines the gentile tribes, independent of one another, developing poetic logic in their different languages. But all had a common "mental language" or natural way of thought and expression, causing them to create their spoken languages as they did. Blake seems to have imagined his ancient poets all speaking the same tongue. But there is, nevertheless, a parallel in Blake to Vico's common mental language. Blake speaks of a "universal Poetic Genius" (1). This genius is the true man, and his "outward form" is derived from it. Men are alike in genius as they are in outward form, and this accounts for the similarities among religions and philosophies. So though, as Blake says in the early tract from which I have quoted, "All religions are One" (1), they are also different. The principle commits the offense of the poetic logic of identity that we find in metaphor.

Elsewhere Blake locates the source of true religion in England, putting to his own synecdochic use some eccentric syncretic ideas current in the eighteenth century. For Vico this would have been an example of the "conceit of nations," which causes every nation to declare its language and religion the original ones. In *The Marriage of Heaven and Hell*, Blake has the biblical prophet Elijah tell how the Israelites followed this pattern. Blake's use of this idea is, in fact, an example of Vico's poetic logic, as it employs synecdoche, making the small, local thing expressive of a larger thing. Thus Blake's Albion, who is England and by synecdochic extension the world, contains everything within his body, as in Vico the world is made by poetic theologians extending their bodies by tropes outward to nature. Albion is an imaginative universal. In Blake's story, Jerusalem, both a city and a woman, was originally inside Albion but externalized by the domination of the reflective or reasoning powers. She is now alien and far away, in other words, objectivized.

Blake's poetical practice and his essay on his picture of Chaucer's Canterbury pilgrims agree with Vico's notion of imaginative universals. The Canterbury pilgrims are the "physiognomies or lineaments of universal human life" (524). Blake does not call them allegorical, at least not the kind of allegory that is merely a code. Vico would have called them allegorical:

> . . . the fables being imaginative class concepts, as we have shown, the mythologies must have been the allegories corresponding to them. Allegory is defined as *diversiloquium* insofar as by identity not of proportion but (to speak scholastically) of predicability, allegories signify the diverse species or the diverse individuals comprised under these genera so that they must have a univocal signification connoting a quality common to all their species and individuals. . . . [12] (*New Science*, 128)

The distinction here between predicability and proportion is also one, as Vico uses it, between concretion and abstraction. It is not surprising that Croce, on the basis of this and other passages, accuses Vico of never really ridding the imaginative universal of abstraction. Vico is in the position of having to describe something in the language of philosophical abstraction that does not fit its categories. His position is ironic, as must be all criticism attempting to do justice to poetic logic.

Therefore, to go beyond Vico's and Blake's notions of the origin of language in poetic logic and to confront the true offense of poetry as such, we must go to poetry itself.

Jerusalem: The Emanation of the Giant Albion

Blake's *Jerusalem* radically surrounds narration with drama; the teller is made into an active character in a scene of visionary poetic creation. This

---

12. Vico is speaking in an Aristotelian way. See *Categories* 1, 7, in Richard McKeon, ed., *Basic Works of Aristotle* (New York: Random House, 1941): " . . . things are said to be named 'univocally' which have both name and the definition answering to the name in common. A man and an ox are both 'animal', and these are univocally so named, inasmuch as not only the name, but also the definition, is the same in both cases: for if a man should state in what sense each is an animal, the statement in the one case would be identical with that in the other" (7).

action identifies what Croce kept apart when, after joining intuition and expression, he separated off what he called "externalization."[13] Everything within the circumference of the telling is actually being envisioned by the teller as he writes. The intuition is being created in the externalizing act of writing. This is true also of Blake's unfinished work *The Four Zoas*, though in it there is only one explicit indication that a dramatized author is telling the story. This occurs in Night Five, where the author writes, "I write not here but all their after life was lamentation" (343), implying his presence composing his poem and also implying another story he chooses to withhold or, rather, not create. This single utterance in that poem requires us to keep in mind the fictive action of the poem's making as the poem's ultimate circumferential form.

In *Jerusalem*, the circumferential drama is more explicitly offered. The character we call Blake refers to himself as at work, including reminders to himself of how to proceed, asides indicating his presence, invocations, and requests for continued inspiration. There are also his own questioning commentaries on what is happening, references to himself seeing what is going on, not merely in the present of the conversation between Jesus and Albion that begins the poem but also in the present of what is going on inside Albion. There is even an anxious exhortation to the characters Jerusalem and Albion, and everyone else, including the social body of external listeners:

> O come ye Nations Come ye People Come up to Jerusalem
> Return Jerusalem & dwell together as of old! Return
> Return! O Albion let Jerusalem overspread all Nations
> As in the times of old. O Albion awake! (227)

It is an interesting moment, in which the narrator confounds narrative decorum and pleads dramatically with his characters and even with his readers.

It works the other way around, too. We learn toward the end of the

13. Benedetto Croce, *Aesthetic, A Science of Expression and General Linguistic* [*Estetica*] (1902), trans. Douglas Ainslie (1909) (New York: Noonday Press, 1963).

poem that one of the story's principal characters, Enitharmon, knows that she is in a poem, for as the climax of *Jerusalem* approaches she remarks that the poem is about to end (252). It is not clear whether she fears for her existence because of this or is concerned about maintaining her fallen alienated selfhood when Albion awakens. Probably both. No matter which, she is in error on this point, for she remains eternal in the poem, her world, whenever it is read. She speaks at this point as a contrary to system. (She steals a march on Molly Bloom in Joyce's *Ulysses*, who seems, apparently unknowingly, to address her author near the end of that book. Enitharmon doesn't address Will as Molly does Jamey, but at this point she has stepped outside the poem while still being in it.)

Enitharmon's moment confounds system by turning the work inside out and back again and indicates that Blake's work is really an antisystem. It thus eludes and, I think, implies the impossibility of any final interpretive commentary of the sort one of its characters, Urizen, would try to make of the world he is inside. An antisystem is contrary to the negation system-disorder. It is what I have described as antithetical, being offensive to desires for a certain order and proper closure. It may be identified with the gesture of the whole poem, not just that of its narrator.

Jerusalem, then, can be said to have its own identity even as it escapes interpretive identification. As an antisystem, *Jerusalem* can include system within itself as one of its own contrary fictive constructions. It can allow the contrary to exist as a fiction like itself. System, which demands belief in its truth, can never contain antisystem but must thrust it forth as an exteriorized, negated, and alien form of untruth. Unopposed, system thrusts the text outside itself in the form of interpretation of the sort Blake called "allegory" addressed to the "corporeal understanding" (730) and Vico regarded as a product of the conceit of scholars.

Jerusalem presents a notion of time antithetical to the objectified time we habitually think of. The poem keeps reminding the reader of the presentness of its writing even as an imagined past is constructed. There is an objectified time that everyone is inside, a spatialized time defined by measurements into units, a linear extension from past to future or creation to apocalypse that everything is moving along, locatable somewhere on it at any moment. But there is also a time that is inside the characters and emanates forth as acts, unmeasurable and eternal in the sense that their ethical implications don't go away. In this latter time, there is no past in the sense of an objective, abstract, alien distance measured in hours, days, and years. The past is constantly created by human beings as history in the present moment. Even in the former case, the past is not externally back there. Rather, back-there-ness is a category of a fictive historical projection going on in the present, contrary to the radical notion of an eternal now and the presence of the act. When Blake elsewhere remarks that "eternity is in love with the productions of time" (36) and "the Ruins of Time build Mansions in Eternity" (705), he projects both views simultaneously, once one recognizes, that by synecdoche, eternity is now. A painting or engraving eternalizes the moment as *now* in the ethical sense, though we can view it in historical projection as a created *then* and as created *then*. One of the principal repeated actions in *The Four Zoas* is the effort of fallen and disoriented characters to remember what caused them to fall. Each constructs a different history. They do not recognize that they are actively making fictions, constructing rather than passively remembering, and they remain trapped inside their constructions. One result is that their stories are not metaphorically identical.

In addition to the radical dramatization and antithetical temporality in *Jerusalem*, there is the offense of the trope. Blake had the courage of his tropes and his commitment to their identicality. He took his metaphors and synecdoches literally. The devouring view of metaphor always privileges the difference in a metaphor, negating sameness as a falsity. In this view, a metaphor declares an indifference even as everyone knows that the poet acknowledges difference as the only reality. In this view, it must be either a decoration or a comparison with respect to a few common characteristics, or it is part of an untrue fiction or phantastic imitation.

For Blake, a metaphor is a contrary to this negation, that is, it claims neither the absolute indifference insisted on in the concept of miraculous mystical unification nor the difference insisted on by hard-headed realism. Rather, it claims identity. It claims both indifference and difference at the same time. In Blake's principal trope of synecdoche, the part is the whole yet remains itself. You can envision it as both. So the Blakean contrary looks like this:

difference/indifference//identity

This is impossible, one responds; you can't see the duck and the rabbit at the same time.[14] But Blake's poem is not an imitation of the natural world, where indeed it would be impossible. Blake's poem is a process or enactment of making an ethical vision, where identity becomes an imperative as a contrary to the natural world of multiplicity or to any world of abstract realism or its negation, a situation of mystical indifference. Blake's poem is not referable, then, to ontological or epistemological formulations. It opposes by contrariety both a differential linguistic philosophy and its mystical negation, and it is neither materialist nor idealist. Further, it resists political readings either individualistically or collectively inclined. The consciousness it projects cannot be adequately described as either an autonomous or a culturally generated subject. Thus Blake puts into ethical practice the trope's principle of identity.

In *Jerusalem*, the creative process dramatized at the circumference of Blake's activity of composing seems to operate on the principle of continuous accretion and invention. That activity has its synecdoche in the poem in the creative activities of the character Los. In the earlier *Four Zoas*, there is continual invention of new characters. The assumption we conventionally make about characters is that they were somehow fictively existent before they came on the stage of the poem. But at the level of the narrator's creative activity in *Jerusalem*, we experience a process of invention, including a stream of new names. *Jerusalem*'s invention includes this new dimension, the sudden appearance of characters as in *The Four Zoas*, and the introduction of what we might call an additional twist requiring us to rethink something we thought we had successfully closed into system. We are unable to rest content with a final act of devouring, in which one would seem to know the terrain as a stage set on which all the action must take place. Our faculties must continue to act, not in order to fit these new elements into a plan but to revise a plan we have wanted to construct in order to give us a place to stand.

14. The reference is to Ludwig Wittgenstein's drawing in his *Philosophical Investigations*, trans. G. E. M. Anscombe (Oxford: Basil Blackwell, 1963), 194e, which can be seen as the head either of a duck or of a rabbit, but not both at the same time.

Blake's major type of accretion is the making of a chain of metaphorical relations. One thing becomes another thing, and another, and another in a chain that would return to the word with which it began, but in an infinite length of time, everything identified:

> All human forms identified, even Tree Metal Earth & Stone, all
> Forms identified. . . . (258)

In the preface to the fourth and last chapter of *Jerusalem*, Blake writes:

> I give you the end of a golden string,
>   Only wind it into a ball:
> It will lead you in at Heavens gate,
>   Built in Jerusalems wall. (231)

This figure is both spiritual advice and advice on how to read the poem. It shows how to extricate oneself from the various labyrinths composing the fallen world that the poem describes. The whole poem as it exists on its pages cannot escape linearity. It must be imaginatively rolled up into a ball so that the reader, like the narrator, can see "past, Present, and Future, existing all at once" within the linearity. The metaphor brings in a contrary to simple narration.

All of *Jerusalem* is to be read, like the infinite metaphorical chain, as a fiction of imaginative possibility, a future that is a state of activity, not a completed stasis. As the poem ends, the four Zoas

> . . . conversed together in Visionary form dramatic which bright
> Redounded from their Tongues in thunderous majesty, in Vision
> In new Expanses, creating exemplars of Memory and of Intellect
> Creating Space, Creating Time according to the wonders Divine
> Of Human Imagination. . . . (258)

Exemplars are models, examples, archetypes. They are makings in the specific sense of fictions. In these conversations, the Zoas are telling one another stories. They are all artists. The problem all along has been the externalizing of fictive stories into objects of obeisance and belief and the attempt to impose them on others as allegories of the law or of a mystery with teller as priest. As fictions, as stories, there is nothing wrong with them. All of them, seen as such, have the capacity to rouse the faculties to act—to create more stories, even when they are cautionary tales such as *Jerusalem* really is. A dramatic action of its speaker, a making of a fiction grounded on synecdoche, a maker of metaphorical chains of identity, *Jerusalem* is a grand verbal gesture. It constantly challenges the reader. An offense all around.

But such conversations can easily break down once again into war within Albion's members. All that is necessary is for one of the Zoas to try to impose his fictive story as objective truth or law. It is not difficult to imagine the poem beginning all over again. This is also to say that *Jerusalem* is always potentially present to be read and reread. It is not surprising that Blake's Zoas are subjected to friendly parody in Joyce's *Finnegans Wake*, which writes us a letter about cyclicity, for that work's technique and cyclic shape has as forerunners Blake's longer poems, relentless in their accretion of perspectives, contraries, and metaphorical chains. Joyce's four—Matt Gregory, Mark Lyons, Luke Tarpey, and Johnny MacDougal—sit in an Irish pub, try hopelessly to interpret the text (world) they are in, and tell stories, with a garrulousness unknown even to Blake's Zoas, in a world inevitably cyclical.

9

Blake and Joyce: Friends in Offense

One of the fundamental events in *Finnegans Wake*, as in *Jerusalem*, is displacement of narrative to drama. In their acts of narration, both narrators (in the case of *Finnegans Wake*, the dreamer) are characters in the drama of their respective acts. *Jerusalem*'s Blake is present, seeing and creating throughout; and the surrounding present of the text is the moving present of Blake's utterance. It is well known among critics of Joyce that in *Ulysses*, the act of, or perhaps acts of, narration takes place under the aegis of what has come to be known as the "arranger," who directs these acts.[1] In both *The Four Zoas* and *Jerusalem*, there is a dreamer. But Blake as describer of his own creative activity and as narrator (and sometimes orator) is quite awake and outside the dream of Albion, whose many interior selves act in the dream. However, the neatness of concentric enclosures surrounded by Blake is, as we have noticed, confounded in *Jerusalem* by Enitharmon's knowledge that she is in a poem, and we have noted also that in *Ulysses* Molly Bloom inadvertently calls on Jamey. *Finnegans Wake* invokes Joyce more than once. This breakdown of discrete differences between circumferences of narrated action is virtually a principle of formal order in *Finnegans Wake*, where there are hapless efforts to interpret the text (or world) from inside it, to read not only the alleged letter that is mentioned in the text but also the spirit of the text, as it were.

Synecdoche and Contrariety: Against Allegory

The ordering principle of all this is synecdoche, though as a formal principle it goes far beyond a simple notion of part standing for whole. Indeed, it goes beyond the usual notion of form to include also theme. In Blake, synecdoche works as whole standing for part and part standing for whole,

1. See note 12, chapter 4.

and it works both ways between the largest unit and the smallest.[2] Furthermore, the largest imaginable unit—in this case, the giant Albion—is unfortunately capable of thrusting what is inside him outside to surround and contain him. Indeed, this is what seems to have happened in the so-called Fall. The Fall in Blake is the fall of intellectual powers into a condition of isolation that threatens solipsism. Each of Albion's Zoas is the whole, that is, identical to the whole, but they have each fallen into degrees of misunderstanding of this fact and, in the most egregious cases of error, act to negate this identity. For Blake, the epistemological problem of subject and object is really the projection of an ethical problem.

Finnegans Wake also operates on a synecdochic principle, though there are interesting differences. Like Blake's Albion in England, Joyce's macrocosmic giant Finn lies dreaming in Ireland, his head at Howth and his feet somewhere near Chapelizod. Blake's Albion is, of course, identified with Britain; his body is located on a rock, which, among many things, is the sinking Atlantis, the cliffs of Dover, and England's material conditions. But at the beginning of *Jerusalem*, he walks in his sleep into his own dark valleys, that is, the valleys of his mental isolation. Finn himself never appears as such in *Finnegans Wake*. The book contains and may be entirely his dream, and the dream remembers and imagines him synecdochically as Tim Finnegan the hod carrier, who is quickly replaced by HCE in Joyce's cyclical Vichian history. Joyce's version of the Fall emphasizes Vichian history in that Finn is the lost poetic or imaginative universal and HCE the present abstract universal or the effort of the dreamer to make an imaginative universal image in the age of men. HCE is the most elusive figure in the text-dream, the best synecdoche left for the new Finn in a history in which the abstract takes over, not without cost. His name is never fully uttered in the text—Humphrey Chimpden Earwicker—and may not be his name at all. He is an acronym. His clothes are described, but his body is constituted mainly by our inferences, and the alleged hump on his back is

---

2. I offer the notion of a "radical progressive synecdoche," both open and closed (or neither), in connection with Blake in "Synecdoche and Method," *Antithetical Essays in Literary Criticism and Liberal Education* (Tallahassee: Florida State University Press, 1990), esp. 27–29.

more a projection of "Humphrey" and its variants than a fact. Nor is HCE's guilty act presented as a particular. Instead, it is a tissue of rumors endlessly repeated and varied, as if the dreamer were seeking to recover some event as an imaginative universal, dreaming back to it, much as Yeats's dead spirits in *A Vision* dream back their lives in order to achieve purgation (an act parodied in *Finnegans Wake*). But the dreamer can't ever quite constitute the original particular. It escapes ever into a chain of linguistic relations where the image gives way to the capriciousness of the pun and homonym and to gossip, which is what Joycean history, at least in *Finnegans Wake*, turns out to be. In parallel, HCE is always trying to escape into a series of evasions of his guilt, only to fall back into a guilt never precisely specified. It is as if that vague object *original* sin is a construction of abstract logic.

The Blakean vision is of a fall into abstract reasoning that is most fully exhibited in the activities of the Zoa Urizen in Nights Six and Seven of *The Four Zoas*. There, Urizen explores the external and alienated world, creation of his own intellectual understanding. It is a world of Locke's primary qualities of experience, among other things, and he is terrified by it, attempting to impose his own laws on it. These laws are fundamentally the laws of measurement and "mathematic form," and his act is a centering of authority in an arbitrarily chosen place and in the tables of the law, his own books.

There is an irony in the Joycean synecdoche, for the dreamer fails to re-create an original imaginative universal as such, there being no origin in a metaphorical chain. Finn is but a vague memory, and Finnegan is dead and prevented from rising by the insistent wakers. HCE, the usurping abstract universal who is everybody and is as abstract as that acronym, seeming to have no particular body, is a signal of the Vichian cyclical movement in which the dream is caught up. The dream contains a family that includes a daughter and the two sons who are together going to be a new version of their father HCE. Finn is not going to return as such, but HCE will return. With every morning, with every erection encouraged by ALP, with every fall of every Finnegan, he will arrive, the usurper, the guilty one. He is replayed microcosmically in the strife of his two sons.

The Blakean synecdoche shows us a somewhat different picture, an Albion whose microcosmic parts can come back into an appropriate relationship with one another under the conditions of conversation described at the end of *Jerusalem*. This would be a productive strife called contrariety. The model of this kind of strife is, as we have seen, the trope, a situation in which things that are not the same are nevertheless also the same, maintaining the offensive tension of tropological identity. This idea of identity is particularly clear in the activity of the matured Los of *Jerusalem*, who, though much put upon by his own spectral self, refuses to negate any of the other Zoas in spite of their outrageous behavior and willingness to suppress him if they can.

Though there is little doubt in my mind that Joyce instinctively sensed the principle of contrariety in Blake and was drawn to it, and though he may have worked it out in what reading of Blake he had accomplished, there is considerable evidence that Joycean contrariety has closer affinity with the principle of joined opposites of Giordano Bruno of Nola, recalled over and over again in *Finnegans Wake* in the many variations played on Brown and Nolan, the Dublin stationers and booksellers. Bruno's conception, as I understand it, is more fluid than Blake's and may have appealed more to Joyce for that reason.

The difference between Bruno's and Blake's contraries is a subtle one, perhaps of emphasis. In *De l'infinito universo et monda*, Bruno writes that his philosophy "maketh contraries to coincide, so that there is one primal foundation of both origin and of end. From this coincidence of contraries, we deduce that ultimately it is divinely true that contraries are within contraries, wherefore it is not difficult to compass the knowledge that each thing is within every other thing."[3] The implication of a cyclical temporal movement from one to many to one is strong here, as is the notion of a marriage of contrariety and synecdoche that works both ways, things turning inside out and back like the great world-egg that Michael Robartes speaks of in Yeats's *A Vision*.

Blake would have been suspicious of a movement that makes contraries coincide and then separate, and, for him, cyclicity was neurotic repetition. He would have thought that the coinciding inevitably results in the

3. Dorothea Waley Singer, *Giordano Bruno, His Life and Thought with an Annotated Translation of His Work "On the Infinite Universe and Worlds"* (New York: Henry Schuman, 1950), 359.

domination of one element in that relationship and the submerging of the other. The coinciding turns out in history, as Blake saw it, to be the replacement of one tyranny with another. There is no "progression" here, merely an endless cyclicity. Contraries do not merge.

But if Joyce's contrariety is Brunovian and submitted to cyclicity, it is also in some respects Blakean, and this is no more clearly seen than in the preposterous lecture on the dime-cash problem in chapter 6 of *Finnegans Wake*. In it, Professor Jones, the lecturer, has it in for the "sophology of Bitchson," or Henri Bergson, who is described as "driven as under by a dime-dime urge" (149: 20–21). Professor Jones is a spatialist, which is also a specialist. He is a stand-in for the Wyndham Lewis of *Time and Western Man* and Lewis's argument against the alleged time obsession of modern Western thought. The exemplars of it, in addition to Bergson, are Samuel Alexander and A. N. Whitehead in philosophy, Albert Einstein in physical science ("the whoo-whoo and where's hairs theories of Winestain" [149: 27–28]), Lucien Levy-Bruhl in anthropology, and Ezra Pound, Gertrude Stein, and James Joyce in literature. An apparently obstreperous student at the lecture is Bruno Nolan or Nolan Brown, who is finally either excused from or asked to leave the lecture hall.

One of the problems with Lewis's attack on space-time is that *he* seems to be obsessed in his own way with time. Lewis insists dogmatically on the absolute primacy of space. Professor Jones favors space, puts down all opposition, and in his telling of the fable of the Mookse and the Gripes favors the Mookse, who can see but does not hear very well, over the Gripes, who can hear but does not see very well. This opposition, based on the fable of the fox and the grapes from La Fontaine, is similar to the contrary of devourer and prolific, user and creator, in Blake. Joyce has some fun with this in that he makes the poetical, antithetical character a griper.

The Mookse plays a role like that of Blake's spatialist Urizen. The Mookse is also Pope Adrian, author of the infamous papal bull *Laudabiliter*, which provided the excuse for the Norman English invasion and colonization of Ireland, an appropriation of space. The Gripes is presumed to be a temporalist, at least he is to the Mookse, who treats him with disdain when he isn't merged with him in the dream. But it may make more sense to see the Gripes as a contrary to the negation that privileges either space or time—as space-time, for the Gripes seems to have no design on the Mookse.

In Professor Jones's lecture, space and time are cash and dime respectively, and this produces the dime-cash problem that is its subject. This conflation connects spatialization with measurement and number and with the enlightenment economics of *laissez-faire*. But Professor Jones can't keep time out of his discourse. He absurdly spatializes the old Heraclitan exposition of the flux. Heraclitus said, "You could not step twice into the same rivers" and "Into the same river we step and do not step."[4] This lurks in Jones's remark, "The cash system . . . means that I cannot now have or nothave a piece of cheeps in your pocket at the same time and with the same manners as you can now nothalf or half the cheek apiece . . . " (161: 7–11). Jones attacks the unskilled singers who subordinate the "space-element" to the "time-factor," which ought to be killed, *"ill tempor"* (164: 33–35). We discover that Jones's ill-tempered anxiety about time has to do with his desire to preserve his "unchanging Word." This word, he says, is his wife: "The word is my Wife, to exponse and expound" (167: 28–29). His notion of the Word, like Urizen's, is the originating word as the law, and the god behind it. Neither Blake nor Joyce accepts this notion. In their works, the word is not law, but there is a kind of law governing the word, and it is the trope. Language is grounded on the trope.

Jones's word is the spatialized word with a meaning lying behind it, subject to priestly and professorial allegorical interpretation. Both priest (in Blake) and professor (in Joyce) are keepers and selective revealers of a mystery, the mystery of meaning that Joyce's hapless four codgers (Matt, Mark, Luke, and Johnny) seek but never find. Jones is wrong to call the spatialized word his wife, even if the dreamer was garbling "life," for Joyce's female figure ALP is identified with time, and her letter is never finished and certainly never finally interpreted. There is always more time, and interpretation is as potentially endless as a metaphorical chain.

In this characterization of time as female, Joyce departs from Blake. In establishing a female time, Joyce would emphasize value in the cycle as

---

4. W. H. S. Jones, trans., *Hippocrates IV, Heraclitus* (Loeb Classical Library) (Cambridge, MA: Harvard University Press; London: William Heinemann, 1931), 483, 495.

such and in the ordinary cyclical life of birth, marriage, procreation, parenthood, and death, over which ALP presides as a sort of muse-deity and the turning of which she endlessly encourages. Joyce also departs from Blake in his treatment of the Fall. For Blake, it is a failure of imagination, a withdrawal of Albion into a state of alienation. In Joyce, it is a rumor that the four old codgers try to constitute as law leading to guilt, which poor HCE is constantly attempting both to confess and to disown. The Fall is a fall from a ladder, a fall into drunkenness, a fall into bed, the fall of a penis. It is always followed by a rising. Sin is a rumor, a form of Blakean error. The last sentence of *Finnegans Wake* turns out to be the first part of the first sentence. The golden string is a ball.

The whole dime-cash lecture in *Finnegans Wake* is an example of Joycean comedy, which is given to good-natured parody. Blake's poem has similar characteristics but not the same degree of comic relentlessness. But sometimes the aims of Blake and Joyce seem very nearly the same. Blake's Urizen is an obsessive engineer whose muse is mathematics. One of the parody scenes in *Finnegans Wake* makes number and geometry play an absurdly ridiculous part. The specific object of parody is not, however, Blake's Urizen but the Yeats of *A Vision*. It is offered in the spirit of Blake's remark that God was not a mathematical diagram. Whether Joyce thought that he was parodying Yeats or the fictive quasi-Urizenic Yeats that the poet created in self-parody is not clear, nor does it matter for purposes here. The Urizenic abstractionist Shaun attempts to understand ALP's sexuality by means of Yeats's favorite terms and geometrical shapes—circle, triangle, cone, and gyre. Joyce parodies the fictive Yeats's search for the ultimate miraculous symbol and, for the two sons of ALP, the ultimate mystery. Urizen is also parodied in that with the tools of measurement he, too, seeks the ultimate truth. Joyce shows how the particular becomes lost in abstraction, just as Finn is lost (and but a rumor) in the Vichian abstract universality of HCE. One of the washerwomen on the bank of the Liffey thinks she sees Finn:

> Is that the great Finnleader himself in his joakimono on his statue riding the high horse there forehengist? . . . Holy Scamander, I sar it again! Near the golden falls. Icis on us! Seints of light! Zezere! Subdue your

noise, you hamble creature! What is it but a blackburry growth or the dwyergray ass them four old codgers owns. (214: 11–33)

The first speaker is wrong, and the second corrects her. The rumor of Finn is garbled in the dreamer's mind, and the first washerwoman's, with the Dublin victualler Findlater and an equestrian statue. Finn has long ago been relegated to history and, like King Arthur or Charles Stewart Parnell, won't return. What she has seen is but a bush or a donkey, just as the harbinger of a new dispensation in Yeats's play *The Herne's Egg* is but a donkey.

We can say that Blake's Urizen, Yeats's Urizenic Yeats of *A Vision*, and the four old codgers of *Finnegans Wake* are all allegorists in the sense in which the romantics used that term. They seek behind the word what the word stands for. In this, they desperately try to negate the chain of metaphor by seeking a first and founding word. They would be Vico's conceited scholars. When Urizen cannot find the ultimate word, he locates truth arbitrarily in his books. Yeats seeks revelation from his mysterious "instructors" and hopes it is in the word or diagram or behind those things, but one instructor tells him they will fool him if they can. In Joyce, the fall into the allegorical attitude is played out in the elaborate, frustrated attempts at interpretation made by the four, including what seems to be a half-hearted dreaming effort to impose Saint Thomas Aquinas's fourfold interpretive scheme on the text of which they are a part, even as they recognize that "the sword of certainty . . . never falls" (51: 05–06).

The most mechanical of these acts is the following:

> . . . we also know, what we perused from the pages of *I Was a General*, that Showting up, Bulsklivism by "Schottenboum", that Father Michael about this red time of the white terror equals the old regime and Margaret is the social revolution while cakes means the party funds and dear thank you signifies national gratitude. (116: 05–10)

This desperate searching for an unrecoverable original, only the most explicitly allegorical of the many attempted, well illustrates Blake's remark distinguishing allegory from vision. "Allegory," Blake says, "is Formd by the Daughters of Memory" (554). Joyce's four are the fathers of memory as

Finnegans Wake sees it, the fomenters of gossip signifying nothing. For Blake, allegory is like what historians do in that allegorization tries to see the word of truth behind remembered events. This is why Blake asked historians just to tell their stories and to leave the reader to reason on the events. The attempt by Joyce's four to reason always ends in verbal chaos, and the stories themselves do also.

Blake criticism for some time consisted of desperate efforts at allegorization in spite of Blake's strictures against it. Joyce's act of dissuasion is *Finnegans Wake* itself, containing the relentless efforts of the four to interpret. They are constant reminders of how not to read the book or world that they occupy. Devoid of irony about their position, the four unintentionally convey Joyce's negative lesson in literary criticism, defending, as did Blake, poetry against the conceit of scholars and generally providing the necessary cultural contrary offensive to single-minded ways of thinking.

Finnegans Wake: Against the Law

Joyce's poetic approach is not antithetical only according to the examples I have given. It is antithetical to notions of poetry that have become hardened and abstracted into external rules. To illustrate Joyce's evasions of or, perhaps, indifference to such systematic approaches, let me contrast the hierarchy of poetic elements in Aristotle's *Poetics*, from which rules were derived, to Joyce's practice in *Finnegans Wake*. I shall not claim that Joyce deliberately reverses Aristotle, nor is it in any case an exact reversal.

As is well known to scholars, Aristotle arranges the principal elements of dramatic art in a hierarchy of six. They are, in order of descending importance, plot, character, diction, thought, melody (including song), and spectacle. Except for thought, which would have to possess a quite different meaning for *Finnegans Wake* in order to be included at all (I shall return to this), *Finnegans Wake* seems to have revised this hierarchy.

In *Poetics*, Aristotle describes plot (*mythos*) as the "structure and incidents" of the play, the arrangement.[5] This indicates that plotting involves

---

5. W. D. Ross, ed., "De Poetica," *The Works of Aristotle*, trans. Ingram Bywater (Oxford: Clarendon Press, 1924), 1453b.

decisions about what is to be presented first, not necessarily what is chronologically first. The classical advice to begin *in medias res* proposes a certain arrangement other than the strictly chronological arrangement of a chronicle. It is clear, however, that plot for Aristotle implies there is a chronological story to be inferred as existing prior to plotting. According to *Poetics*, the events are acted out by characters or what Aristotle calls "personal agents" (1450b). In the typical novel, the plot is narrated either by an agent or a third person or a third person who is an agent.

In *Finnegans Wake*, the narration, if that is what we can call it, tends to be antithetical to these conventions. We cannot locate a narrator in the usual senses. There seem to be various voices, or thoughts, or a dreaming that plays many parts. There is an enormous amount of what seems to be neurotic verbal repetition standing in for plot. A sense of underlying story seems to fade away quickly. Some critics, notably John Gordon, claim to have unearthed the story beneath the narration, but only by heroic acts of inference that the surface obviously frustrates.[6] The temporal structure of this story is evasively presented and seems at best, when its details sporadically appear, balanced against a variety of other elements—gossip, hearsay, a family situation, a letter, a heap of refuse, a fall from a height, an event in a park, and efforts at interpretation, to name a few—some of these, as in letter-litter, the product of wordplay and metaphorical chains.

The repetitions involving these elements are laid out not only temporally (as we usually think of repetition) but also by synecdoche, the major one being the repetition of Finn in Finnegan and HCE (or Finnegan and HCE in Finn), and subsequently Shaun in HCE (or HCE in Shaun), the synecdoches in *Finnegans Wake* working both ways. Whereas in most novels repetition enhances the narrative, endorsing it with events that resonate in one another or with reappearing objects and types, in *Finnegans Wake* repetition has little to do with plot or chronology; yet it seems fundamental to everything that one can isolate for discussion. The reader does not come away from *Finnegans Wake* with experience of a *peripeteia*. The plea-

---

6. John Gordon, *Finnegans Wake: A Plot Summary* (Syracuse, NY: Syracuse University Press, 1986). In Aristotle's terminology, what Gordon is talking about is not the plot but the story behind it.

sure is not that of *catharsis* or of all passion spent, but rather the satisfaction of a developed recognition, as, for example on a small scale, when "hesitancy" is repeatedly misspelled "hesitency" and one recognizes that this misspelling was a critical piece of evidence exonerating Parnell of the murders in Phoenix Park, scene also of the alleged guilty act of HCE. Recognition occurs also when "hesitency" is finally spelled correctly during a period of the text in which the ass, a trustworthy voice on the whole and without guilt, seems to be speaking.

Finnegans Wake's repetitions often appear to be contributing to some recognizable structure, but it is more accurate to view them as consistently unstable, recalling Aristotle's notion that if characters are to be inconsistent they should be consistently so. The text constantly breaks with itself, seeming to embark on a new structural tack just as the reader begins to attain a sense of order. Thus, one chapter suggests a mime, another an annotated text, still another a television skit, and another a dialogue. Woven in and out are stories never quite told but instead recalled in bits, fits, and starts: Kersse and the Norwegian Captain, Buckley and the Russian General. Inside these *as if*s, the structure collapses. At the level of the sentence, the same thing occurs. Often one reads a sentence with the expectation of closure, but then something in the process of thought and of syntax goes "wrong," and the sentence trails off into an irrelevance that may include motifs repeated from something that has seemed quite distant from anything at hand. Plot is constantly giving way to something else.

The usual way to talk about this is to evoke the notion of a dream structure, and, of course, there is a lot to this. But *Finnegans Wake* may not be quite all dreaming; perhaps it is better described as occurring somewhere between dream and consciousness or moving back and forth in a half-light. It is perhaps best simply to call it, as John Bishop has, Joyce's book of the dark.[7] In any case, it is neither a Freudian nor a Jungian dream in any strict sense, though it contains a certain amount of "fraudstuff," present perhaps for the "yung and easily freudened" (7: 13; 1 15: 22–23). One could argue that the cyclic nature of *Finnegans Wake* replaces Aris-

---

7. John Bishop, *Joyce's Book of the Dark: Finnegans Wake* (Madison: University of Wisconsin Press, 1986).

totelian plot. Cyclicity can be seen, as I shall later suggest, as the outcome of total commitment to the logic of tropes, which connects it perhaps with Aristotle's "diction." But it is better to see *Finnegans Wake* as antithetical to the opposition between plot and absence of plot.

In some ways, character (ethos) is more important than plot in *Finnegans Wake*. In another way, it may be said that there are no characters in *Finnegans Wake* other than characters in the sense of signs or *sigla*, as they are called by Roland McHugh.[8] Or perhaps there is but one recurring character who is many. Yet even if we recognize that neither HCE nor ALP are ever physically described and that in no place in the text are their full names given except in a multitude of displacements from a source we as interpreters infer but cannot find, we do come to know them through a mist of language. This is because we want to and do work them back from their states as Vichian abstract universals represented only by initials to make them distinct individuals. It is then that they become characters in both senses of the word.

There are, of course, other *sigla* in *Finnegans Wake* that take on similar kinds of characteristics—Shem, Shaun, Izzy (who becomes two), and the four (Matt, Mark, Luke, and Johnny) who merge synecdochically into one known as Mamalujo. Finally, there is the ass who pulls their cart. We do get brief descriptions of the four, but on the whole we learn about their characters through their voices, which are also by synecdoche one voice. *Finnegans Wake* opposes the absolute division between one character and many characters, between character (*ethos*) and character (*siglum*).

Aristotle identifies thought (*dianoia*) with rhetoric. It is "the fact of saying whatever can be said, or what is appropriate to the occasion" (1450b: 4–5), and he proceeds to think of thought in connection with effect on the audience. It includes "everything to be effected by [the characters'] language—in every effort to prove or disprove, to arouse emotion pity, fear, anger, and the like, or to maximize or minimize things" (1456a: 37–1456b: 1). He goes on to assert that both incidents and speeches should contribute to the same end. Thought is seen then as what is expressed by characters, but it is by extension what is conveyed by the whole.

Finnegans Wake is both thoughtful and thoughtless. It is thoughtless

---

8. Roland McHugh, *The Sigla of Finnegans Wake* (London: Edward Arnold), 1976.

in that it offers no voice not filtered through or created by a semiconscious "speaker." Or, perhaps, it is just a speaking that seems to be garbling potential thought or is often incapable of sustaining it for the duration of an entire sentence. Thought (was it ever really thought?) is corrupted by neurotic incursions and repetitions. Yet from the whole of *Finnegans Wake* there emerges something like, though also different from, an Aristotelian rhetorical effect. It sets off in the reader Keats's "momentous depth of speculation."[9] This is really quite different from Aristotle's "thought," the conception of which is tied (unfortunately for the discussion of diction in *Poetics*) to the aim of persuasion. Much of Aristotle's discourse on this matter refers to the parts of speech and the nature of sentences. He does not concern himself with questions of language's constitutive power, but he does acknowledge the importance of metaphor, pointing out that a command of metaphor is more important for a writer than propriety of diction, which is nevertheless a "great thing." (1459a: 1–8). *Finnegans Wake* would persuade us of nothing, yet we speculate on many things that are, in the end perhaps, one thing.

In *Finnegans Wake*, words are characters in the sense of *sigla*, and they are characters in the sense of *ethos*, so it can be said that diction (*lexis*) contains character even as characters use diction. In *Finnegans Wake*, there are two drives, as I shall call them, that diction expresses. There is the reasoning drive that wants a structure of logic and a linearity standing behind and ordering the plot. There is the imaginative drive that interferes with the desire for that order. These are in a contrariety that constitutes a perpetual *agon*, with each requiring the other. From this point of view, the difficulty of *Finnegans Wake*, including the onslaught of garbling, punning, and linguistic motifs, is the arena of a struggle to liberate the reader from total dependence on analysis and differentiation at the expense of synthesis and sameness. *Finnegans Wake* negates neither side of this opposition but instead lets them exist in a tension. This contrariety in its linear or historical form falls into time as cyclical. The model for it is metaphor, where sameness and difference coexist in relation.

We come now to the notion of melody or, as Aristotle called it, *harmonia*. Aristotle actually has little to say about song in *Poetics*. Melody "is

9. John Keats, letter to George and Thomas Keats, 28 December 1817.

the greatest of the pleasurable accessories of tragedy," he writes (1450b: 16–17). Melody and song occur in tragedies; *Finnegans Wake* is (metaphorically at least) a song, the title coming from an Irish ballad. The song title, with the apostrophe dropped, is in a synecdochic relation to the whole of the book's contents.[10] In addition, of course, many song titles and lines play into the texture of the whole.

Spectacle (*opsis*) is for Aristotle the least important of his six, partly (but by no means more than partly) because Aristotle wavers between thinking of the essence of drama as that which can be read and regarding it as performance. For him, spectacle belongs only to the latter. It "has, indeed, an emotional attraction of its own, but to produce [the effect of pity and fear] by means of the Spectacle is less artistic, and requires extraneous aid," than to produce it by the arrangement of the incidents (1453b: 3–9). If we take "spectacle" in a metaphorical sense, it becomes in *Finnegans Wake* the most important of the six and connected the most to poetry. Of course, *Finnegans Wake* is a written text, but it is also one of the most oral of written texts. I would like to connect it to the notion of verbal gesture already discussed. *Finnegans Wake* as a whole is like *Ulysses* in that it is a showing off, a highwire act in which the arranger of the text is exhibiting an eclectic virtuosity meant to be viewed with astonished pleasure: "Watch me as I do this and then this." There are many performances (mime, interview, dialogue, story, etc.) and yet one performance, the total gesture of the text, which has no verbal equivalent.

The gesture is an antithetical one. It contains and allows oppositions: order and disorder, reason and imagination, writing and speech, thought and desire, and so on. The antithetical poem can and must include that which is apparently opposed to it, refusing to repeat the crime of negation. Thus, *Finnegans Wake* takes all of preceding European literature as the type to which it is, in one sense, the antitypical fulfillment; and it negates none of its predecessors, making no claim to replace them. It would both point to and contain the whole tradition. A bold effort. A spectacle. An offense not only to good Aristotelian dramatic behavior but also to good old common sense.

10. On titles as synecdoches, see my "Titles, Titling, and Entitlement To," *Antithetical Essays*, 111–43.

10

Joyce Cary's Antitheticality and His Politics of Experience

This chapter considers dramatization as the characteristic offense of Joyce Cary's trilogies and proceeds to a consideration of how his work performs an engagement with politics. The aim of the chapter, as well as that of the next, on Seamus Heaney's criticism, is to show, as I suggested in the preface, that poetic offense or friendliness to it produces an antithetical politics.

Antithetical Dramatics

Gesture, as indicated early in chapter 4, can be silent and without movement, as in prayer or contemplation. There is a metaphorical parallel to this in the trilogies of Joyce Cary where the "author" never speaks in his own voice. I shall return to this, but first it must be acknowledged that authorial gesture in these novels *seems* to be displaced to the narrators. They exist as dramatic characters in their monologues. They gesture in language, and their gestures constitute much of what interests us. Each one is a performer who practices a different rhetoric with a different purpose. In the first, or so-called art, trilogy, Sara Monday of *Herself Surprised* is writing a "true confession" for money under commission from a scandal-mongering newspaper. In *To Be a Pilgrim*, Thomas Wilcher, for whom Sara was a cook, housekeeper, and mistress, is writing a confessional diary. In *The Horse's Mouth*, Gulley Jimson is speaking his memoir to someone who will edit and publish it. There are, of course, countless novels in which narrators are recognizably dramatic characters, but there are few, if any, in which narrators view narrators in other novels. The trilogy suggests to us the presence of another character, the arranger or director of the total drama.

The second, or so-called political, trilogy takes a similar shape. There again, the rhetoric of the three speakers is different. The central figure, the liberal politician Chester Nimmo, is a complex of background and per-sonality. His story, as he tells it in *Except the Lord*, has a design on his read-ers, principally his former wife, now Nina Latter, narrator of the first book, *Prisoner of Grace*; this very fact adds an important dimension that would otherwise be lost. It reveals Nimmo's combination of confession and rhetorical guile, which in turn reveals his complexity and comments on itself. At the same time, the novel as a whole explores the life of politics. As read-ers, we must keep amending or qualifying our view of Nimmo as we are challenged to evaluate his acts, his interpretations, his confessions, his self-justifications, his ways of persuasion, and finally our own responses.

But this does not end our involvement, because we must also bal-ance the Nimmo of *Except the Lord* against the view of him offered by Nina in *Prisoner of Grace*; and then we must go on to *Not Honour More*, where he appears in Jim Latter's formal narrative confession of murder. Are we supposed to be sympathetic to Latter, who has gruesomely slit his wife's throat and seems at least a borderline paranoid psychiatric case? Well, yes and no. Latter is a man of honor, but of honor gone wrong, a man of truth, but of truth too narrowly conceived and acted on. He has swum against the current of what he sees as corruption, but he is close to incompetent. His is an imagination enslaved to moralistic abstractions. Nimmo, on the other hand, is a man of imagination so strong as occasionally to overwhelm reason, making him sometimes appear, as Latter sees him, a charlatan.

Who is right and who is wrong? Who has done right and who has done wrong? These are questions, but they are not the questions Cary directly answers. Nor are they the questions that the drama of much poetry answers. Are these the questions answered by Browning's "My Last Duchess"? Have we closed that poem when we have ruled that Brown-ing's duke is evil? Does the envoy of the count get off scot free? In a rush to judgment, do we ignore Browning's evocation of a world? It is clear enough that in *Prisoner of Grace* Nina vacillates, that in *Except the Lord* Nimmo conveniently prevaricates, and that in *Not Honour More* Latter has murdered, and that these are all wrong in ascending order of grievousness. No poem or person has to tell us this. The trilogy tells us other things or asks other things of us by setting in motion an intricate dance of words and gestures. The trilogy's total gesture is one of juxtaposition.

We have entered the realm of poetic antitheticality and its risk of offense, opposed to but not negating the opposition of right and wrong. The poetic interest is in successes and failures of the imagination. Cary makes more challenging our movement from the particularity of his dramas to universals than some would like it to be. Yet this vivifies questions we ponder, requires that we not avoid genuine problems, and rouses the faculties to act.

The first trilogy is about the imagination, the art of making. *The Horse's Mouth* is specifically about artistic imagination. The imagination, for Cary, is the power by which we each create our own idea of things, that is to say, our own world. Cary is not, however, an epistemological idealist. For him, the world is here, we are in it, and our imaginations must work on the brute facts of nature. Our lives are composed of a laborious building up of our ideas of the world. We must engage in this activity on our own; we must do it for ourselves. Human beings, even the worst of us, are immensely ingenious at it, too clever often for our own good.

Because the imagination is relatively unfettered, it is also potentially dangerous and often resists being put to good uses. It is capable of evil. Cary fears sometimes for what man will do with the freedom imagination bestows. He once wrote in an essay: "I am not afraid for freedom, I am afraid for the world if it cannot manage freedom. For it is a most mysterious and terrible power, secret and eternal. It is born in every child and sets to work at once to create a world according to that child's desires. It uses every weapon to achieve its aims, and is infinitely cunning in the invention of new weapons."[1]

Cary dwells not only on danger but also on the power of the individual human mind to confront a reality consisting of "highly obstinate facts,"[2] to contend with it, and to create a situation conducive to the realization of the good and the beautiful. All such acts must begin with the individual, for, as Cary says, "We are almost entirely cut off from each other in

1. Joyce Cary, "Liberty or Freedom," unpublished essay, the Bodleian Library, Oxford.

2. Joyce Cary, *Art and Reality: Ways of the Creative Process* (New York: Harper & Brothers, 1958), 6.

mind, entirely independent in thought, and so we have to learn everything for ourselves" (9). But we are not cut off in feeling. From his insistence on the role of the individual imagination in making a life comes the structure of the trilogies. I shall risk bifurcating content and form, theme and structure in order to simplify the discussion, but I shall try to show in the end that both are one, emerging from a single concern.

First, the theme of artistic creation. The theme is appropriate for a trilogy on the imagination because, of all human activities, art symbolizes most intensively the creativity, or imagination, of human beings. Gulley Jimson is an artist—a painter, and, further, he is an obstinately independent and original painter who is constantly abandoning his old style for a new and, he is convinced, better expression. He even abandons paintings for which he has had immense enthusiasm in order to begin new ones. One of the major motifs in *The Horse's Mouth* is Jimson's repeated quotation from and reference to Blake, who takes on the role of Jimson's spiritual mentor—a painter who stubbornly insisted on a style that was not *in* style and preached the gospel of art in such remarks as "Prayer is the Study of Art" and "You must leave Fathers & Mothers & Houses & Lands if they stand in the way of Art."[3] Jimson has followed these precepts as best he can and to a fault, leaving his secure job, his wife, and child to pursue painting. The narrators of the other two novels of the trilogy are also, of course, possessed of imagination, but of lesser degrees of power and self-awareness. Each copes with reality from his or her position; each builds up a world, or seeks to protect a world. Sometimes the latter is impossible; Thomas Wilcher of *To Be a Pilgrim* suffers in this situation, and there is an air of loss and tragedy about his life, though in the end he seems redeemed by his hard-won ability finally to accept change, even welcome it as he regrets it. Sara Monday's creativity is chiefly domestic. She is a natural artist at making a nest. In fact, Jimson identifies her with Mother Nature herself.

Second, structure. We the readers observe how each narrator constructs his or her world and how each has designs on the reader. This means

---

3. David V. Erdman, ed., "The Laocoön," *The Complete Poetry and Prose of William Blake*, rev. ed. (Garden City, NY: Anchor Press/Doubleday, 1982), 273.

that Cary never speaks directly to us and that we must depend entirely on the narrators for our understanding even of simple fact. This has bothered some critics because, as I have indicated, it appears to them that he abdicates making judgments on people or events. Furthermore, some say, we cannot be sure of what really happened. We do not know whom to trust, if anyone. There is a sense, I suppose, in which this is true; there is a stubborn reality against which we all come up. But there is also a sense in which the human world is always being made by those who participate in it. In fact, "in it" is not quite correct. We would have to make "participate" a transitive verb and say that Cary's characters participate a world in the way that players of games make the game, though not the rules. Judgment of Cary's people can be made by asking the questions: How full a world is each able to make? What judgment does each individual consciously or unconsciously make on himself or herself through establishment of the limits of his or her vision? The judgment Cary invites us to make is on imaginative power in the face of the real.

Each novel is written from a different point in time as well as by a different imagination, each includes the appearance, however brief (but telling), of the two others, and each concentrates on a different period of time. The events that come before us exist only through these narrators, and each constructs the other two narrators in his or her way. This triple form, of which *The Horse's Mouth* is chronologically the third, Cary illustrates in his preface to *Herself Surprised* by commenting on Sara as follows:

> . . . as she sees herself [she is] the victim of mysterious events and her own soft heart; as Wilcher sees her . . . , the devoted and unselfish servant and mistress; as Jimson sees her . . . , cunning, vain, lecherous, self-deceiving, a man-catcher, whose devotion is a cloak for her secret instinctive and everlasting design to build herself a nest somewhere in the world, even if she has to murder a man's soul to christen the foundation.[4]

4. Joyce Cary, "Prefatory Essay," *Herself Surprised* (1941), Carfax ed. (London: Michael Joseph, 1951), 11.

Usually when we are confronted with different views of the same object, we fall back on the venerable idea that each view is subjective and there-fore either wrong or woefully partial, like those of the blind men feeling the elephant. Further, we tend to assume that there is possible an objective stance that will transcend the subjective and reveal the truth. But Cary's novels are good examples of a dramatic contrary to object-subject. Cary treats all three views of Sara as correct; they are not objective, nor are they subjec-tive. They express relationships—between Sara and herself, Wilcher and Sara, Jimson and Sara. Some of these views are larger than others, more expressive of imaginative power. One notices that even in Cary's prefaces, written well after the novels first appeared, this seems implied.

The Horse's Mouth

Jimson's view is imaginatively the largest of the three. He also has the largest ego and the most complex view of things. Further, he is the most single-minded, the most self-conscious, the wittiest, the most exuberant, the most mercurial, and the most verbally inventive. As a result, he seems to be the most masked, an actor on a stage who knows his part and knows he is act-ing. He is the one who makes language work for him, while the other two tend often to fall victim to the limitations of their thought and language. One of the most impressive things about *Herself Surprised* and *To Be a Pil-grim* is how Cary invests the narrative voices with clichés that reveal char-acter. Their tropes are different from Jimson's. Sara's are homely and rarely surprising. Though she has her design on the reader, her manner is so habit-ual that it seems unconscious of its craftiness. Wilcher's characterizing of himself on the very first page as an "unfaithful servant" tells much of his certain kind of piety. The metaphorical limitation of each does not in the end diminish the speakers; it reveals them sympathetically; we enter into their lives through their languages.

Jimson's tropes are far more varied, often hyperbolical, and, as might be expected of a painter, visual. He is more interested in scene and the mask he has made for himself than in narrative. Cary presents this to us in the very first sentences of the novel: "I was walking by the Thames. Half-past morning on an autumn day. Sun in a mist. Like an orange in a fried fish shop. All bright below. Low tide, dusty water and a crooked bar of straw, chicken-boxes, dirt and oil from mud to mud. Like a viper swimming in skim milk."[5] Jimson does not specify a date for this event, though we later learn he was just out of prison when it occurred. To specify a time would be for him abstract. His eye is on constructing his memory as scene, the particularity of the experience, the detail and the suggestivity of it. When he is not giving us the object, he is inventing the symbolic possibilities of the scene. The verbal simile of the "viper swimming in skim milk" leads him to "the old serpent, symbol of nature and love," the serpent of Eden seen in Gnostic tradition. The movement in the passage is a microcosm of Jimson's artistic career, from his early "lyrical" stage, as he calls it, where he tried to see things clearly as they are, so to speak, to his epic stage, in which he created huge symbolic works based on the Bible under the inspiration of Blake.

Jimson's gesture as a whole is not conventionally autobiographical. He tells us only in asides about certain things that we would want in the foreground of an autobiography. We only very sketchily learn about his father, his first job, his early marriage, his son, and so forth. The actual temporal duration of his narrative is less than a year in 1938–39, the last months of his life, though there are flashbacks. The memoir apparently stands adequately in his own mind for what he is, like a self-portrait that fixes on a moment but expands symbolically—as the viper becomes the Gnostic serpent—to include by synecdoche his whole being and meaning. His memoir is entirely a dramatic performance.

For Jimson, the verbal equivalent of a painting (at least his kind of painting) is a highly figurative piece of verbal exuberance. For example, the following is the way Jimson describes Thomas Wilcher in their first meeting:

> Wilcher was a rich lawyer, with a face like a bad orange. Yellow and blue. A little grasshopper of a man. Five feet of shiny broadcloth and three inches of collar. Always on the jump. Inside or out. In his fifties. The hopping fifties. And fierce as a mad mouse. Genus, Boorjwar;

5. Joyce Cary, *The Horse's Mouth* (1944), Carfax ed. (London: Michael Joseph, 1951), 11.

species, Blackcotius Begoggledus Ferocissimouse. All eaten up with
lawfulness and rage. . . . (183)

And here is a moment of their conversation:

At this Mr. W. sprang clean through the ceiling, turned several som-
ersaults in mid air, sang a short psalm of praise and thanksgiving out
of the Song of Solomon, accompanied on the shawm, and returned
through the letter box draped in celestial light. That is to say, he raised
his right toe slightly from the carpet, said "indeed". . . . (184)

The description moves to greater and greater feats of exuberance. It makes
light of Wilcher's careful reserve by claiming to have discovered beneath
it the epic violence of Wilcher's suppressed feelings. It takes an apparently
trivial moment and opens it up to reveal its possibilities. The passage is a
friendly parody of Blake, whose exuberant hyperbole Jimson endeavors to
equal in the paintings of his later epic style. It is this style that is characteristic of the memoir as a whole.

When Jimson parodies Blake, he consciously parodies himself. This
self-parody is one way Jimson plays a role, masks himself, expresses an ironic
view of his own situation, and frees himself of anxiety. It is part of a deliberate means he has of coping with a world that has little interest in art and
cares as little for the fate of those who produce it. Jimson could express
bitterness about this situation, but in fact he deliberately makes a comedy
of it in order to save himself from the self-destructiveness he sees in bitterness. Bitterness can only prevent him from getting on with the next painting. It is his effort to concentrate on the possibilities of the future that enables
him to survive the substantial disappointments of the present. When his
huge epic work in progress called "The Fall" is destroyed, his young idol-
ator Nosy Barbon is outraged, but Jimson calms him and declares himself
full of new energy. Why? He has learned to protect himself in this way, by
means of an eccentric self-discipline: "I almost burst out laughing at Nosy's
indignation. And I decided to give way to my gaiety. It's not an easy thing
to do when you have a real grievance, and if I had been fifty years younger
I shouldn't have done it. But for some time now I had been noticing that

on the whole a man is wise to give way to gaiety, even at the expense of a grievance" (169). Here Jimson has deliberately created the idea that gaiety is the fundamental human emotion. It is implied that other emotions, including bitterness, are merely suppressions of this basic human quality, which is good. Whether this is so or not (and probably for Jimson it is not), his insistence declares at least that it should be so and man should try to make it so. This is consistent with the idea that man can, to some extent at least, create the conditions of his existence. But it is at an enormous expense. A certain sadness is revealed behind the mask of exuberance, which is a defense against that large part of the real that he cannot control.

Jimson's response to the painting's destruction illustrates the tyranny that a work in progress can perpetrate on the artist, for as it begins to take shape, it also begins to dictate the range of moves an artist can make, narrowing that range with every artistic act. With the painting destroyed, Jimson is released to savor the full freedom of beginning a new work. The first stroke of the brush is the best: "It must be one of the keenest pleasures open to mankind. It's certainly the greatest that an artist can have. It's also the only one. And it doesn't last long—usually about five minutes. Before the first problem shows its devil face" (170). As the artist must struggle to deal with his picture, so also must the man struggle to make true his idea of gaiety as the fundamental emotion. He must create that reality. One senses in Jimson's gaiety, therefore, a certain desperation. After all, in order to pursue his art, he must steal or hoodwink so that he can obtain canvas and paint. As Sara Monday knows, he is subject to fits of temper. He eventually causes her death by pushing her down a stairway in an effort to get back from her an old sketch he thinks he can sell to obtain more materials.

Jimson constructs an offense against a society to which an artist is profoundly alien. That offense, in the end, goes badly wrong. Far better a poetic offense. It is an offense that has its gaps. Just as Jimson cannot always control his temper, he cannot always control his despair. His manner is therefore, when it is successful, an accomplishment, a product of imagination, though some might call it a piece of chicanery, and Jimson does turn to chicanery at times. Since his concept of creation is always directed toward the future, there is no doubt that he likes to think of himself as perpetually being made.

Cary apparently had in mind locating in the travails of Jimson some of the problems of the artist in the modern world as well as some of the artist's eternal problems. Of these latter, the gap between intuition and expression is one that most interests Cary. He devoted a considerable amount of space to it in his book *Art and Reality*.[6] Jimson constantly laments that his intuition is too great for his technique. In the process of trying to express his intuitions, he loses them. The work in its unfinished state asserts its own life and drags the artist in directions he did not intend. And the artist is at the mercy of external forces. He is lucky if he can obtain a patron, but this patron will probably soon ask him to return to an earlier style that he has outgrown and come to detest. For the modern artist, the gap between the popular and what he himself regards as worth doing is critical.

The Horse's Mouth can be regarded as not merely about art in the specialized modern sense of the word but about the whole life of imagination—the artist at life in each of us. Jimson provides an extreme example. His career raises all the issues, and he knows that it does. He has deliberately constructed his story to do so. Yet he perseveres through laughter and through a disciplined ability to see things clearly and in a light unencumbered by cliché. He is, at sixty-eight, able to express the wonder of things in the world around him, which never goes stale. Yet this is a quality of mind that he has to re-earn every day of his life. He fondly recalls lines from Blake's notebook, which he creatively misquotes as follows:

> The Angel that presided at her birth
> Said, little creature, born of joy and mirth
> Go love without the help of anything on earth. (129)[7]

We are all alone in mind, Cary says, but not in feeling. The imagination must take us out of ourselves into others, commit antithetically the metaphor

6. See also my *Joyce Cary's Trilogies: Pursuit of the Particular Real* (Tallahassee: Florida State University Press, 1983), 5–7, which quotes from unpublished material by Cary.

7. Also 297. Blake wrote in his notebook: "The Angel that presided oer my birth / Said Little creature formd of Joy & Mirth / Go love without the help of any King on Earth" (502).

of identity and relation against all negations. This is the ethic art presents. It is to run risks. Sometimes we fail (and some of Jimson's offensive defenses lead to failure). Sometimes no one is listening. Yet the imagination is all that we have by which we may declare ourselves formed of joy and mirth. It was very nearly all that the world gave to Jimson, and he made something of it, though he suffered for it, too. In the end, he killed someone out of desperation and by mistake. We could say that the comedy of *The Horse's Mouth* is a mask, that it is a tragedy. But it is both. As Blake said, "Joy & Woe are woven fine" (491).

It is well at this point to remind ourselves of the presence of the arranger who has juxtaposed these narrations and their narrators. The lack of authorial voice has been a stumbling block for some critics of Cary. He has been accused of creating a world of indeterminacy. Another criticism, connected with this, expresses the reviewer's puzzlement as Cary's fault. In 1944, *The Horse's Mouth* was described by a reviewer in the *Times Literary Supplement* as "portentously trifling and fatiguing to read." In 1952, the complaint about *Prisoner of Grace* was that "The reader is never quite clear whether the story illustrates the incredible complications of human relationship where love and marriage are concerned, or whether our attention should be concentrated on the course of a typical political career during the last fifty years." Chester Nimmo's career is hardly typical, and the reviewer seems incapable of reading a novel that resists reduction to an abstract idea.

In 1958, the *Times Literary Supplement* was unsympathetic to Cary in a review of the first book published about his work, Andrew Wright's *Joyce Cary: A Preface to His Novels*. Cary had character and imagination but lacked intellect, and his themes were inclined to "get lost or tangled up under the multicoloured tumble of words deliriously and often splendidly out of hand." The second trilogy failed quite seriously in "other than human terms." This is astounding, for one wonders what other terms there are for a novelist or poet. Then we discover what the reviewer really disliked: Cary had no "real grasp of the politics of the first quarter of this century." The confusion here is compounded by a literal-minded demand for historical accuracy, based probably on the reviewer's own political views. He wants to pigeonhole Cary and his work. But Cary seems to have rejected such critical approaches.

To those on the left, Cary must have seemed uncomfortably out of step and his colonial service enough evidence to solidify suspicion. They must have been more than nervous when Cary saw ineradicable evil, when he analyzed profoundly and prophetically for his time the problems of Africa and expressed skepticism about sudden wholesale change there. Those on the right must have thought him a dangerously independent thinker, a critic of colonialism, the attributer of at least some evil to law and order, the employer of the word "God" in an unfamiliar and suspect way, and a preacher of what seemed to be ethical relativism. It is no surprise that Alan Bishop in his biography of Cary remarks that he has always been a controversial novelist.

It will also come as no surprise to learn that I regard this situation to be the result of Cary's antithetical offense as a thoughtful writer on the themes of both art and politics.

Antithetical Politics

I have just observed that Cary was sometimes criticized from a political position as a result of his antithetical position opposed to the usual political oppositions. This will take me into Cary's treatment of childhood and the Blakean states of innocence and experience, for politics begins in childhood.

In an essay of 1955 written for a French periodical and titled "L'influence britannique dans la révolution libérale," Cary discusses the development of British liberalism and its powerful global influence. He observes that the great nineteenth-century political figures of Europe thought that the British were anarchists "tearing Europe to pieces." All this time, the British "saw themselves not only as liberators, but as the one reasonable people in Europe. For them, absolutism, repression, were supreme follies which perpetrated disorder."[8] Cary asserts that he is not saying that the British were right in what they thought or did; indeed, he holds that they were often as naive as Herzen or Tolstoy, and he goes on to observe that the early British liberals were unable to realize that "votes and popu-

---

8. Joyce Cary, "Britain's Liberal Influence," *Selected Essays*, ed. A. G. Bishop (London: Michael Joseph, 1976), 215.

lar assemblies" didn't cure everything: " . . . they do not even begin to cure ignorance, and . . . they are very likely to increase poverty" (215). Democracy Cary sees as the product of a "long process of industrial and social development . . . a balance of powers between forces all capable of fighting the central government; but held in some kind of unity by a common history, common ambitions, especially common fears" (215). But in a primitive community, this balance does not work because the community lacks the trade and professional forces that can stand up to governmental power and the education to foresee the consequences of actions. Cary concludes that, for good or evil, an undeveloped society has to have a strong government. The earliest revolutionary liberals did not understand this, but they did know that human beings seek freedom and hate restraint, accepting control only for some convincing reason that it will increase freedom from ignorance and want.

For Cary, there are principally two kinds of ignorance: the ignorance of the primitive and poverty-stricken, of which he had seen much during his time with the British colonial service in Africa, and the ignorance of childhood, the emergence from which he considers in numerous works but especially in *A House of Children*, *Charley Is My Darling*, and the posthumously collected *Spring Song and Other Stories*.

With ignorance go naïveté and innocence. Blake's distinction between innocence and experience is significant for Cary, but he gives it an individual twist, creating a corollary, darker negative distinction between ignorance and abstract power. Cary looks back with great interest on his own childhood, and in *A House of Children*, based in part on it, he recalls childhood with a certain affection, but neither the innocent nor the experienced state is sentimentalized. Innocence is, at once, the beginning of experience. Certain characteristics of the child persist in adults. The two contrary states, as Blake called them, threaten to negate each other in the sentimentalization of one and a granting of the only firm grasp of reality to the other. In *A House of Children*, Cary's narrator remarks:

> I don't know when my childhood ended or if it is all ended now. The only certain distinction I can find between childhood and maturity is that children grow in experience and look forward to novelty; that

old people tend to be set. This does not mean even that children enjoy life more keenly than grown-ups, they are only more eager for experience. Grown-ups live and love, they suffer and enjoy far more intensely than children; but for the most part on a narrower front. For the average man or woman of forty, however successful, has been so battered and crippled by various accidents that he has gradually been restricted to a small compass of enterprise.[9]

Childish eagerness for experience Cary also speaks of as will. Finally he connects it with power.[10] It is not so much a will to power as a power to will and of will; this power he identifies with imagination.

Cary's children are unique individuals with innate imaginative power. As he observes in the preface to the Carfax edition of *Charley Is My Darling*, children are already possessed of complex motivations that are not different in kind from those of adults.[11] But they have only a little experience and are therefore often deeply confused. They have "powerful imaginations and weak control" (8), and these imaginations and wills to experience put them into situations in which they are always testing the real and the law: " . . . it has always seemed to me that every ordinary child is by nature a delinquent, that the only difference between us as children was the extent of our delinquency, whether we were found out in it and how we were punished for it" (5).

This remark is followed by an account of a crime Cary himself committed at the age of seven. It was the tearing out of doorbells of the houses of various townspeople in the Donegal village of Moville. In the child, temptation, inspiration, and the desire for experience are not far apart. When combined with confusion or boredom, they can become criminal.

9. Joyce Cary, *A House of Children* (1940), Carfax ed. (London: Michael Joseph, 1951), 66.

10. See Cary's *Power in Men* (1939), 2nd ed., with my introduction (Seattle: University of Washington Press, 1963). Cary identifies power with creative imagination. For further discussion of this, see my *Joyce Cary's Trilogies*, esp. 52–58.

11. Joyce Cary, *Charley Is My Darling* (1940), Carfax ed. (London: Michael Joseph, 1951), 7.

In the preface to *Charley Is My Darling*, Cary observes that the child faces a world that is also a "moral structure" and that nature has equipped him with parents for the purpose of providing him with experience and judgment. If they fail to do so, he suffers, and the imagination goes wrong: "I am ready to bet that a good deal of what is called neurosis and frustration among young children is due to nothing but the failure of parents and teachers (often the most conscientious) . . . to give a clear picture without uncertainties. Without such a picture, children don't know where they are, and they do all kinds of evil (because it is just this sphere of good and evil that is puzzling them) to find out" (9).

At the same time, children have "great powers of putting away and ignoring fears or even actual sufferings" (*House*, 135). Cary saw the same capacity in the destitute Africans he observed during times of famine and disease. In a position similar to a child's, they had no alternative but resignation: "They were so completely ignorant and unable to help themselves, that their only defence against what seemed to them the cruel fantasies of chance and the mysterious injustice of nature, was resignation" (*House*, 135-36). But this attitude was not the resignation of the defeated; it was more like "a magic cloak of the soul, put on to make the wearer invisible and impregnable" (*House*, 136). It was a tragic expression of imagination in a situation of ignorance and want. Cary isn't claiming, as the early revolutionary liberals might have, that the African primitive tribesman is a child. He is saying that he is deprived by ignorance and poverty of the freedom that imagination can generate under better conditions. To Cary, these Africans were no different from the British in their fundamental human traits, in their will to freedom. Both children and adults would fight against authority, defy law, some even to death.

Cary observes that the primitive tribe tends to disintegrate when tribal authority is relaxed and there is a means of escape into a life that seems to promise greater freedom. Part of this is the result of the desire to satisfy curiosity, to gratify frustrated desires, ambition, love, and family hopes. These are things that bind all people together.

But the imagination is a power for evil as well as good. It is not the innocence of the "noble savage," and there is for Cary absolutely nothing in the least sacrosanct about the state of nature, which is a fantasy form of innocence, not its reality. Writing in the preface to *Charley Is My Darling*, Cary remarks,

> The wrecking of the house in this story was taken from fact, when even younger boys did greater damage. And such raids were not at all uncommon. They are sometimes expressions of boredom; sometimes of hatred, a rage against beauty and dignity by those who have neither but feel the want; sometimes they arise from the ordinary dynamics of gangster politics (which now rule half the world), the leader's need to invent new and exciting enterprises for his band, but I think above all from the secret hunger of a starved imagination, not only for aesthetic but moral comprehension. (10)

In *Charley Is My Darling*, Charley Brown is a fifteen-year-old Londoner evacuated to the west-country village of Burlswood during the Second World War. He is small for his age, discovered to be infested with lice, of shaved head as a result, and without friends. His stepmother has been ineffectual. Yet he possesses an imaginative power well in excess of those into whose presence he has been intruded. He marshals this power in defense against the other evacuated children, whom he sees as threats to his well-being, even his survival. In time, by means of many daring escapades, he achieves a tenuous hold on leadership of a small gang of "vackies," but he must continue to invent new plans in order to maintain that hold on them. Beginning with the release of a farmer's bull and the theft of beer, Charley proceeds through a series of ever more daring thefts to the wrecking of the interior of the manor house of Burlswood itself. This is the beginning of his undoing, for he is apprehended; but even then he escapes from the remand house and rejoins his fourteen-year-old girlfriend Lizzie, only to be apprehended once again and to face three years' incarceration.

Charley's is a case of an imagination that outstrips maturation, in part because it is under severe stress, an imagination so active as to be starved for experience, an imagination both fantastical and practical, but under the rule of boredom and resentment at a bewildering world of adult law and convention. When he and Lizzie, now pregnant, are captured, each is separately accused of ill treatment of the other. Both reject this interpretation, but neither has words or experience with which to express their deeply held feelings for each other. I quote at length from near the end of the novel, where Charley is before the magistrates:

"Do you realize, I wonder, what a terrible wrong you have done her?"

Charley feels again the impact of that will to shame him, to drive him down into the pit of remorse and despair. Startled, he turns red and looks at the woman; from her to the two kind gentlemen who have been talking to him in so friendly a manner. In all these faces, but more plainly in the woman's, he sees the same resolution. He exclaims: "But, Mum, Lizzie and me, we was—" He stops and tries to hold down a sudden impulse to weep, to allow himself to be shamed.

But angry and obstinate nerves within him stiffen against surrender; he feels he is not really guilty at all, that Lina and the nice magistrates still don't understand the situation. He can't explain it, but it isn't in the least like their idea of it. He frowns at them, looks sullen and defiant.

"To be honest, Brown," the eldest and kindest of the gentlemen, with a little white moustache and round spectacles, speaks to Charley: "Your attitude toward the whole affair strikes us all," he looks at the others who look acquiescent, "strikes us all as extraordinarily cool, to say the least of it, even callous, though I don't like to use the word. I am thinking not of the wanton destruction at Burls House, though that was bad enough, but your treatment of this poor girl, Bessie Galor. We are trying to help you, you understand—but it is difficult to do anything for you if you take up this attitude that nothing much has happened and that you've done nothing to be ashamed of."

"If you take that view," the lady said, "but I hope I'm wrong, there's no hope for you at all. None whatever."

In two minutes Charley is once more in tears. He can't speak. But now, underneath this violent hysterical emotion, there is fury like steel, a deep resolute anger. It is the protest of all his honesty against a lie, and a defilement. (328–29)

Lizzie, for her part, is anxious to defend Charley against these incomprehensible adult judgments and is herself accused of leading him on. Their affection for each other finds itself antithetical to two opposed versions of their relationship, in both of which one is guilty of treating the innocent other badly. These versions are abstract. One is that of the aggressive male, the other that of the seductive female. The children's mode of experiencing is highly concrete. They are together in feeling without developed intellects. The adults possess relatively developed minds and waning capacities for empathetic identification with another. The result is that Charley wishes to strike out in defense against the world, and the adults cannot understand the feeling in the children's relationship. When he and Lizzie are finally separated and Lizzie faints, the policeman thinks it is from hunger.

One senses in Cary's writings from the beginning, but gradually intensified in the second trilogy, representation of an inexplicable evil that lurks always in the process of gaining experience, a possible product of the inevitable struggle between the desire for unbridled liberty and the restraint necessary to convert it into freedom, which for Cary is a condition of ever-expanding knowledge and absence of want. The liberals erred: "I was myself a liberal, like most of the young people of my time. In fact, like so many at that time, I overlooked the enormous power of evil working incessantly to destroy happiness and peace anywhere in the world. I had forgotten how many people take actual pleasure in evil, in spreading lies, and building hatred, and that they are incurable."[12]

In addition to the cruel, there are the misguided, who, seeing lies and evil all around them, turn to repression, revenge, and law as simple answers. Such a one is the hapless Jim Latter of *Not Honour More*. Of him, Cary remarks,

> He is a perfectly honest man and he is not a cruel man. He is like those people who hate drink, which is a real evil, and who say why don't we stop it by law. That is to say . . . they're people who want to make the world good by law. The only way is by education and

12. Joyce Cary, "Joyce Cary's Last Look at His Worlds," *Selected Essays*, 246.

by trusting them and giving them a sense of responsibility as free men to behave like good citizens and they won't have a sense of responsibility if you push them around by law.[13]

But this does not in any way mean that Cary glorifies the notion of freedom simply as an absence of restraint. Such would be a prolongation of a corruptible innocence, a monstrosity. Nor do Cary's claims for education imply some possible perfectibility for man even in the very distant future. There will be no eradication of evil, even though it is usually man-made. As for the idea of a final shape for society, " . . . if it ever arrived, [it] would be one not of peace and justice, security and comfort, but of limited insecurity, limited physical misery on the one hand, and on the other, richer possibilities of experience, both in fulfilment and despair. The tragic dilemma of freedom is incurable."[14] There would be no sentimentalized renewal of innocence here, nor any synthesis of innocence and experience.

Political acts are played out from childhood through old age. The child's earliest politics are anarchic, then tribal. He can express imaginative power in opposition to external restraint, but his freedom comes not in the triumph over restraint but in achievement of a condition of tension between liberty and restraint that is productive of greater knowledge and greater freedom from want. Freedom is antithetical to the negation liberty-restraint.

The principal political drama played out in Cary's works is the personal struggle, frequently a blind one, to gain some such antithetical tension, but often in conditions that thwart the attempt. This is one of the issues in Cary's best-known novel of Africa, *Mister Johnson*, in which Johnson, a poor African clerk in an isolated British colonial office, is ultimately destroyed by the strength of his own imagination in a condition of ignorance and want as well as the limitations of those from whom he takes his orders. He glimpses a better life and cannot keep that golden world separate from the conditions that surround him. Clearly far more imagina-

---

13. Joyce Cary, "The Political Novel," broadcast on the BBC series *Window on the World*, July 1955, quoted by Malcolm Foster, *Joyce Cary: A Biography* (Boston: Houghton Mifflin Co., 1968), 489.

14. Joyce Cary, "Prefatory Essay," *Castle Corner* (1950), Carfax ed. (London: Michael Joseph, 1952), 7.

tive and inventive than the dull and fixed colonial officers for whom he works, he invents illicit ways to doctor the office books in order to free money for his boss Rudbeck to build a road connecting his area to the larger world of commerce. Johnson does this in spite of the duplicitous opposition of the local emir and his "Waziri," and with only the dogged, mindless persistence of Rudbeck, who condones his transgressions without really understanding them. Johnson endures enormous suffering and causes much of it himself. Along with a certain charisma and imaginative power that determines him to build the road, he has a reckless inability to prevent his imagination from overwhelming his sense of reality. As events conspire against him, mostly as a result of his own bold schemes, he takes to simple theft in order to carry them out. Ultimately he murders a white store-owner in a moment of panic. We recognize that he has possessed insufficient knowledge to accompany his imagination. His white boss Rudbeck, who is his executioner, has more knowledge but is deficient in imagination. At the end, it is possible that Rudbeck knows Johnson has in certain ways been his leader. He comes to recognize that he himself bears some responsibility for what has happened. In the last few pages of the novel, a magnanimous Johnson refuses to allow Rudbeck to take blame, but part of the reason for this is that Johnson wants to preserve his golden and totally unrealistic notion of Rudbeck. It is unrealistic, but, at the same time, it is Johnson's imaginative power that has brought Rudbeck to some minimal imaginative activity.

The vision of an achieved freedom, a sustaining contrary to the tension between liberty and restraint, is also Cary's contrary to the negating opposition of liberalism to conservatism, without which there will be, in his neo-Blakean view, no progression. The tension opposes the threat of fall into either anarchy or totalitarianism. It is the vision not of a golden world but of a livable one. In his last essay, published posthumously in 1957, the year of his death, Cary observed,

It is quite certain that in twenty-five years the present day will seem even more remote than 1900 does now. For the revolution of the free mind goes faster as that mind invents new tools. We live, literally, in the creation, and every year there are more creative imaginations at work. And more, much more, for them to feed on. The world grows more tense, more dangerous, but also infinitely richer in experience. There is no more happiness, perhaps less, but very much more intensity of living, more occupation for the mind and the senses.[15]

It is a world of incessant human desire for experience and the struggle of good and evil that results from it.

Cary always wanted to look at particulars, and this, no doubt, led him to the dramatic presentation of his narrators in the trilogies. In them, one senses the identity of the arranger with his narrators. Cary was deeply interested in fairness to individuals, even to politicians: "Before we call any statesman a fool or a crook we should ask what problems he faced, what kind of people he had to handle, what kind of support he got, what pressure he withstood, what risks he took."[16] I add: what recognition in his actions he gave to individual imagination and how he sought to increase freedom—in Cary's sense of the word. Cary's is an antithetical politics of experience, in which identity with others is an ethical imperative.

15. Joyce Cary, "Joyce Cary's Last Look at His Worlds," *Selected Essays*, 247.
16. Joyce Cary, "Political and Personal Morality," *Selected Essays*, 232.

11

Seamus Heaney's Criticism and the Antithetical

Inquiry into Joyce Cary's antitheticality took us into questions of the relation of art to politics. Not deeply involved in politics as we usually think of it, he did contribute a book, *Power in Men* (1939), to the short-lived Liberal Book Club. Seamus Heaney, on the other hand, was born and educated in Northern Ireland, experienced the "troubles" there, and was closely associated with the Field Day Theatre group, which included a number of artistic and intellectual activists. It is not too much to say that his was the kind of situation that can create a crisis for a poet and his art. Heaney recognized this and put the demands of art prior to but not apart from politics. Best known as a Nobel Prize–winning poet, Heaney has also published collections of his critical essays and lectures, and they take a stand antithetical to abstract political doctrine, even as they recognize that politics is a part of the poet's experience and thus material for poetic expression.

Recently the critical discourses of poets have not been taken very seriously in academic halls. Indeed, it is difficult to discover theorists well-acquainted with such discourses. And it is a little more difficult than an outsider might think to discover a theorist deeply interested in poetry. This last phenomenon has to do with the impatience of many theorists with literary values, techniques, and traditions that seem to them irrelevant to political content or at least difficult to assimilate to it. Seamus Heaney was forthright about this matter in a 1991 essay:

> Nowadays, undergraduates are being taught prematurely to regard the poetic heritage as an oppressive imposition and to suspect it for its latent discriminations in the realm of gender, its privilegings and marginalizations in the realms of class and power. All of this suspicion may be salutary enough when it is exercised by a mind informed

by that which it is being taught to suspect, but it is a suspicion which is lamentably destructive of cultural memory when it is induced in minds without any cultural possessions whatever.[1]

All of this is by no means entirely the fault, if one thinks it a fault (I do), of some academicians, but some of it is.

Through the early career of T. S. Eliot, most of the principal critical and even theoretical statements written in English that we highly value and anthologize were made by poets, novelists, and dramatists tacitly or explicitly defending what they regarded as their own practices. As any anthology of criticism and theory will show, the situation is now radically different. Hardly any contemporary poet, dramatist, or novelist now gains entry into the academic anthologies of criticism and theory, and the estrangement between poets and theorists is pronounced except in a few special cases where a writer has deliberately created works that live on the border. All of this has occurred in spite of assertions by many theorists that the line between imaginative literature and theoretical discourse has been effectively erased, even that "literature" is an obsolete word. One notes that it is theorists who say these things (I know few poets who do), which suggests that the line may have been only theoretically erased and that what has been happening among some theorists is the attempt to develop a new and different sort of theoretical discourse—a new category, but one that seems more hermetically sealed and specialized even as it seems to claim the disappearance of all boundaries.

Place and Identity

Heaney is not easily fitted into the scene I have described. He has published five collections of critical essays including *Preoccupations: Selected Prose 1968–1978* (1980), *The Government of the Tongue* (1988), *The Place of Writing* (1989), and *The Redress of Poetry* (1995). Recently, parts of these

---

1. Seamus Heaney, "On Poetry and Professing" (1991), *Finders Keepers: Selected Prose 1971–2001* (London: Faber and Faber, 2002), 71–72.

have been collected along with later essays in *Finders Keepers, Selected Prose 1971–2001* (2002). All of these essays were written in the decades in which the developments to which I refer have taken place. Although in recent years Heaney has spent a certain amount of time in the United States (principally when he was Boylston Professor of Rhetoric and Oratory at Harvard), his criticism reflects the Irish situation, though he has been aware of the more general issues involving trends in criticism and theory to which I have referred. Indeed, it is the strenuous relation between his sense of vocation as a poet and the depressing political events in Ireland that has given to his critical essays a thematic center, sometimes directly, sometimes tacitly expressed. His criticism is engaged, though he is always cautionary about the nature of that engagement, as I shall try to show, and his cautionary statements seem to have been frequently directed by implication at other Irish critics (often friends), though they are also meant as comments on the general situation of the critic and the poet beyond the boundary of purely local concerns.

There is very little reference to recent critical and theoretical discourse familiar to American academics in Heaney's essays (virtually none in *The Redress of Poetry*), and almost no use of its jargon, though what little there is indicates acquaintance with some of it—the work of Roland Barthes and of Deconstruction in general. One indirect reference to Barthes occurs in a discussion of a poem by Patrick Kavanagh, in which Heaney describes his own response: "What was being experienced was not some hygienic and self-aware pleasure of the text but a primitive delight in finding world become word."[2] This is not, I think, meant to be critical of Barthes's assumptions about the pleasure of reading so much as to try to isolate Kavanagh's particular value (about which more later), a recasting of Friedrich Schiller's old distinction between naive and sentimental poetry, not at the expense of the sentimental so much as in the interest of expressing a need in Irish poetry that Kavanagh fulfilled or at least nearly fulfilled. Another more recent mention of Barthes invokes him in sup-

---

2. Seamus Heaney, "The Placeless Heaven: Another Look at Kavanagh," *The Government of the Tongue* (London: Faber and Faber, 1989), 8.

port of Heaney's own long meditation on the stressful relation of poetry to politics.[3]

The other references or implied allusions to recent theory involve Deconstruction and are rather general and loose with respect to any rigorous understanding of theoretical practices. In a discussion of Yeats and others in *The Place of Writing*, Heaney views Yeats as a heroic self-deconstructionist of sorts, arguing for Yeats's process of unwriting his previous writings and indicating that "any writing is to some extent an unwriting not only of previous writings but even of itself" (*Place*, 56). He observes that since this has always been the case, the elaboration of the awareness of unwriting into "systems of reading" has resulted more or less in New Critical procedures rather than a new perception (*Place*, 56). Many would regard this view as unexceptionable, even though there is a little edge to it, similar to Blackmur's bemoaning of the decline of the New Criticism into mechanical method. Heaney is nothing if not evenhanded in such remarks. He is even deliberately somewhat self-effacing in the foreword to *Preoccupations* when he characterizes his own critical work as "the slightly constricted utterance of somebody who underwent his academic rite of passage when practical criticism held great sway in the academy."[4] In *The Government of the Tongue*, he praises the critical procedures of Geoffrey Grigson on Auden. They are not so up-to-date as Stan Smith's deconstructive readings, which, he observes, "yield many excellent insights," for Grigson is not so strictly analytical. Nevertheless, his kind of activity is "not superseded, because it is so closely allied, as an act of reading, to what happens during the poet's act of writing" (*Preoccupations*, 120). I shall turn to this as exemplary of an interest Heaney never abandons, but it must first be observed that his account of Yeats in *The Place of Writing*, the Richard Ellmann Lectures given at Emory University in 1988, is not easy to imagine apart from a critical climate in which Deconstruction was a significant force. This is true even though Heaney's account emerges from consider-

3. Seamus Heaney, "The Pre-Natal Mountain: Vision and Irony in Recent Irish Poetry," *The Place of Writing* (Atlanta: Scholars Press, 1989), 37.

4. Seamus Heaney, Foreword, *Preoccupations: Selected Prose 1968–1978* (London: Faber and Faber, 1984), 13–14.

ation of some remarks by Ellmann, hardly a postmodernist, on Yeats. Heaney's thesis in the Ellmann lectures is twofold: " . . . that the poetic imagination in its strongest manifestation imposes its vision upon a place rather than accepts a vision from it; and that this visionary imposition is never exempt from the imagination's antithetical ability to subvert its own creation. In other words, once the place has been brought into written existence, it is inevitable that it be unwritten" (*Place*, 20). In the end, though, it is more important to see Heaney's discussions of Yeats in the context of the debates about him that recently raged in Ireland and were highly politically motivated.

There is nothing nostalgic about Heaney's praise of Grigson and no implied criticism of deconstructive methods, but clearly what interests Heaney and what he regards as "not to be superseded" is a criticism that is centered on the problems of the writer. For him, these are in great part technical and "expressive," that is, pertaining to the *way* something is presented, not exactly what M. H. Abrams in *The Mirror and the Lamp* characterized as typically romantic self-expression, the inner self made outer, though it does not exclude this. Technique and the "genetic laws" of poetry are involved, and it is these matters that poets, and presumably critics as well, should put first.

As a result, one of the major themes of Heaney's critical writings is the relation of art to life, reflecting the existence of political tension in Northern Ireland. He obviously inherited the theme from Yeats, but it is expressed specifically in relation to Heaney's own time and place every bit as much as Yeats ever made it relevant to Yeats's. The place is Northern Ireland, and the time is the summer of 1969: "From that moment the problems of poetry moved from being simply a matter of achieving the satisfactory verbal icon to being a search for images and symbols adequate to our predicament" (*Preoccupations*, 56). I doubt that the problems of poetry had ever been that simple, but the statement is understandable given the situation in which Heaney was writing

"Verbal icon" recalls the time of the New Criticism, it being the title of W. K. Wimsatt's well-known book of essays. "Predicament" suggests place, but place is not invoked only because of the political situation as such. Place has a deeper yet connected significance in that Heaney does not think of poetry without the implication of either rootedness or displacement. His accounts of Kavanagh, Montague, Hewitt, Mahon, Muldoon, and Longley, to say nothing of Yeats, begin in an assessment of each poet's relation to place. He discriminates among them on the basis of this relation. Not only does the matter of place have a more or less political aspect for the poet; it also, and more fundamentally, is a ground for feeling and identity with a natural environment even prior to words. It is where poetry finds its "entry into the buried life of the feelings" (*Preoccupations*, 52) and provides a point of exit or expression for them in the form of a personal mythology. Place is never far from Heaney's discussion of the roots of poetry, which begins in crucial "unconscious activity, at the pre-verbal level" (*Preoccupations*, 62). His criticism covers a range that, if laid out as a continuum, moves from what he admits is the "slightly predatory curiosity of a poet interested in the creative processes of another poet" (*Preoccupations*, 79) to his deep concern with what he calls "the tail-end of a struggle in a province between territorial piety and imperial power" (*Place*, 57). As for poetry itself, "on the one hand, [it] is secret and natural, on the other hand it must make its way in a world that is public and brutal" (*Preoccupations*, 34). I shall return to these matters. Here I can remark that the opposition Heaney sets forth is not one he can easily take a side in, for though he is clearly against "imperial power," he has deep reservations about Irish "territorial piety" and those sacred mysticisms believed in and exploited by the Irish Republican Army. His own sense of place, and his notion of a poet's proper sense of it, has nothing to do with such mystifications. It must be antithetical to both sides. For him, poetry is a sort of "divination, . . . a revelation of the self to the self, . . . restoration of the culture to itself" (*Preoccupations*, 41). Poems are "elements of continuity." In emphasizing place, Heaney identifies himself with continuity. The Celtic sensibility, he observes, has a strain that expresses "love of place and lamentation against exile"; and he notes that the Irish God of the monasteries has for poets always shared importance with "another god in the tree, impalpable perhaps but still indigenous," and with which early Irish poetry affiliated itself (*Preoccupations*, 186). The early poets especially made the sense of place "more or less sacred," performing a "marriage between the geographical country and the country of the mind" (*Preoccupations*, 132). Heaney's sense of identity with these early poets is an expression of his search for *poetic* roots. In one essay, he speaks of his desire to "see how far we can go in seeking the origins of a poet's characteristic 'music'" (*Preoccupations*, 61). Elsewhere he insists on the power of poetry emerging from a depth always below "declared meaning," a force that is "elusive, archaic and only half-apprehended by maker and audience" (*Preoccupations*, 186). He wishes to go far deeper than patriotism or nationalism or the programmatic tendencies that, for example, conscious applications of Gaelic techniques to poetry reveal (*Preoccupations*, 36). These lead to rhetorical, not poetic, gesture.

Heaney sees himself in terms of place and what has happened in it, but he recognizes the complexity of doing so in Ireland. He has found himself "symbolically placed between the marks of English influence and the lure of the native experience" (*Preoccupations*, 35), between the demesne and the bog, as he put it in 1972. And he has found himself between the political and cultural traumas of Ireland and the world beyond them. He observes that one identifies with "a place, an ancestry, a history, a culture," but there are quarrels with the self in which the "voices of [one's] education," as D. H. Lawrence remarked, figure decisively (*Preoccupations*, 35). All of the Irish poets on whom Heaney comments he sees in the light of one or more of these oppositions, and he consistently seeks a third, antithetical position from which to view both them and himself. It is not easy, and a certain dramatic tension is the result.

Life (Politics) and Art

The overriding concern of Heaney's criticism is the traditional and universal one of the relation of the poet's art to his and all life. Both *Preoccupations* (1978), the title of which indicates the theme's importance, and *The Government of the Tongue* (1988), with the ambiguity of its title, begin by stating the theme; and the second of these beginnings acknowledges tacitly the stress of Northern Irish political conditions that has required Heaney to reaffirm certain principles. In 1978, Heaney asked simply how a poet should live and write and what his relation to his own voice, his place, his literary heritage, and the world should be (*Preoccupations*, 13). In 1988, his views on these matters had not changed, but the stress was greater and the discussion more intense. Can art, should art, go on under the conditions of violence being experienced in the North? Heaney invoked his remembrance of lecturing on Wilfred Owen some twenty years before and his awareness on the one hand of Owen's tendency to "over-write" against the sense that "the need to call for verbal restraint felt prissy and trivial when you considered what lay behind the words" (*Government*, xv). Poets, too, not just critics, are in most situations embarrassed by their art, for "lyric poetry, however responsible, always has an element of the untrammelled about it. There is a certain jubilation and truancy at the heart of an inspiration. There is a sense of liberation and abundance which is the antithesis of every hampered and deprived condition. And it is for this reason that, psychologically, the lyric poet feels the need for justification in a world that is notably hampered and deprived" (*Government*, xviii). The view expressed here, which dramatizes the antithetical condition, was later developed at length in *The Redress of Poetry*, to which I shall eventually come.

The poetic model Heaney chose to help overcome this embarrassment was Osip Mandelstam, in whom obedience to the poetic impulse was identical with obedience to conscience. Heaney had some trouble explaining by definition what "obedience to the poetic impulse" is, but the example of Mandelstam takes us a certain distance. It is the "urge to sing in [one's] own way" (*Government*, xx), and this may involve to "witness" (*Government*, xvi), when the "compulsion to identify with the oppressed becomes necessarily integral with the act of writing itself" (*Government*, xvi). In such situations—Owen's, for example—the poet may feel compelled to abjure conventional artistic expression and assert his freedom to employ the language, but in any case his art, if at all genuine, will involve an expression of the determination to speak out freely. Yet that freedom requires a certain detachment from one's own emotions so that a separation from both self-justification and self-obliteration is perhaps fleetingly achieved. The stance would be antithetical to such oppositions.

Much of what had been happening in Northern Ireland was blatantly clear to Heaney and did not require working out, appraisal, revelation, or even accusation: "Sectarian prejudice, discrimination in jobs and housing, gerrymandering by the majority, a shared understanding that the police were a paramilitary force . . ." (*Government*, xxi). His generation, he thought, saw itself as part of a possible change for the better: "The fact that a literary action was afoot was itself a new political condition, and the poets did not feel the need to address themselves to the specifics of politics because they assumed that the tolerances and subtleties of their art were precisely what they had to set against the repetitive intolerances of public life" (*Government*, xxi). For Heaney, there were moments in which the tongue rejected governance by the conditions of obeisance to one loyalty or another: "It gains access to a condition that is unconstrained and, while not being practically effective, is not necessarily inefficacious" (*Government*, xxii).

But this faith was constantly tried, and Heaney's criticism made the stress on it central to his essays. The pages of *The Government of the Tongue* restated the propositions about poetry that appeared ten years earlier in *Preoccupations*. "They are," he now said, "symptomatic of an anxiety that in arrogating to oneself the right to take refuge in form, one is somehow denying the claims of the beggar at the gate" (*Government*, xxii). Yet, with the example of Mandelstam before him, he chose that freedom.

Examples: Yeats and Kavanagh

The theme took Heaney to repeated meditations on his great predecessor Yeats, whose poem "Ego Dominus Tuus," preeminently among others, sets forth a distinction between men of action and poets, and who made the poet's relation to action one of his many subjects in his ambitious sequence "Meditations in Time of Civil War." Poets of the generation after Yeats and before Heaney were certainly preoccupied with Yeats, who for them represented a spectral force overwhelming in power. Heaney is neither slavish follower of nor Orcan rebel against Yeats. He is free enough of Yeats to point to him as an example. Yet an example of what? Thus the title of the essay, "Yeats as an Example?" ends with a question mark. It is not just a question of what Yeats is an example of. It is also a question of whether Yeats can be an example at all without overwhelming. Yeats is not present in Heaney's essays as a stylistic influence or an object to be opposed at any cost. But as a certain kind of example, Yeats is everywhere. As an object of meditation he appears twice in *Preoccupations* and very strongly in *The Place of Writing*. Heaney returned to Yeats in an important moment of *The Redress of Poetry*.

The example of Yeats to be deeply respected was his stubbornness on behalf of the poetic and of "creative action," his deliberate assertion of freedom. In Heaney's view, Yeats, who worried the anxiety of the relation of art to life into some of his greatest poems, managed to make a tense marriage of the two:

> I admire the way that Yeats took on the world on his own terms, defined the areas where he would negotiate and where he would not; the way he never accepted the terms of another's argument but propounded his own. I assume that this peremptoriness, this apparent arrogance, is exemplary in an artist, that it is proper and even necessary for him to insist on his own language, his own vision, his own terms of reference. (*Preoccupations*, 101)

To the practicing poet, Yeats offers the example of "labour, perseverance" (*Preoccupations*, 110). It is to be noted that these remarks do not engage in the Yeats-bashing that became popular at about the same time. The difference is grounded first on Heaney's respect for Yeats's commitment to the "absolute validity" (*Preoccupations*, 99) of the artistic process and second on Yeats's "large-minded, wholehearted assent to the natural cycles of living and dying" (*Preoccupations*, 110). For Heaney, Yeats's intransigence and commitment to both of these things evoke a great admiration that runs entirely counter to the fairly common tendency in Ireland, among Catholic intellectuals at least, to treat Yeats as "poor silly Willie" or to regard him as a bit cracked. Finally, Heaney sees Yeats as an example to others in "the way his life and work are *not* separate but make a continuum, the way the courage of his vision did not confine itself to rhetoric but issued in actions" (*Preoccupations*, 100). Heaney's Yeats was well aware of, made a theme of, the problem of life and art and plied "the effort of the individual work into the larger life of the community as a whole" (*Preoccupations*, 106). For Heaney, the popular notion of Yeats as an impractical dreamer is belied by the facts not only of his life but also of his poetry and drama. His intransigence and commitment were toward a goal, from which he seldom wavered: a campaign "with the idea of conquest, not of territory perhaps but of imagination" (*Preoccupations*, 104). This is Heaney's Yeats of a 1978 lecture.

Ten years later in *The Place of Writing*, the question of place is paramount. Yeats as a poet who imposed his own vision on a place and thereby revealed a "country of the mind" is contrasted to Thomas Hardy, whose country seemed to have created his mind and whose houses somehow defined *him*. But this notion of imaginative domination and making is given a further twist with the idea that Yeats finally unwrote the place he made his ground or at least unwrote its ultimate efficacy as an insurance against the absurd. This for Heaney was Yeats's greatest triumph—the acknowledgment, indeed the necessary embrace, of limitation, the return to earth, the rejection of the temptation of triumph itself. Heaney's Yeats possessed an implacable artistic drive that would shape and discipline his materials, always trying out new voices, assuming theatrical masks, overcoming difficulties. He is contrasted to a Wordsworth who seems mesmerized by his own voice and by natural forces and prescribes a wise passiveness.

But the poet whom Heaney most contrasts to Yeats—in an entirely different way—is Patrick Kavanagh. In *Preoccupations*, it is as if an essay on Yeats generates one on Kavanagh. Ten years later, Heaney looks at Kavanagh again and feels that he has better come to understand why he is drawn to Kavanagh's work. Heaney contrasts Kavanagh to Yeats, but not at the expense of a Yeats deemed irrelevant, a Yeats who must be overthrown in order to get on with the task of an Irish cultural politics that would transcend nationalism. Kavanagh has a strong appeal to critics and poets of the left in Ireland for at least two reasons. First, he rejected the "matter of Ireland." He refused to serve the traditions and forms of the Irish Literary Revival, of which he was entirely suspicious. They have become suspect on the left because of their alleged connection with middle-class culture and nationalist jingoism. Second, as Heaney points out, Kavanagh expressed "a hard buried life that subsisted beyond the feel of middle-class novelists and romantic nationalist poets" (*Preoccupations*, 116). Kavanagh was a "new, authentic and liberating" voice (*Preoccupations*, 116) and spoke for a consciousness not before given articulation. Kavanagh's *The Great Hunger* was a rebuke to the idea of the peasant as a noble savage and a dramatization of what its author called "the usual barbaric life of the Irish country poor" (*Preoccupations*, 124). For Heaney, Kavanagh expressed social commitments in spite of himself, even as he rejected any form of nationalism. Yet his work "probably touches the majority of Irish people more immediately and more intimately than most things in Yeats" (*Preoccupations*, 137).

The essay in *Preoccupations* expresses, however, some reservations about Kavanagh's work. I shall turn to these after observing that, in the essay ten years later in *The Government of the Tongue*, Heaney somewhat revised his opinion. In the earlier essay, Heaney valued Kavanagh for his bringing an aspect of Irish life to expression. In the later, Heaney identified himself to some extent with that life. "One felt less alone and marginal as a product of that world now that it had found its expression" (*Government*, 9). He described himself as responding to Kavanagh from a "comparatively bookless background," presumably like Kavanagh's own. Heaney also valued Kavanagh's work because, though it was deliberately antipolitical in intention, it had political effect, even an effect that Kavanagh probably would have hated: "Whether he wanted it or not, his achievement was inevitably co-opted north and south, into the general current of feeling which flowed from and sustained ideas of national identity, cultural otherness from Britain and the dream of a literature with a manner and a matter resistant to the central Englishness of the dominant tradition" (*Government*, 9–10). It is ironic that Kavanagh, then, has been read in the light of the aims of the Irish Literary Revival, which he had called "a thoroughgoing English bred lie."

The result in the second essay was an assertion of a high personal evaluation. Heaney saw Kavanagh as having achieved a style appropriate to "his universal ordinariness" (*Government*, 14). He would then rewrite the conclusion to his earlier essay: "I said then that when Kavanagh had consumed the roughage of his Monaghan experience, he ate his heart out. I believe now that it would be truer to say that when he had consumed the roughage of his early Monaghan experience, he had cleared a space where, in Yeats's words, 'the soul recovers radical innocence' . . . " (*Government*, 14). Yet Heaney admitted even here, I think, Kavanagh's definite limitations and alluded to his too often "wilful doggerel, writing which exercised a vindictiveness against the artfulness of art" (*Government*, 14). Thus Heaney, though appreciating Kavanagh, did not abandon the criticism he made in the earlier essay, where he drew a distinction between technique and craft and faulted Kavanagh for a paucity of the latter.

By "technique," Heaney refers to a way with words, meter, rhythm, and verbal texture in general. "Technique is what allows that first stirring of the mind round a word or an image or a memory to grow towards articulation" (*Preoccupations*, 48). But this also involves "stance towards life, towards [one's] own reality," and discovering ways to "raid the inarticulate" (*Preoccupations*, 47). Craft, on the other hand, involves what one can learn from other verse; it is skill. What Heaney calls "poetic music" he identifies with technique more than with craft (*Government*, 109). Craft is for Heaney what Blake called the learning of the "language of art." Though Blake hated imitation of nature, he argued that all artists copied a great deal. It was part of their learning the language.

Heaney's second essay on Kavanagh did not depart from his earlier judgment with respect to this distinction:

> There is, we might say, more technique than craft in his work, real technique which is, in [Kavanagh's] own words, "a spiritual quality, a condition of mind, or an ability to invoke a particular condition of mind . . . a method of getting at life," but his technique has to be continually renewed, as if previous achievements and failures added up to nothing in the way of self-knowledge or self-criticism of his own capacities as a maker. (*Preoccupations*, 116)

In spite of a failure of craft, Kavanagh is still to be admired.

In *Preoccupations*, a personal statement in behalf of his own way seems half apologetic in the context of Northern Ireland's political troubles: "It would wrench the rhythms of my writing procedures to start squaring up to contemporary events with more will than ways to deal with them" (34). Momentarily Heaney apologizes for his antitheticality. Ten years later, he is less apologetic, more forthright in defending the necessity of the poet's hard-won freedom, even as he recognizes the tension. By this time, he is convinced that poetic commitment must come first, and the ethical, moral, or political vision must be fashioned within it, for better or worse. He concedes the danger: "I do not in fact see how poetry can survive as a category of human consciousness if it does not put poetic considerations first—expressive considerations, that is, based upon its own genetic laws which spring into operation at the moment of lyric conception. Yet it is possible to feel all this and still concede the justice of Czeslaw Milosz's rebuke to the autocracy of such romantic assumptions" (*Government*, 166). These dangers acknowledged, Heaney nevertheless returns frequently to the assertion that poets must be faithful to the demands of the "poetic event" in spite of how much they feel they must "concede to the corrective pressures of social, moral, political and historical reality" (*Government*, 101). Poets must stand by what they write, "stand [their] ground and take the consequences" (*Government*, 39). Heaney is explicitly critical of "poets who dwell in the conditional," and he comments on the frequency of such poetry, particularly in the United States (*Government*, 38–39).

It is worthwhile for a moment to return to Heaney on Yeats, the connection between Yeats's life and art that Heaney perceives, and the relation of that connection to Yeats's aggressively creative tendencies. Yeats, Heaney observed in *Preoccupations*, started and carried through a countercultural movement at which it is now fashionable to smile indulgently. But it was grounded, for Yeats, on place, a place actively made, though it also involved what he looked on as restoration of a body of legends and folklore. Yeats would create a "new country of the mind" (*Preoccupations*, 135). Yeats came under attack from the materialist critics for the falseness of this country. Heaney did not make this attack. He was interested in the accomplishment rather than its content and relevance to the contemporary situation. He therefore made no explicit quarrel with others over Yeats. However, he did issue warnings against judgments so completely centered on political ideology and the situation of the moment: "We live here in critical times ourselves, when the idea of poetry as an art is in danger of being overshadowed by a quest for poetry as a diagram of political attitudes. Some commentators have all the fussy literalism of an official from the ministry of truth" (*Preoccupations*, 219–20).

He also raised interesting questions about poets in the United States who live with "anxious over-the-shoulder glance[s] at a world of grants, fashions, and schools" (*Government*, 40). Poets in his view should not consciously respond to a "demonstrable literary situation" lest their brains be turned into "butterfly nets" (*Preoccupations*, 190). Heaney holds out against fashionability, a certain literary politics, ideological commitments oversimplified by the pull and stress of the moment, and, perhaps above all, the jingoism of the extremists on all (both) sides. From the outset of his career, or at least from the moment when he defined his task as "the search for the images and symbols adequate to our predicament" (*Preoccupations*, 56), he has held to the notion that he could be a poet and, with the artistic commitments which for him this implies, still "encompass the perspectives of a humane reason, and at the same time . . . grant the religious intensity of the violence its deplorable authenticity and complexity" (*Preoccupations*, 56–57). In *The Government of the Tongue* ten years later, he insisted that if no lyric poem has ever stopped a tank, it ought to be possible to write poetry that is like "the writing in the sand in the face of which accusers and accused are left speechless and renewed" (*Government*, 107).

Redress

The Redress of Poetry (1995) is a collection of Heaney's Oxford lectures delivered between 1989 and 1993. Its title takes advantage of some of the meanings that lurk in "redress," particularly the idea of reparation or compensation and an obsolete meaning Heaney gleans from the Oxford English Dictionary: "To set (a person or thing) upright again to an erect position. Also *fig*. To set up again, restore, re-establish."[5] The former refers to poetry's potential social role, which is to bring to consciousness new possibilities, even ideal impossibilities. The compensation would be a bringing into the picture what is lacking or only lurking unperceived. This is why, for Heaney, in poetry "enough is never enough" (*Redress*, 121). He is fond of Keats's memorable phrase "a fine excess," which he takes to refer to "that more radiant and generous life which the imagination desires" (*Redress*, 115). The definition refers to Heaney's implicit defense of poetry on these grounds. His insistence on putting the demands of poetry first is an adoption of antitheticality as the poet's proper stance, often a hard-won antitheticality in a situation of political urgency.

Through ten lectures that center on specific poets, or even specific poems, technique and craft are intertwined as themes, but always with cer-

5. *The Redress of Poetry* (London: Faber and Faber, 1996), 15.

tain warnings directed mainly at those who demand ideological assertion from poems. On the first page of the first lecture, Heaney sets forth a view that persists throughout: " . . . governments and revolutionaries would compel society to take on the shape of their imagining, whereas poets are typically more concerned to conjure with their own and their readers' sense of what is possible or desirable or, indeed, imaginable" (*Redress*, 1). Thus there can be a certain troubling (need I say offensive?) unpredictability in poetry, even an unruliness with respect to doctrinal expectations. But unpredictability "gets converted into inevitability" in critical hindsight (*Redress*, 20). Heaney's possible, desirable, or imaginable are more than Sidney's golden world of poetry. They are nearer to Northrop Frye's concept of poetry as working the whole range from the limit of repugnance to the limit of desire.

It is important to notice that Heaney sets up a third force antithetical to the struggle between government and revolutionary, both of whom, according to Blake, adopt the same story. This third force would meet the need to "respond," to "answer," in all of the senses of the latter. In order to achieve this, there must be a line between daily life and imaginative representation. The latter performs by transforming and in so doing "brings human existence into a fuller life" (*Redress*, xvii). On the outside of conventional oppositions or on the other side of a frontier, the poem is potentially able to offer to consciousness "a chance to recognize its predicaments" (*Redress*, 2). Sometimes Heaney sees such poetic acts as "counterveiling gestures" or "counterweighing" as if the aim is to achieve a balance: " . . . to place a counter-reality in the scales—a reality which may be only imagined but which nevertheless has weight because it is imagined within the gravitational pull of the actual" (*Redress*, 3). Such an alternative may be only "glimpsed" (*Redress*, 4), but that itself is of value, because of its power of attraction, even of attractiveness to human social desires. But to perform this social role, poetry must remain poetry and not become something else; it must be "its own category" (*Redress*, 6), which is not to say that it cannot effect or contribute to effecting political change. It must express its integrity as poetry and avoid simplistic and possibly transitory commitments. Heaney offers Thomas MacDonagh and Joyce as writers neither of whom " . . . considered it necessary to proscribe within his reader's memory the riches of an Anglophone culture whose authority each was, in his own way, compelled to challenge. Neither denied his susceptibility to the totally persuasive word in order to prove the purity of his resistance to an imperial hegemony" (*Redress*, 7). "Purity" here recalls Robert Penn Warren's championing of "impure poetry" on related grounds fifty years before.

Through the ten lectures, the emphasis is on motion and countermotion. In a fine essay on Christopher Marlowe's "Hero and Leander," Heaney speaks of " . . . a motion countered by an implicit acknowledgment of repression and constraint. This dialectic [which is without synthesis] is expressed formally by the co-existence of a supple voice within strict metrical pattern , and tonally by a note that is modulating constantly between the scampish and the plangent" (*Redress*, 33). Heaney's insistence is on what one might call the intellectual function of form, for poetry "answers" in meter, syntax, and tone as these things infuse anything that might be called content. All of this is in the interest of affirming Marlowe's value, even as his works are "bound up with a particular moment in English history, and are thereby implicated with the late-Tudor project of national consolidation at home and colonization abroad" (*Redress*, 22). We remember that a Northern Irish Catholic is saying this.

Marlowe's *Doctor Faustus* forces into one play a "psychological realism" that "insists that too much should not be expected from people, or from life in general, while its artistic virtuosity insists that too much is the least we should expect" (*Redress*, 36). This is not a fault in the play. Rather, it is its strength in that it forces into relation two things that seem incompatible, dissuading us from too easy a choice of one over the other. This illustrates a necessity that Heaney elsewhere connects with Yeats: "The poet who would be most the poet has to attempt an act of writing that outstrips the conditions even as it observes them" (*Redress*, 159).

Heaney's criticism is a "writerly" criticism in contrast to recent academic criticism that has been "readerly" and descriptive. The latter has given way to a theoretical discourse tending to dwell incessantly on its own problems. This has been followed by an ideological discourse that has little patience with the niceties either of technique or of craft and approaches poems from a fixed external set of presumptions that are a projection of the theorist's own will. As a critic, Heaney attempts first to see the poem from its own point of view, as ultimately impossible as this critical effort finally may be. Heaney's critical writings frequently offer a paragraph about a particular poet or particular lines that achieve what is lacking in most discussions of literature—an insight into another's work, expression of a capacity to edge up to the poem in words without burying it in either paraphrase or jargon, an appreciation of gesture. With the credentials of his experience, he returns to insistence on the necessity of art's having its own role generated and regenerated by the poet's properly stubborn commitment to a special sort of freedom, offensive as it may be to cherished methods and jargons.

12

The Double Offense of Great Bad Poetry;
or, McGonagall Apotheosized

We have observed that some metaphysical works based on the synecdoche of macrocosm and microcosm turn out to seem poetical once they are perceived to have no scientific value.[1] Can bad poems over time sometimes turn into good ones? Witness the popularity over the past seventy-some years of the anthology of bad verse *The Stuffed Owl*.[2] It is my thesis that certain bad poems rise to greatness by committing a double offense, including the offense against poetry itself that all bad poetry commits. The great bad poem, in contrast to the embarrassingly dull, simply bad poem, causes us to confront the offense of badness and makes it possible for us to pass through it in spite of ourselves. There is something unsettling about this passage, and it is not surprising that some of us successfully resist it. At the first public reading of bad poetry in which I participated, we readers were surprised at the angry response of a young student poet who, I suppose, was offended by our cavalier treatment of apparently serious purpose, which he must have regarded as solemnly to be respected. He may have thought he was expressing solidarity with working-class people, showing a consciousness that some of the poets from whose work we read expressed tacitly a desire to rise up intellectually on the wings of poetry. Perhaps he saw us as looking down on sincere effort. Maybe he thought we had perpetrated violence on the sacred,

1. Another group of works, in what seems to be prose, falls into this class: mainly eighteenth-century works of syncretic mythology, containing do-it-yourself etymologies and speculations on the sources of languages and myths. These works (for example, Jacob Bryant's *New System* [1774], mainly known now because Blake did for it an illustration of a great egg with a serpent wrapped around it) await the critic with the necessary dogged devotion.

2. *The Stuffed Owl: An Anthology of Bad Verse*, selected and arranged by D. B. Wyndham Lewis and Charles Lee (1930) (New York: Capricorn Books, 1962). Some of the examples I offer, but not including those of William McGonagall, come from this book.

and he brought moral judgment down on us. Or was he suddenly reminded of the peril of writing poetry, of the false step, of the word that goes its own way, and in a moment of panic feared for himself?

The Greatly Bad

The redoubtable Horace said, "A lawyer, pleading an ordinary suit, may fall short of the eloquent Messalla, and know less than Aulus Cascellius, but he is still respected. But neither gods, men, nor booksellers tolerate a mediocre poet."[3] Horace does not take account of poets who, beyond mediocrity, are greatly bad, whose work, like that of William McGonagall, has somehow managed in spite of everything to stay in print.

All forms of human expression are products over long periods of time of cultural development and have grown into cultural forms, or, as Cassirer called them, "symbolic forms,"[4] providing contexts for what is created in them. Each form, we might say, has its own language in which the world is constituted according to that form. Thus physical science expresses itself and its world in mathematical language. Musical art expresses itself in notes of sound, and so on. I have been discussing four things that contribute to the poetic form of expression and are, as I have tried to show, offensive, particularly to those who cannot enter the poetic context, by virtue perhaps of a wholesale commitment or bondage to another cultural form. Within its own cultural form, poetry is astonishingly free to invent new things. Its circumference is flexible, and it can surprise the reader, but it can do this only because its cultural form allows flexibility. Joyce's work, as we have seen, is a good example, having opposed the law of the dramatic at least as Aristotle saw it. This is always a risk, taken by choice. It requires a great writer, who can reveal possibilities for expansion. It requires a tacit understanding of and faithfulness to the poetic cultural form. It also requires

3. Quintus Horatius Flaccus, "Art of Poetry" ["Ars Poetica"], trans. W. J. Bate, *Critical Theory Since Plato*, ed. Hazard Adams and Leroy Searle, 3rd ed. (Boston: Thomson Wadsworth, 2005), 84.

4. Ernst Cassirer, *The Philosophy of Symbolic Forms*, trans. Ralph Mannheim, 3 vols. (New Haven: Yale University Press, 1953–57), and *An Essay on Man: An Introduction to a Philosophy of Human Culture* (New Haven: Yale University Press, 1944).

resistance to those external measures that any external law might impose. If poetry seems disorderly and perhaps dangerous from that point of view (as Plato's Socrates thought it was), great bad poetry offends even against that perceived disorder, against the poetic cultural form itself. This transgressive behavior sometimes turns the serious into the comic, the solemn into the ridiculous. Sometimes an oratorical gesture is so in excess of the fiction presented that the presentation itself is overcome, forcing the reader to embarrassment and then at the moment of greatest seriousness, if the stumbling block is passed, to laughter. Often a metaphor has its way with the poem, rather than the other way around; or the fiction attempted cannot overcome even for a moment our disbelief. Great bad poetry shares in a perverse way something with Greek comedy or the comedy of Molière, the symbolic driving out of a culprit, but here it is not a miser or a misanthrope but the unfortunate poet who is victimized. Just as a comedy is a tragedy for the one driven out, so is it for the bad poet with an honorable ambition. We who enjoy the often barely suppressed savagery that is the ground of comedy may honor the hapless poet with a touch of our guilt, but the greatly bad poet becomes the principal character in a comedy. Sensing intention somehow gone wrong, we are happy to ignore a fundamental principle of the dramatic—that the speaker is a fictive construct made by the poet.

There is thus an element of the awful in humor, so close to malicious raillery as it is. But, in the greatly bad, something is redeemed. The greatly bad poem becomes not something more but something less than its apparent intention. Perhaps it succeeds by redirecting the best of intentions or deflating a possible pomposity with brilliant infelicities no one could have deliberately invented as such. Great badness is a sign of a poem's freedom from its author's moment of amazing incompetence. More than our wishing to have fun at the poet's expense, we are enlivened by moments of destabilizing surprise, what, as I have previously mentioned, Koestler called "bisociation," the clash of incompatible things. The poem has strayed into a continuing life. We might say it has made of itself the best of a bad thing. If it turns out that we are offended and cannot pass the stumbling block of double offense, either the student poet would be right or we would be without sense of humor—or the poem would not be greatly bad but merely bad.

Merely bad poetry inevitably employs some of the offenses that occur in good poems, but it succeeds only in the dullness that helps line shelves of poetry sections in used bookstores. Merely bad poetry fails to rouse the faculties to act. A great bad poem may commit poetic offense, but something goes spectacularly wrong. Gesture often wanders away into an astounding poverty of significance rather than a surplus, although sometimes there is a concomitant surplus of stylistic eccentricity. Keats's "momentous depth of speculation" gives way to momentary astonishment. Speakers in poetic drama lose a struggle to control their words and end up conveying something they wouldn't want to say or, often more spectacularly, something they actually and unfortunately want to say. On the whole, fiction is rejected for the embrace of hard truths of self-expression or the solemn, didactic conveyance of fact. As for tropes, rhetoric overwhelms poetics, and the poet in either enthusiasm or ineptitude or both mixes metaphors, performs apostrophes to and animates inappropriate objects, succumbs to clichés in the name of propriety, or would abandon tropes entirely in the name of honest talk, were this possible. Much of all this involves a cultural form not poetic invading the poetic context and wreaking havoc with what Wilde called "careless habits of accuracy."[5]

The fundamental difference between merely bad poetry and great bad poetry is that merely bad poetry is not bad enough and great bad poetry succeeds in failure. There is a curious connection between great bad poetry and parody, the difference being that great bad poems seem to be parodies of originals that never existed, originals that are impossible to imagine. For the most part, I shall not classify the passages I present according to the categories I have already mentioned, for many of the selections blend one with another to include both, and classification would not adequately call attention to the scope of their great badness.

The editors of *The Stuffed Owl* valiantly offer a distinction between bad verse and good bad verse, but I believe it is inadequate: " . . . good Bad Verse," they write, "is grammatical, it is constructed according to the Rubrics, its rhythms, rimes, and metres are impeccable" (ix). I can see why they say this. They want to clear out of their enterprise work that has no

---

5. "The Decay of Lying," *Complete Works of Oscar Wilde* (London and Glasgow: Collins, 1966), 973.

connection to verse as we usually think of it. However, some of the best bad poetry, perhaps the greatest (as I shall later show by example), is characterized by rhythms that simply peter out into prose, rimes undelivered when expected and delivered when unexpected, and excruciatingly dogged repetitions—dogged especially when in the form of refrains that evade making any impression of musicality. The editors are more accurate, though they have soared from *terra firma* and tested the circumambient gas, when they claim, "It would, indeed, be a permissible exercise in dialectic to prove here conclusively and inclusively, if we had the time, that good Bad Verse has an eerie, supernal beauty comparable in its accidents with the beauty of Good Verse" (ix). The term "accidents" is accurate both in its Aristotelian sense and in the more modern sense of calamity. The editors go on to claim that the best bad verse is that by esteemed poets, the fall of a Tennyson being perceived greater than that of a Cornelius Whur. Perhaps this is so to the connoisseur, but a certain relativity enters here that, if insisted on, would lessen unfairly the absolute bad greatness or great badness of the astonishing McGonagall, who to my knowledge never wrote a good poem. But, then, McGonagall was a great, not just a good, bad poet, surpassing in his greatness even the Sweet Singer of Michigan, the redoubtable Julia A. Moore.

Wayward Tropes

Bad poetry achieves greatness partly by means of many of the tropic devices (not deliberately offered, of course) of comedy. One of these is that dogged repetition I have already mentioned. Northrop Frye commented on John Synge's tragedy *Riders to the Sea* as follows: "In Synge's *Riders to the Sea* a mother, after losing her husband and five sons at sea, finally loses her last son, and the result is a very beautiful and moving play. But if it had been a full-length tragedy plodding glumly through the seven drownings one after another, the audience would have been helpless with unsympathetic laughter long before it was over."[6] Such a play might have its delights, our laughter perhaps not exactly unsympathetic, but not sympathetic either—perhaps

6. Northrop Frye, *Anatomy of Criticism: Four Essays* (Princeton, NJ: Princeton University Press, 1957), 168.

disinterested, as Matthew Arnold might have said. As for teaching, the great bad poems surely teach other poets what not to do. But in order for bad poetry to be great bad poetry, it must offend, then by means of a second offense provide the perilous pathway to gaiety. It does so with its unexpected and, we trust, unintended comedy. It is as if chance and not causality has prevailed.

I leave good or even great bad poetry as undefined as I would leave poetry, having referred to its offensiveness, and now take note of the somewhat random list of characteristics offered by the editors of *The Stuffed Owl*: bathos, windy splurges, bombinating, sentimentality, banality, the prosaic, *style pompier*, anemia, obstipation, and insufficiency of emotional content for material form (ix). To which I add insufficiency of material form for emotional content. Beyond all of this, there lies the supreme ingredient absolutely necessary to great bad poets in their unintentional creation of the comical, an apparent lack of a sense of humor or of self-awareness, at least their desertion in a crisis.

The mixed metaphor, surpassing the ridiculous, is a staple of great moments if not whole poems. An example is a quotation from an anonymous young poet joyfully made by Coleridge in *Biographia Literaria*:

> No more will I endure Love's pleasing pain
> Nor round my heart's leg tie his galling chain.

The gesture of the trope of apostrophe Coleridge himself was capable of desecrating in his "Hymn Before Sunrise":

> So long he [the sun] seems to stop
> On thy bald awful head, O sovran Blanc.

This fails, in my opinion, to equal the offhand gesture of Julia A. Moore in her masterpiece "Lord Byron's Life," the result being ambiguity of a type unimagined even by William Empson:

> "Lord Byron" was an Englishman
>   A poet I believe

His first works in old England
    Was poorly received.
Perhaps it was "Lord Byron's" fault
    And perhaps it was not.
His life was full of misfortunes,
    Ah, strange was his lot.

Is Byron a poet in whom Moore believes (that is, admires), who she believes existed, whose assertions she believes; or is she ironically questioning whether he is a poet at all? Or is she simply uncertain? After all, his works "was" (on occasion) poorly received. Or was she saying only that she believes that his works in England were so received? The ambiguity surpasses that of the title *Finnegans Wake*, in that she leaves out the comma after "poet" in her line as Joyce left out the apostrophe after "Finnegan" in his title. There is also the problem of interpreting Moore's decision to put Lord Byron's name twice in quotation marks along with "Englishman." Perhaps Moore had learned something hidden from Byron's biographer Leslie Marchand, that Byron was not really Byron, or that he was not a lord, or that he was not English at all. Or perhaps she was telling us that Byron was a Scot (he was Scottish on his mother's side), and her remark, far ahead of its time, is in support of Scottish devolution. Or perhaps Moore's use of quotation marks raises vexing speculations about fictionality that are best passed over here.

    In the concluding stanza, Moore anticipates the diction of the postmodernist G. W. Bush before proceeding to her stunning conclusion:

He had joined the Grecian Army
    This man of delicate frame;
And there he died in a distant land,
    And left on earth his fame,
"Lord Byron's" age was 36 years,
    Then closed the sad career
Of the most celebrated "Englishman"
    Of the nineteenth century.

Here the poet's uncertain hold on rime results in a demand on the memory of the reader, who, coming to "century," must vaguely remember "army" and be satisfied with it.

Wayward Diction

What Moore does or does not do with rime is decentering, but no more so than her way with words as in "The Temperance Army":

> Ah, from the Temperance Army,
> > Your feet shall never stray,
> Your mind will then be balmy
> > If you keep the shining way.

These lines rival but do not eclipse the following by an anonymous housemaid poet, who also suffers a dictional indisposition:

> O Moon, when I gaze on thy beautiful face,
> Careering along through the boundaries of space
> The thought has often come into my mind
> If I ever shall see thy glorious behind.

Some great bad poetry comes to us by fortunate chance after linguistic change has introduced new and sometimes unwelcome meaning that the poet could not foresee. The following by Tennyson expresses such an accumulation of unanticipated significance:

> Form, Form, Riflemen form!
> Ready, be ready to meet the storm!
> Riflemen, Riflemen, Riflemen form!
>
> Let your reforms for a moment go!
> Look to your butts, and take good aims!

Or Mrs. Browning's lines:

> Our Euripides, the human
> With his droppings of warm tears.

The unparalleled McGonagall's lines in his funeral elegy on the death of the indomitable Lord Dalhousie commit an offense not pardonable by time and change. The opening stanza has its own way with sentiment:

> Alas! Lord and Lady Dalhousie are dead, and buried at last,
> Which causes many people to feel a little downcast;
> And both lie side by side in one grave,
> But I hope God in His goodness their souls will save.

The poem goes on to praise the Dalhousie marriage in a mysterious rhythm that succumbs to scansion only after a struggle:

> 'Twas in the year 1877 he married the Lady Ada Louise Bennett,
> And by marrying that noble lady he ne'er did regret;
> And he was ever ready to give his service in any way,
> Most willingly and cheerfully by night or by day.

She did not outlive him.

Now that we have heard briefly from McGonagall, we can summarize: Poetry so bad as to commit the crime of greatness offends against poetry itself with creative syntax, uncalculated ambiguity, heroically mixed metaphor, dogged literality, the highest seriousness at the lowest moments, the unexpected collapse of established rhythm or rime scheme, and imbalance or utter disrelation of form to content and of subject matter to rhetorical gesture.

As I have indicated, when Joyce offends, he enlarges the context of the poetic and forces the recognition, on those of us who are reluctant to recognize it. What he is doing fits the flexible poetic context he has enlarged. When the sentences of *Finnegans Wake* wander into irrationality, we note that he has made these oddities (which cease after a while to be oddities) contribute to a whole. When he leaves out the apostrophe in the title *Finnegans Wake*, we know, or come to know, that all the readings we can concoct fit the whole. When Blake mixes a metaphor, we come to learn that it is part of a chain that makes each connection good. With great bad poetry it is heroically different: The poetic context disappears or is clouded, and we seize in spite of ourselves on the moments of infelicity.

The Technological Muse

Making a massive rhetorical gesture seems to be the tendency of poets of a neoclassical bent and of nineteenth-century ones bewitched out of the poetic into the embrace of science. The cultural powers of scientific and technological advance triumph. All of this is reflected in a line Coleridge quotes in *Biographia Literaria*: "Inoculation, heavenly maid, descend!"

Even earlier, the metaphysical poet Abraham Cowley provided an excellent example of such enthusiasm in a poem densely memorializing, with the application of classical myth, Harvey's discovery of the circulation of the blood:

> Coy Nature (which remain'd, though aged grown,
>   A beauteous virgin still, enjoyed by none,
>   Nor seen unveil'd by any one),
>   When Harvey's violent passion she did see,
>   Began to tremble and to flee,
>   Took sanctuary, like Daphne, in a tree:
>   There Daphne's lover stopt, and thought it much
>   The very leaves of her to touch,
>   But Harvey, our Apollo, stopt not so,
>   Into the bark and root he after her did go. . . .

Here I mercifully skip a few lines and then resume:

> What should she do? Through all the moving wood
> Of lives endow'd with sense she took her flight;
> Harvey pursues, and keeps her still in sight.
> But as the deer long-hunted takes a flood,
> She leaps at last into the winding stream of blood;

Of man's Neander all the purple reaches made,
>   Till at the heart she stay'd,
>   Where, turning head, and at a bay,
Thus by well-purged ears, was she o'erheard to say:
"Here sure shall I be safe," said she;
"None will be able sure to see
>   This my retreat, but only He
>   Who made both it and me.
The heart of man, what art can e'er reveal?
>   A wall impervious between
>   Divides the very parts within,
And doth the heart of man ev'n from itself conceal."
>   She spoke, but ere she was aware,
>   Harvey was with her there. . . .

I happily give over commentary on extended metaphor gone wild to the editors of *The Stuffed Owl*: " . . . we perceive Dr. Harvey, discoverer of the circulation of the blood, chasing Nature, that coy and aged spinster, across country with all the gusto of a Jorrocks . . . and finally whooping her down" (24).

Nineteenth-century poets were entranced by the glory of steam, both at sea and on land. One of the great, bad poems devoted to this subject is T. Baker's "The Steam-Engine; or, the Power of Flame, an Original Poem in Ten Cantos" (1857), which stretched to two hundred pages. I quote from the heroic measure of Canto X, where a certain factual directness is a gesture that blithely wanders out of poetry toward cold utilitarianism:

The trains are stopp'd, the mighty Chiefs of Flame
To quench their thirst the crystal water claim;
While from their post the great in crowds alight,
When by a line-train, in its hasty flight,
Through striving to avoid it Huskisson[7]

---

7. On this event, see Simon Garfield, *The Last Journey of William Huskisson* (London: Faber and Faber, 2002). Huskisson died on 15 September 1830.

> By unforeseen mischance was over-run.
> That stroke, alas! Was death in shortest time;
> Thus fell the great financier in his prime!
> This fatal chance not only caused delay,
> But damped the joy that erst had crown'd the day.

As above, the nineteenth century married technology to violence and death in some of the best of its bad poems. It is a subject matter even more often addressed than another favorite, the dangers of too much drink taken. The editors of *The Stuffed Owl* note that Julia A. Moore's penchant for violence covers a wide range. She is "concerned to a large extent with total abstinence and violent death—the great Chicago fire, the railway disaster of Ashtabula, the Civil War, the yellow fever epidemic in the South. She sings death by drowning, by smallpox, by fits, accidents by lightning-stroke and sleigh" (234). Her following included the great in both creation and criticism. She was revered by Mark Twain. Northrop Frye was particularly taken by her lines in defense of herself against hostile reviewers and once recited them to me:

> Some reporters and editors
>   Are versed in telling lies.
> Others it seems are willing
>   To let industry rise.

Her first book was a best seller in spite of her tormentors.

Wary and Unwary Modernity

Lest you think that great bad poetry, at least in fits and starts, has disappeared with enlightened modernism and the present day, let me evince lines from "The Invasion Handbook," a long poem by the contemporary Irish poet Tom Paulin. The reviewer for the *Times Literary Supplement*, Nicholas Laird, valiantly seeks to justify some lines from Paulin's poem. Paulin seems "convinced that if a chancy rhyme can be made, something true must be discovered. He has a faith in etymology or vernacular connections, in the wisdom of the language itself, and that its internal connections are not arbitrary but ordained."[8] The lines are the following:

> as if it was a man full
> of drink—but as the sea
> is also known as the drink
> there may be more to this than you think.

A nice try, Laird, but a trifle too solemn, I fear.

On the whole, the bad poetry of modernism lacks the comic quality that might have achieved greatness. Dylan Thomas, who wrote many fine poems, never met a modifier he didn't like, and if one did not come immediately to mind, he made one up by splicing two words. The repetition of this device leaps out of the poetic whole to demand an excess of attention:

> In the mustardseed sun
> By full tilt river and switchback sea
> Where the cormorants scud
> . . . .
> This sandgrain day in the bent bay's grave
> He celebrates and spurns
> His driftwood thirty-fifth wind turned age.

But the bad poetry of the twentieth century, an age schooled in the self-protective armor of irony, mistrusts the medium too much to let it rip and create memorable badness. It may not delight, and it does not doubly offend.

Among bad modern poets there are, of course, dire exceptions to the attitude of mistrust. I offer the Cypriot poet Ali Sedat Hilmi, who wrote in English and Turkish in the mid-twentieth century. His book, auspiciously titled *Verse at Random*, was published in 1953. In the preface, he argued as follows:

8. Review of *The Invasion Handbook* (London: Faber and Faber, 2002), *Times Literary Supplement*, 5 July 2002: 7.

I believe that once a thought is crystallized, it is no more poetry—not even verse. Poetry must be the product of instantaneous free imagination unlimited or natural inspiration uncontrolled. Its poetic value is lost when thoughts or feelings are crystallized. Real poetry represents instantaneous sentiment, observation or mood—not controlled or limited to the extent of squeezing all sentiment, thought or observation for the sake of not contradicting one's own ideas in the long run. In my opinion contradiction is essential in all consistent poetry. . . . It is my hope that *Verse at Random* will speak to its readers at random.[9]

(Here I must pause to remark that a logical contradiction has nothing to do with what Blake called contrariety, the latter involving two things logically independent of each other.) No poet known to me is truer to his own strictures than Hilmi is.

His poem "Nirvana," from which I draw the lines below, dramatizes the dying of a young girl:

> . . . There laid, behold!
> A girl in bed about to say good-bye.
> Her dad concealing tears: "You'll live, not die!"
> Cried she: "Don't let night fall! I'm growing cold!
> Oh, God, I'm coming fast. No fears—I'm bold."

Hilmi was most notable for single unforgettable lines and couplets that raised poems of simple badness to greater heights:

> The world is ours, let's smile.

> You're ethically sound, nice men.

> The moon means nothing now at all.

---

9. Ali Sedat Hilmi, *Verse at Random* (Larnaca, Cyprus: Ohanian Press, 1953), 16. I am indebted to X. J. Kennedy for alerting me some years ago to Hilmi's book.

> Come, oh come to me to be
> My homely happy bride.

> The earth turned normal now, the Hand of Fate
> Had somehow brought the Peace at any rate.

> Your eyes talk sweetly, smile at me so sweet,
> I am in love with you from head to feet!

And there are the touching lines on the death of King George VI:

> The poet left his beard to grow,
> He mourns in Mother Nature's way.

In his preface, Hilmi expressed his tropic boldness with respect to publication: "*Verse at Random* is published despite all the soaking discouragement of so many wet blankets all around it" (14).

The Great Age and Its Contents

Perhaps the age of the best bad poetry, the nineteenth century delivers much comedy, often from its best good poets. Witness one of the poets who ushers it in. Wordsworth, in his poem "The Thorn," provides a dragon's treasure trove of badness, complete with tarn, small though it be:

> High on a mountain's highest ridge
> Where oft the stormy winter gale
> Cuts like a scythe, where through the clouds
> It sweeps from vale to vale;
> Not five yards from the mountain path,
> This thorn you on your left espy;
> And to the left, three yards beyond,
> You see a little muddy pond
> Of water—never dry,
> I've measured it from side to side;
> 'Tis three feet long and two feet wide.

One could hardly do worse except to produce a twelve-and-one-half-foot dragon emerging, or perhaps to determine that the pond was in fact hexagonal. The muse of mathematics has triumphed over that of the poetic. Coleridge criticized these lines in *Biographia Literaria*. Henry Crabb Robinson confessed that he "dared not read them out in company." Wordsworth replied, "They ought to be liked," providing the pomposity the poem lacks. But he revised the arithmetic out for later editions.

Thomas Hood was always dependable for badness and reached it in "The Bridge of Sighs," which is on the subject of a woman who committed suicide by drowning:

> In she plunged boldly,
> No matter how coldly
> The rough river ran.
> Over the brink of it,
> Picture it, think of it
> Dissolute Man!
> Lave in it, drink of it
> Then if you can!

Or Edgar Allan Poe in his "Faerie-Land" (I believe he is describing fairies), where what we may call the desperation of descriptive simile takes over:

> And their moony covering
> Is soaring in the skies,
> With the tempests as they toss,
> Like—almost anything—
> Or a yellow Albatross.

Nineteenth-century Canadians take no second place to Americans in the production of bad poetry, some of which rises to greatness. By way of example, I offer the entire "Ode on the Mammoth Cheese" by James McIntyre, written probably about 1866, when a gigantic cheese was produced in the town of Ingersoll and was displayed on a tour around Ontario and even into the state of New York:

ODE ON THE MAMMOTH CHEESE
Weight Over Seven Thousand Pounds

We have seen thee, queen of cheese
Lying quietly at your ease,
Gently fanned by evening breeze,
Thy fair form no flies dare seize.

All gaily dressed soon you'll go
To the great Provincial show,
To be admired by many a beau
In the city of Toronto.

Cows numerous as a swarm of bees,
Or as the leaves upon the trees,
It did require to make thee please,
And stand unrivaled, queen of cheese.

May you not receive a scar as
We have heard Mr. Harris
Intends to send you off as far as
The great world's show at Paris.

Of the youth beware of these,
For some of them might rudely squeeze
And bite your cheek, then songs or glees
We could not sing, oh! queen of cheese.

We'rt thou suspended from balloon,
You'd cast a shadow even at noon,
Folks would think it was the moon
About to fall and crush them soon.[10]

10. From *Musings on the Banks of the Canadian Thames, including poems on local, Canadian, and British subjects, and lines on the great poems of England, Ireland, Scotland,*

McIntyre outdoes almost all bad poets in the comparisons he offers in the name of similes that approach complete irrelevance. His flirtation with the sublime as well as the sexually risqué is impressive. McIntyre was by profession a cabinetmaker and undertaker and may have confused avocation with profession, thinking every poem should have or perhaps be like a decent burial.

The Great McGonagall

With respect to consistency of badness, intense concentration of subject matter, and genius of repetition not imagined even by Søren Kierkegaard, no one approaches the greatest and certainly the most sublime of bad poets, William McGonagall, whose voice is as immediately recognizable as those of his contemporaries Tennyson, Browning, and Swinburne.[11]

William McGonagall was born in March of 1825 to Irish parents in Edinburgh, the youngest of five children. His father was in the weaving trade and later a salesman of hardware. It is said of his schooling that young William, like Shakespeare, learned more from nature than from books. He did learn to weave, and he made several appearances on the stage in Shakespearean roles. It is reported that, playing Macbeth, he refused to fall down dead and had to be persuaded by Macduff, "Lay doon, McGonagall, lay doon."[12]

---

and America, with a glance at the wars of Victoria's reign (Ingersoll, Ontario: H. Rowland, 1884), 111–12. I am indebted to Nicholas Halmi for alerting me to this poem and through him to Todd Webb for bibliographical information. The latter informs me that McIntyre is discussed by William Arthur Deacon in his *The Four Jameses* (Toronto: Ryerson Press, 1953). Deacon reprints the poem on pp. 60–61. Both Halmi and Webb hold out the tantalizing suggestion that this was not the only dairy ode that McIntyre wrote, but I have not seen others, if they indeed exist.

11. How it was that McGonagall was omitted from *The Stuffed Owl* should be, when the time is ripe, the subject of inquiry by some scholar of bad poetry and no doubt will be, now that I have blazed the trail.

12. "Scots Hail Their Bard of Bad Verse," *Orlando Sentinel*, Sunday, 5 July 1987: p. A-15. There is some ambiguity about whether Macbeth dies onstage or offstage. Generally it seems that Macduff dispatches him offstage, then enters carrying his head, but a few texts are not clear about this. In McGonagall's performance, Macbeth seems to have died excruciatingly slowly with the combat and death in full view.

McGonagall, a master of repetition or rather mastered by it, came to poetry only in his forties, but from that time onward there issued from his pen a long march of poetic gems in seven volumes of verse with the following titles: *Poetic Gems, More Poetic Gems, Still More Poetic Gems, Yet More Poetic Gems, Further Poetic Gems, Yet Further Poetic Gems*, and, not least, *Last Poetic Gems*.[13] The first of these included his important "Ode to the Queen on Her Jubilee Year," sent to Queen Victoria in a letter. McGonagall followed it on foot to Balmoral, but there he failed to gain admission and was threatened with arrest. He had hoped to be appointed poet laureate on the death of Tennyson, whom he eulogized with words that may covertly express a certain envy and disparagement:

He was a man that didn't care for company,
Because company interfered with his study,
And confused the bright ideas in his brain,
And for that reason from company he liked to abstain.

Even the poem to the queen betrays a disturbing ambivalence, perhaps even subversiveness, as discussed by Professor Edward Rosenheim at a Victorian Festival at the University of Chicago. Alas, the paper is to my knowledge unpublished. Rosenheim notes the ominous tone of the lines

I hope her subjects will show their loyalty without fear.

And

She has been a good Queen, which no one *dare* gainsay. (my italics)

And

13. The volumes have been published under one cover, *McGonagall: A Library Omnibus* (London: Gerald Duckworth and Co., 1980). The publication was hailed in a *Times Literary Supplement* review by Alan Hamilton, which begins as follows: "Success to Mr. Duckworth of London NW1! For a great service to literature he has done, which in the world of bad verse must be second to none; he has published the works of William McGonagall in seven volumes instead of one."

> She is noble and generous,
>> Her subjects must confess.

Yet McGonagall seems also to be praising her, which leads to Professor Rosenheim's shrewd observation that McGonagall's ambiguity is "calculated."

> Oh! It was a most gorgeous sight to be seen,
> Numerous foreign magistrates were there for to see
>> the Queen;
> And to the vast multitude of women and men,
> Her majesty for two hours showed herself to them.

Death and calamity are McGonagall's major subjects, as an examination of his titles reveals. Here is a selection: "Death of Lord and Lady Dalhousie," "Death of Prince Leopold," "Funeral of the German Emperor," "Burial of the Rev. George Gilfinnan," "Death of the Rev. Dr. Wilson," "Death of Fred Marsden, the American Playwright," and "Tragic Death of the Rev. A. H. Mackonochie." Poor Mackonochie perished in the snow,

> Because for the last three years his memory had been affected
> Which prevented him from getting his thoughts collected.

No disaster on land in Britain escaped his pen. Here is a list of titles selected at random: "Calamity in London," "The Clepington Disaster," "Burning of the Exeter Theatre," "Disastrous Fire at Scarborough," "The Terrific Cyclone of 1893," "The Sunderland Calamity." Occasionally events far away caught his attention: "The Great Yellow River Inundation in China," "The Pennsylvania Disaster," which memorializes the Johnstown flood. Yet McGonagall's interest is by no means ghoulish. Rather, his attitude is fatalistic and stoical with a fastidious empathy for the dead:

> Oh, heaven! It was a horrible sight, which will not be forgot,
> So many people drowned and burned—oh hard has been their lot!
> But Heaven's will must be done, I'll venture to say,
> And accidents will happen until doomsday!

I am not implying that McGonagall's range is limited. He can be recommended to feminists for his support of women's suffrage:

> But the time is not far distant, I most earnestly trust,
> When women will have a parliamentary vote,
> And many of them, I hope, will wear a better petticoat.

He was of interest to advocates of temperance for his poetic campaign against the demon drink, and to Irish nationalists for his excoriation of the infamous Richard Pigott, false accuser of Parnell. Pigott, as McGonagall writes, was "a very bad man / And to gainsay it there's nobody can." McGonagall was, then, nothing if not politically correct.[14] Yet audiences were known to pelt him with tomatoes.

McGonagall is a poet of recurring form. I draw the following from various poems and note that they stand in for images of sight, which are entirely absent: "most beautiful to be seen," "most gorgeous to be seen," "a most gorgeous sight to be seen," "most wonderful to be seen," "most handsome to be seen," "most gigantic to be seen," "most awful to be seen," "unequaled to be seen," "obvious to be seen," "visible to be seen." These and certain syntactical deviations suggest to me that McGonagall anticipates the Russian Formalists' theoretical notion of defamiliarization. They have led one critic, Professor Joseph Williams of the University of Chicago, to declare that there may in fact be no deep structure at all of McGonagall's language or alternatively that some dead language, perhaps Old English, may actually have been McGonagall's first language.[15] But of all subjects, violence at sea or waters emptying into it most arrested McGonagall's tal-

---

14. If not for my vigilance, McGonagall might well have insinuated his way into chapter 3 above because of his stirring "Lines in Defense of the Stage," in which he claims morality for plays, "vice punished and virtue rewarded." Like Sir Philip Sidney, he extols the example over the precept and displays his modern theoretical correctness: "The theatre ought to be encouraged in every respect, / Because example is better than precept, / And is bound to have a greater effect / On the minds of theatre-goers in every respect."

15. From the University of Chicago Victorian Festival. Alas, the essay, like Rosenheim's, is also unpublished, which leads me to observe that the best McGonagall scholarship and criticism known to me are not in print, perhaps out of deep respect for double offense and fear of repercussions or even reprisals.

ent. A select list of poems reveals an unusual intensity of concentration. No report of a wreck at sea seemed to have escaped his notice: "Wreck of the Steamer 'London'," "Wreck of the 'Thomas Dryden'," "Grace Darling, or the Wreck of the 'Farfarshire'," "Wreck of the Barque 'William Patterson of Liverpool'," "Wreck of the Schooner 'Samuel Crawford'," "Burning of the Steamer 'City of Montreal'," "Wreck of the Whaler 'Oscar'," "Wreck of the 'Columbine'," "The Albion Battleship Catastrophe," "Wreck of the Steamer 'Stella', "Wreck of the Steamer 'Storm Queen'," "Wreck of the 'Abercrombie Robinson'," "Loss of the 'Victoria'," "Burning of the Ship 'Kent', "Wreck of the 'Indian Chief'," "Death of Captain Ward," "Wreck of the Barque 'Lynton'," and (two for one) "Collision in the English Channel."

In histories of Scottish literature, McGonagall has a mixed reputation. Roderick Watson, in *The Literature of Scotland*, does not mention him.[16] In *The Scottish Tradition in Literature*, Kurt Wittig remarks, "The poetic gems of the Great William McGonagall, Poet and Tragedian, and shabbiest of public-house rhymesters, are still reprinted almost every year; and their continuing popularity would indeed be an interesting problem for a psychiatrist to study."[17] On the other hand, Alan Bold, near the beginning of *Modern Scottish Literature*, offers McGonagall as exemplifying one of three "indigenous" Scottish poetic traditions, the one he calls "broadside primitivism."[18] He remarks of the unpleasant treatment the poet received and of the "orthodox opinion" of McGonagall as a "sublimely bad poet: a posturing clown who got the hostility he deserved" (17–18). But McGonagall, he argues, was in the tradition of the broadside ballad. His poems adhere to "a metrical tradition" and abide by "a rigid set of

---

16. Roderick Watson, *The Literature of Scotland* (Basingstoke: Macmillan, 1984).

17. Kurt Wittig, *The Scottish Tradition in Literature* (Edinburgh and London: Oliver and Boyd, 1958), 253.

18. Alan Bold, *Modern Scottish Literature* (London and New York: Longmans, 1983), 15. Bold, I think, would be sympathetic to the displeasure of the student poet whom I mentioned at the beginning of this chapter: "McGonagall's achievement has been ridiculed by those who despise his lowly origins and humble verse" (17). But I wonder whether the student would have been willing to say, with Bold, that McGonagall was "an absolutely outstanding primitive poet" (18).

rules" (18). Bold recognizes what he regards as McGonagall's faults, but he points out that the poet's style—"do-it-yourself syntax (complete with inversions to force the sentences into the rhyming pattern), the metrical padding . . . to drag out the linear movement, the matter-of-factual tone"— is typical of narrative broadside ballads (19). Bold goes so far as to compare McGonagall's primitive poetry to the primitive painting of Henri Rousseau: "What Rousseau is to painting, McGonagall is to poetry" (19). But I must say that I agree with other readers who find something mysterious in McGonagall's style beyond the broadside qualities that Bold makes so much of.

The Tay Bridge Trilogy

Critical common sense has always warned that excessive quotation is a mistake, but I nevertheless intend to present part of McGonagall's trilogy at some length and for the following reasons: First, beyond Scotland and the reach of English connoisseurs of his verse, his poems are not as available as one might wish. Second, some of his poems' greatest badnesses reveal themselves only over a large space, where his capacity for the inflated apostrophe, dogged repetition, creative riming, and solemn bathos can be adequately appreciated. Third, with such presentation I admit to trying to protect myself from the crisis any critic of the comic confronts: explanation of a joke. To put it another way, just a touch of solemn explanation risks drowning the unintentional comic spirit of double offense.

The object that most challenged McGonagall's muse was the one that led to his much admired trilogy of poems, which redefines all notions of the expected and unexpected in poetic art. Near his home city of Dundee on 12 May 1879 was dedicated the great railway bridge over the river Tay, the "beautiful silvery Tay," as he had sung in another poem. This and subsequent events inspired his masterpieces "The Railway Bridge of the Silvery Tay," "The Tay Bridge Disaster," and "Address to the New Tay Bridge."

Here now are the apostrophic first poem of this trilogy and the second with its tropic heights. In offering them, I accept all responsibility, reminding you again that these poems triumphantly respond to the stricture of many critics over the centuries that poetry should delight and teach:

THE RAILWAY BRIDGE OF THE SILVERY TAY

Beautiful railway bridge of the Silvery Tay!
With your numerous arches and pillars in so grand array,
And your central girders, which seem to the eye
To be almost towering to the sky.
The greatest wonder of the day,
And a great beautification to the River Tay,
Most beautiful to be seen,
Near by Dundee and the Magdalen Green.

Beautiful Railway Bridge of the Silvery Tay!
That has caused the Emperor of Brazil to leave
His home far away, *incognito* in his dress,
And view thee ere he passed along *en route* to Inverness.

Beautiful Railway Bridge of the Silvery Tay!
The longest of the present day
That has ever crossed o'er a tidal river stream,
Most gigantic to be seen,
Near by Dundee and the Magdalen Green.

Beautiful Railway Bridge of the Silvery Tay!
Which will cause great rejoicing on the opening day,
And hundreds of people will come from far away,
Also the Queen, most gorgeous to be seen,
Near by Dundee and the Magdalen Green.

Beautiful Railway Bridge of the Silvery Tay!
And prosperity to Provost Cox, who has given
Thirty thousand pounds and upwards away
In helping to erect the Bridge of Tay,

Most handsome to be seen,
Near by Dundee and the Magdalen Green.

Beautiful Railway Bridge of the Silvery Tay!
I hope that God will protect all passengers
By night and by day,
And that no accident will befall them while crossing
The Bridge of the Silvery Tay,
For that would be most awful to be seen
Near by Dundee and the Magdalen Green.

Beautiful Railway Bridge of the Silvery Tay
And prosperity to Messrs Bouche and Grothe
The famous engineers of the present day,
Who have succeeded in erecting the Railway
Bridge of the Silvery Tay,
Which stands unequalled to be seen
Near by Dundee and the Maudlin Green.

THE TAY BRIDGE DISASTER
Beautiful Railway Bridge of the Silv'ry Tay!
Alas! I am very sorry to say
That ninety lives have been taken away
On the last Sabbath day of 1879,
Which will be remember'd for a very long time.

'Twas about seven o'clock at night,
And the wind it blew with all its might,
And the rain came pouring down,
And the dark clouds seem'd to frown,
And the Demon of the air seem'd to say—
"I'll blow down the Bridge of Tay."

When the train left Edinburgh
The passengers' hearts were light and felt no sorrow,

But Boreas blew a terrific gale,
Which made their heart for to quail,
And many of the passengers with fear did say—
"I hope God will send us safe across the Bridge of Tay."

But when the train came near to Wormit Bay,
Boreas he did loud and angry bray,
And shook the central girders of the Bridge of Tay
On the last Sabbath day of 1879,
Which will be remember'd for a very long time.

So the train sped on with all its might,
And Bonnie Dundee soon hove in sight,
And the passengers' hearts felt light,
Thinking they would enjoy themselves on the New Year,
With their friends at home they lov'd most dear,
And wish them all a happy New Year.

So the train mov'd slowly along the Bridge of Tay,
Until it was about midway,
Then the central girders with a crash gave way,
And down went the train and passengers into the Tay!
The Storm Fiend did loudly bray,
Because ninety lives had been taken away,
On the last Sabbath day of 1879,
Which will be remember'd for a very long time.

As soon as the catastrophe came to be known
The alarm from mouth to mouth was blown,
And the cry rang out all o'er the town,
Good Heavens! The Tay Bridge is blown down,
And a passenger train from Edinburgh,
Which fill'd all the people's hearts with sorrow,
And made them for to turn pale,

Because none of the passengers were sav'd to tell the tale
How the disaster happen'd on the last Sabbath day of 1879
Which will be remember'd for a very long time.

It must have been an awful sight,
To witness in the dusky moonlight,
While the Storm Fiend did laugh, and angry did bray,
Along the Railway Bridge of the Silv'ry Tay.
Oh! ill-fated Bridge of the Silv'ry Tay,
I must now conclude my lay
By telling the world fearlessly without the least dismay,
That your central girders would not have given way,
At least many sensible men do say,
Had they been supported on each side with buttresses,
At least many sensible men confesses,
For the stronger we our houses do build,
The less chance we have of being killed.

Some readers have observed everything from relaxation to laxity in the third poem, "Address to the New Tay Bridge." I cannot entirely agree with these judgments. That is because of the unparalleled success of its first two lines, though I admit that McGonagall may have expended his best energy on them and could not rise to their level in the remainder of the work.

Beautiful new railway bridge of the Silvery Tay
With your strong brick piers and buttresses in so grand array.

I wish as a critic to express sympathetic identification with these poems: I do not venture without fear beyond these immortal verses, which are both delightful to be read and educational amid their fitful rimes and stresses. I point out only that they most triumphantly offend against both readers and poetry itself in the end. In fact, many more gems of the poet I might glean, certain they would be most astonishing to be heard or to be seen, but more

buttressing examples are not needed for my argument, unless you the preceding have not heeded, and I without hesitation, fearlessly, and for all the
world to hear do say: "This is not a lay; it is a critical essay." No more need
or should be said by me or by William McGonagall, poet and tragedian of
Dundee.

Epilogue: Reminders Not Quite Gentle

In 1977, Mary Louise Pratt published a persuasive summary account of arguments against the notion, popular among many critics in the twentieth century, of a special poetic language and a special nonpoetic one.[1] She declared, among other things, that any attempt to define literature in the terms of special linguistic characteristics fails because the characteristics always turn out to be present in other forms of linguistic expression. In the wake of the so-called "linguistic turn," it is important to be so reminded.[2]

The foregoing offense of poetry has not sought to define poetry, only to indicate some of its means of offense and to identify poetry's cultural value or potential value as a product of them. These means can and frequently do appear to belong to texts and acts that we do not think of as poetry (even in the broad sense used in this book), but they play a different role in poetry, usually to different ends. Each of the four offenses about which I have written stands antithetical to and confounds a binary opposition that the culture identifies with logicality and common sense. This poetic antitheticality is desirable and even necessary to a tolerable culture, not in order to overthrow and annihilate the binary oppositions but instead to oppose them and foster continued movement of thought, avoiding the potential tyranny of one-dimensional belief.

My reminders, mainly in the form of repetitions, follow upon Pratt's:

Gesture: In the old handbooks of oratory, physical gestures supported meaning and/or ornamented its delivery. The abstractable meaning of an oratorical "text" was one thing, the gesture another. They joined together in intent. The purpose of the latter was to help the language

---

1. Mary Louise Pratt, *Toward a Speech Act Theory of Literary Discourse* (Bloomington: Indiana University Press, 1977), esp. 3–37, 79–99.
2. See Richard Rorty, ed., *The Linguistic Turn: Recent Essays in Philosophical Method* (Chicago: University of Chicago Press, 1967).

employed to convince and/or move to action, offering the addendum of an allurement. In most conversation and in much written discourse, this is the case.

Poetic gesture, a metaphor itself, opposes the difference between meaning and addendum. The poetic gesture encompasses and is the whole of the text. It makes meaning untranslatable, being more than any abstractable message, persuasion, or conveyance of fact. A test case is Pope's *Essay on Criticism*. It may well be that in Pope's day most readers saw it principally as a handbook for critics. Today, perhaps, most readers see it as a document in the history of literary criticism. It is both, of course, but it is also a gesture opposing a form-content opposition, and this gesture encompasses its past and perhaps current uses. That gives it a poetic force outlasting those uses.

Drama: Pope's poem has a dramatic characterizable voice. It may or may not be Pope's, but, if we think it is, we have at least to concede that it is Pope's created persona or mask. Poetry as drama stands against any simple notion of authorial relation to a text. In drama, the author is both present and not present. The author is present in that someone or some people composed the poem. But the author is absent in that the voice or voices heard or read are those of created characters. Plato's Socrates is not Plato (or Socrates, for that matter), though they may often seem to agree with each other. Cary's trilogies have no third-person narrator to be confused with the author, and this has confounded or irritated some readers, who want to know what Cary thinks at the expense of experiencing what the novels present.[3] There is, of course, a sense in which almost all discourse is a kind of acting, the projection of a persona; also there are poems that put the dramatic voice to use with the end of persuasion or inquiry in mind. Lucretius's *De Rerum Natura* is an example. However, Lucretius's poem is usually read today not for its science but for its presentation of an imagined world. Coleridge, as is well known to critics and

3. I again use "present" in the sense of "presentational form" offered by Susanne K. Langer in her *Philosophy in a New Key* (Cambridge, MA: Harvard University Press, 1951).

scholars, remarked of his "Rime of the Ancient Mariner" that in it there was probably an "obtrusion" of a moral too "openly" on the reader.[4] That risks separating the drama from the message, gesture from fixed moral interpretation. It would frustrate what Keats seems to have regarded as the proper end of art, the setting in motion of a "momentous depth of speculation," freeing the mind from easy conclusions and opening it to continued thought.[5] We recognize that drama can be used in the pay of rhetoric in advertising, politics, and the like, where its purpose is to achieve tangible external results. When Cary's Chester Nimmo surreptitiously saw the play at the carnival, the effect on him was not alone, or maybe not at all, that of a moralistic message but of the opening of a new world that changed his life.

Fiction: Hans Vaihinger came to conclude that almost everything is a fiction.[6] However, literary fictions do not pretend or even want to be anything else, while our scientific and other fictions seem to make a pretense of corresponding to reality, or at least seem to in the public eye. Literary fictions are not simply statements of experimental or empirical fact or theory, not persuasive arguments for moral virtues; nor are they false statements. Historical novels, which may be full of the report of actual events and real people, depend for their value on something more than fact. Even Mallarmé recognized something more than a scientific approach in Zola's novels. Literary fictions are presentations, whether intended as such or not, for contemplation, worlds antithetical to our other constituted worlds, material for imagination to work on, images of desire and repugnance that may extend beyond our sense of fact.

Trope: Tropes, dead or alive, are everywhere in language, but poems are particularly courageous about their tropes. They oppose the popular and sensible opposition of sameness and difference, subject and object. Indeed, poets cannot help it, so fundamental to their works are tropes.

The antithetical stance of poetry toward the common binary oppo-

---

4. In his *Table Talk*, 31 May 1830.
5. John Keats, letter to George and Thomas Keats, 28 December 1817.
6. Hans Vaihinger, *The Philosophy of "As If"* [*Philosophie des Als Ob* (1924)], trans. C. K. Ogden (New York: Harcourt, Brace and Company, 1925).

sitions (the modern idols) of the tribe, which so often shut off speculation and deny forms of ethical identity, constitutes poetry's prime offense. In the antithetical world of Blake's *Marriage of Heaven and Hell*, angels are identified with what Blake called "fixities and definites" and devils with energy and prolific activity. Poetry's offense is of Blake's devil's party, and poetry knows it, even if some poets may not.